ARSENE
WENGER

ARSENE WENGER

THE UNAUTHORISED BIOGRAPHY OF LE PROFESSEUR

TOM OLDFIELD

JOHN BLAKE

Published by John Blake Publishing Ltd,
3 Bramber Court, 2 Bramber Road,
London W14 9PB, England

www.johnblakepublishing.co.uk

www.facebook.com/johnblakebooks 🔲
twitter.com/jblakebooks 🔲

First published in paperback in 2009
This revised edition published in 2014

ISBN: 978 1 78418 024 9

British Library Cataloguing-in-Publication Data:

A catalogue record for this book is available from the British Library.

Design by www.envydesign.co.uk

Printed in Great Britain by CPI Group (UK) Ltd

1 3 5 7 9 10 8 6 4 2

Papers used by John Blake Publishing are natural, recyclable products made from wood
grown in sustainable forests. The manufacturing processes conform to the
environmental regulations of the country of origin.

Every attempt has been made to contact the relevant copyright-holders, but some were
unobtainable. We would be grateful if the appropriate people could contact us.

For Noah and Melissa

CONTENTS

ACKNOWLEDGEMENTS

Anna Marx and the team at John Blake Publishing – Thank you for your dedicated work in making this edition a reality. Your patience and diligence are greatly appreciated.

My friends (KES, Nottingham and beyond) – Thank you for your support and sense of humour. We watched many of the games featured in this book together.

My work colleagues, past and present – You have been a priceless source of advice and feedback. I continue to rely heavily on the lessons you have taught me.

Betty, Mike, Phil, Eric, Mary, Mike and the whole Mastrocola-Nicopoulos gang – Mille merci. Fesia, zarta, tors!

Mum and Dad – Thanks for always being there. Looking forward to the family adventures to come!

Matt – I can't thank you enough for all your contributions. You are so talented – big things ahead!

Melissa – Your love and strength amaze me every day. I cannot imagine life without you.

Noah – One day soon, we will read this book together. You are the most amazing blessing and we can't wait to see the young man that you will grow up to be.

INTRODUCTION

In an era where the managerial carousel is turning at a dizzying rate, Arsène Wenger's 18-year tenure as Arsenal boss is a remarkable achievement. While critics will point to a frustrating nine-season trophy drought, which ended last season with FA Cup glory, Wenger's impact in north London goes beyond silverware.

All good managers possess the quality to extract the maximum from a group of players but greatness comes from transforming an entire club, just as Arsène has for the Gunners. The Frenchman has been the key constant for Arsenal over the past two decades, redefining the manner in which players prepare for games, overseeing a move to a new stadium and developing the Gunners into one of the most entertaining sides on the planet.

Make no mistake, Wenger has the trophies to support his status as one of the best managers of all-time – but overlooking his aura, steady hand and stabilizing effect would undersell his role in overall impact in north London.

Wenger's journey to the top has shown him to be a true football man, earning him the nickname 'The Professor'. Starting in France, he began to build his reputation with stints at first Nancy and then Monaco, where he won the French championship and the French Cup and enjoyed good runs in Europe before the Marseille match-fixing scandal marred Arsène's time at Monaco and the club parted company with the Frenchman in 1994.

To the surprise of many, Wenger then accepted the vacant manager's post at Nagoya Grampus Eight in the Japanese JLeague and, after a tricky start, he helped the club enjoy one of its best ever seasons. In the process, he learned plenty about himself and about new coaching techniques.

But when Arsenal came knocking, the offer was too good to turn down. When he first arrived in London, he certainly brought a decent CV with him but he received a rather hostile reception from supporters expecting a bigger name as the new Arsenal manager. He had plenty to prove but did not take long to win over the Gunners fans, and his subsequent achievements at Arsenal have pushed him into the category of world class managers.

The Frenchman's time at the club falls into two distinct chapters – Arsenal as a title-chasing powerhouse; and Arsenal as eye-catching title outsiders. However, throughout it all, Arsène has stayed true to his football principles.

Taking a Gunners team that was off the pace in the Premiership, Wenger transformed the squad into league champions and FA Cup winners in his second season, outwitting

Sir Alex Ferguson in the process. His savvy dealings in the transfer market unearthed bargain signings like Patrick Vieira, Emmanuel Petit and Nicolas Anelka.

Three league titles in seven years put Wenger in elite company, with only Ferguson able to better that record during the Premier League era. The unbeaten league season of 2003/04 is a feat that is unlikely to be repeated for many, many years and is a testament to Wenger's ability to motivate and get the best out of his players.

His Gunners teams established a reputation for playing some of the most stylish football in Europe, with crisp one-touch passing and creative running off the ball. In 2006, a surprise appearance in the Champions League final provided another reminder of Arsène's tactical nous but the Gunners were narrowly beaten by Barcelona on a night that will haunt him for years.

But the second half of Wenger's tenure at the club – which more or less coincides with the move to the Emirates Stadium – has had a somewhat different feel to it, even though the quality of football has often been equally breath-taking.

With Manchester United refusing to take a step back, Chelsea establishing themselves as perennial contenders under Jose Mourinho and, more recently, Manchester City emerging as a serious title threat, Arsenal were suddenly outmuscled and outspent. In the blink of an eye, Wenger's men were forced to face their new reality: securing a place in the top four – and, with it, a place in the Champions League – was the primary objective.

For players impatiently chasing silverware, this proved to be a problem. A host of players, including Emmanuel Adebayor, Gael Clichy and Samir Nasri, joined the Manchester City revolution while Cesc Fabregas returned to Barcelona, and Robin van Persie completed a controversial move to Manchester United.

Wenger has refused to panic in the transfer market – at times, to the dismay of supporters. He prides himself on ushering in new phases in his career at Arsenal by nurturing talented (and often unproved) replacements for big-name departures. For instance, in attack, Ian Wright was replaced by Nicolas Anelka who was followed by Thierry Henry and then Emmanuel Adebayor and van Persie. Marc Overmars gave way to Robert Pires and Freddie Ljungberg, with Theo Walcott, Mesut Ozil and Alex Oxlade-Chamberlain the latest stars on the flanks.

Yet the formula has let him down in the title race. Time and again over the past eight years, Arsenal have looked like promising contenders, only for a couple of injuries or a disastrous month to prove costly. The 2007/08 season is a perfect example, with the Gunners on their way to securing the fourth title Wenger craved before the campaign petered out in the face of Manchester United's flawless finish.

The 2009/10 and 2013/14 campaigns proved to be a similar story. Instead of celebrating silverware, Arsenal fans had to settle for fourth place finishes, followed by limited activity in the transfer market. As frustration mounted in the stands, there was the unfamiliar sight of 'Arsène Out' signs and protests from a small portion of Gunners fans.

But Wenger refused to throw in the towel. He continued to develop his players and stayed true to his football principles. And the trophy drought finally ended last season as Arsenal fought back to beat Hull and capture the FA Cup, a competition that Wenger also won in 1998, 2002, 2003 and 2005.

And there could be more to come. Wenger confirmed that he is not ready to call it quits at the Emirates just yet by signing a three-year extension to his Arsenal contract this summer, keeping him at the club until 2017. 'We are entering a very exciting period,' the Frenchman told the media. 'We have a strong squad, financial stability and huge support around the world. We are all determined to bring more success to this club.'

FA Cup glory lifted a heavy burden from Arsène's shoulders but his thirst for silverware remains unquenched, especially the Premier League and Champions League trophies. Those will be the targets as Wenger looks to end a hugely successful managerial career on a high note.

FROM PLAYER TO MANAGER

Arsène Wenger was born on 22 October 1949 in Strasbourg, France, to parents Alphonse and Louise. The family lived in the small village of Duttlenheim and Arsène grew up there along with older brother Guy. Duttlenheim's tiny population of 2,500 gave Wenger a quiet upbringing, away from the distractions of a big city. The Alsace region of France, in which Strasbourg is situated, offered a pleasant setting for family life and provided Arsène with a solid foundation for his future career.

Such is Wenger's current standing in world football, it is hard to believe that he was brought up in this sleepy village, rather than one of the bustling cities. But perhaps it worked in his favour. He had to work harder and had no choice but to aim higher. It gave him the urge to explore other areas and broaden his horizons. Visitors to Duttlenheim will find little to get excited about. Surrounded by agriculture, this rural setting is the polar opposite to the glamorous lifestyles of today's professional footballers. It is easy to see why the young Arsène would not have been overly influenced by the wealthy, celebrity circuit.

Wenger's father, Alphonse, ran an automobile parts business, called Comptoir de l'Est, as well as a local restaurant-cum-bar called La Croix d'Or. It was hoped that Arsène would follow in Alphonse's footsteps and take over Comptoir de l'Est in due course, but their son had other ideas. He had developed an interest in football that would increase year by year. Due to the size of the village, there was a distinct lack of organised local football and so Wenger had to wait before his first taste of team sport. Aged 12, he joined the village side and his path to the top in football began.

Football had a significant role in Alsace. Being on the border between France and Germany – and at one time a German province – the region took an interest in both leagues. However, it was the Bundesliga that held higher prestige and the likes of Bayern Munich and Borussia Dortmund caught Wenger's attention more than the French clubs. Arsène's favourite team as a boy was Borussia Monchengladbach and he admired the way that the German league was played with such pace and movement. Even at such a young age, he was taking note of these things. His early heroes included the great Franz Beckenbauer of Germany and Brazilian legend Pelé.

Learning more and more about the game, Wenger took a greater interest in the tactical side of football than most youngsters. His curiosity made him a serious young man rather than 'one of the lads' and his lifestyle was far from exuberant. He studied the strengths and weaknesses of teams and his mind absorbed football statistics and information like a sponge.

At this stage, though, Arsène still dreamed of a long and distinguished playing career as he continued to represent the local village team and sought to progress towards playing for a professional club.

He certainly had talent. Max Hild, a well respected coach and still a close friend of Wenger, first spotted Arsène's ability in a match between nearby villages. Wenger's Duttlenheim were playing AZ Mutzig – managed by Hild – and Arsène shone in a midfield role. As Hild told Jasper Rees: 'He was 18 and playing for his village. That was the first time I noticed him. He was a midfielder. He played very well. He made such an impression that I got in touch with him and the next year he came to play for Mutzig.' In years to come, Hild would prove to be a major influence on Wenger's path in football as he helped shape the Arsène who graces the Premier League today.

The influence of religion – namely Catholicism – in Alsace often had an impact on Wenger's football activities. As Arsène himself explains: 'The area I grew up in was steeped in religion. In those days you had to receive permission from the priest to play football because that meant missing vespers.' It would take more than this, though, to keep Arsène away from the pitch. As he has admitted, football has always been his primary focus.

Arsène's reputation as a player was growing steadily but his loyalties were divided between football and his studies. In this sense, he was far from a typical footballer. He was not throwing every ounce into the game because he had his education to consider too. This is not to say, however, that he lacked commitment. His childhood friends recall Arsène's tendency to shut himself away from all distractions in order to concentrate on achieving his aims. One claims that even now, if he phones Arsène, he has to make the conversation to bring Wenger out of his shell. The Frenchman was certainly willing to make the necessary sacrifices in life.

First, though, Wenger signed for Mulhouse, a semi-professional outfit with a proud, lengthy history. He would spend three years at the club as he furthered his football education. He was earning the equivalent of about £50 a week and he enjoyed the camaraderie within the dressing room. The team struggled, though, as they were constantly involved in relegation dogfights.

At the same time, Wenger was studying at Strasbourg University. He managed to combine the two different career paths and graduated with a degree in economics. This would prove very handy in years to come. Amongst all his other achievements, Arsène's appearances for the French university representative side have always gone rather unnoticed. The team travelled to various different destinations, with the highlight being a trip to Uruguay for a tournament in 1976. Injury kept Arsène on the sidelines throughout but the mere fact that he was included in the squad proves that Wenger was a young player with talent.

It was not an easy balance, however. Arsène did not live a typical student life as he found himself forever dividing his time between football and his studies. It was exhausting but it taught him to work efficiently under pressure. He had to make sacrifices in his social life as a result and certainly appeared reclusive due to the devotion with which he chased his goals.

Yet Xavier Rivoire refers to Wenger's days in the representative team in his biography on the Frenchman and includes a story from one of Arsène's friends and closest team-mates, Jean-Luc Arribart, which shows a different side of Wenger's character: 'What he did do was keep us all amused with a never-ending string of jokes. By the end of that trip, Arsène had almost taken on the role of assistant coach and team joker rolled into one. There was always another prank just around the corner.' It made Arsène a very popular member of the team and his colleagues certainly appreciated his selfless nature.

When Wenger decided that he needed a fresh challenge in football, he turned again to Max Hild, who was now coaching at AS Vauban. Hild's assurances were enough to convince Arsène to make the switch and Wenger looked forward to benefiting from more of his mentor's wisdom. It was an interesting decision because Vauban were a new club working their way up the leagues and it was certainly less prestigious. But, on the plus side, it meant that Arsène was closer to his home in Strasbourg. Vauban might not have hit the heights yet but there was plenty of promise for the future and Wenger wanted to be a part of it.

He did not really have a specialist position and this worked against him. Wenger had proven himself capable of performing solidly in defence or midfield and had never complained but at the same time he had not cemented his place in the team. The general consensus was that while Arsène could read the game well, his pace was limited and his distribution with his left foot was almost non-existent.

He did not stay long at Vauban but in his spell there he enjoyed the team's continued development. The club climbed further up the leagues and Wenger was proud to have been a part of the success. However, Hild had been the key factor in Arsène's move to Vauban and, when Strasbourg head-hunted the Vauban boss, things became more complicated. Hild, naturally, could not refuse the offer to join the set-up at Strasbourg but it left Wenger in a tricky situation. His motivation for staying at Vauban had suddenly disappeared.

As luck would have it, Strasbourg then came calling for Arsène. Hild had been appointed as reserve team manager but his expertise was often focused on the first team instead. The reserves needed a coach and Wenger's name was mentioned in conversations within the club, particularly by Hild, who knew Arsène was capable and hoped that the bond between the pair would help to tip the scales in favour of him accepting the proposition. Wenger became aware of the opportunity to work with the Strasbourg reserves and was left with the dilemma of whether to pursue his playing career or begin to explore other avenues within football.

Whilst he consulted others regarding the matter, his eventual move to Strasbourg was very much his own decision. After all, he was still a semi-professional footballer and he saw no obvious route into making the sport a full-time career as a player. Coaching, on the other hand, would give him a new challenge to tackle. Added to the persuasive case in favour of the change was Wenger's love for Strasbourg – his home city and his favourite French club as a child. How could anyone expect him to turn down this offer?

His responsibilities at Strasbourg were far from straightforward and, surprisingly, did not bring an end to his playing days. From time to time, Arsène would be called up to the senior squad and he was a regular in the reserves team, even though he was heavily involved in selecting and organising the troops. It gave him the chance to pit his tactical nous against other top bosses.

The meticulous manner in which he prepared for training and matches was an early indicator that he was cut out for the strains of management. No time was to be wasted idly. He might have shared few interests with the reserve team squad – mostly made up of youngsters – but he quickly earned everyone's respect for his unquestionable authority and professionalism. Rather than balancing football and his studies, Arsène now had football as his focal point yet this time he was combining playing with management. He still had little time to socialise or relax but he was happy.

In general, his time at the club was memorable and his achievements at Strasbourg gave him great pride. Hild used Wenger in the first team as a sweeper (or *libero*) and, despite scepticism from the press and a number of supporters, he had been an adequate replacement when senior players were unavailable. He just did not have the ability to hold down a regular place in the line-up.

Arsène was part of the Strasbourg side that won the French title in 1979, though his was very much a background role; he also tasted European football with the club when the team competed in the UEFA Cup. However, this foray into the elite of Europe was certainly a forgettable experience for Wenger. After missing the o-o home leg against Duisburg, Arsène was selected in central defence for the away leg in Germany and suffered the embarrassment of a 4-o defeat – a major lowlight in his brief playing career to date. Then-manager Gilbert Gress recalled it as 'an absolute disaster'. The glory of the competition, though, was not lost on Wenger and he vowed to return to the European stage again.

The biggest problem for Wenger was that he had never truly fitted in at Strasbourg. His personality and character were alien to some of his team-mates and, though he remained popular, he was noticeably different from the other players. One particular incident illustrates the cultural and intellectual contrasts within the Strasbourg squad. In Myles Palmer's biography of Wenger, the Frenchman explains: 'When you are a professional footballer, you spend your holidays at Club Med. Me, I bought an air ticket to London. A friend advised me to go to Cambridge where I hired a bike and enrolled on a three-week English course. My team-mates thought I was mad.'

When his playing opportunities at Strasbourg continued to be limited, Arsène began to think about his future in the game. The general consensus was that Wenger was not good enough to be a professional, despite his application and versatility. His love for the game remained as strong as ever but the Frenchman had grown frustrated with the lack of first team chances.

He was enjoying his work with the reserves at Strasbourg and the idea of coaching as a full-time job started to take shape in his mind. He is not alone in falling short as a player and then turning to management as an alternative. Sir Alex Ferguson and Jose Mourinho, amongst others, had modest playing careers yet have enjoyed great success as managers. Perhaps this is the secret. Wenger reluctantly agreed when speaking to *FourFourTwo*: 'You have a bit of frustration from your career and that can help the motivation. I did not have complete recognition as a player and maybe I felt that could be forgotten.'

For years, Arsène had expected to choose between running the family business and being a professional footballer. Yet Wenger opted for neither as he committed himself to a career as a manager. His role at Strasbourg had shown him that he was ready. He made his final appearance for the senior side in 1979 and then set off on the journey towards a management post.

It was an opportunity for Wenger to stay in football and, having whetted his appetite with the Strasbourg reserves, he went on to study for a manager's diploma in Paris. The process began at the Regional Centre for Popular Sports Education (CREPS) as he collected the necessary qualifications for a coaching career. His fellow applicants could only marvel at Arsène's intensity and the devotion with which he approached the courses. He came out of the programme with plenty of new ideas and an even keener interest in finding the perfect match preparation. The mental side of the game intrigued Wenger, as did the study of isometrics. As Rivoire explains: 'He was fascinated by isometrics – the system of strengthening muscles and tuning up the body, whilst not necessarily changing a player's bulk.'

As Wenger later revealed, he had also taken a keen interest in plyometrics – a form of jumping training designed to improve power and mobility. As he revealed: 'The idea is to increase the explosive strength of the muscles. It makes the players stronger, more powerful, more agile. It involves all kinds of jumping, one leg, two legs, long jump, high jump. I try to get as near the game as possible in terms of intensity. I try to work the players in match conditions.' Such techniques were relatively untried in football and would certainly be revolutionary when Wenger employed them later in England. His work with psychiatrists and nutritionists was also hugely beneficial in future years.

Armed with this qualification, Arsène continued to impress at Strasbourg, where he took a central role in the youth set-up as well as coaching and playing for the reserves. By this stage, Wenger already possessed many of the vital managerial attributes. His ability to stay calm under pressure would prove very useful and his knowledge of the game was excellent – both in terms of tactics and players. He had always been a football man and the day-to-day running of a club appealed to his work ethic. His language skills – Arsène spoke German, French and English fluently and in addition could converse in Spanish and Portuguese – also made him a man in demand and allowed him to appeal to all sections of the assembled media. With this in mind, it is hardly surprising that his profile grew and grew.

After impressing many with his knowledge and man-management skills at Strasbourg, he moved on to join the coaching set-up at AS Cannes, another French club. It was a sad moment for Wenger when he said farewell to Hild, bringing an end to his Strasbourg adventure, but he was excited for the future. The first-team coach at Cannes at the time was Jean-Marc Guillou, who Arsène knew well and respected, and the switch appealed greatly.

Guillou and then general manager Richard Conte worked hard to persuade Wenger to join Cannes and eventually got their man after lengthy negotiations one evening in Nice. As Conte reveals in Rivoire's book: 'I remember that meeting as being quite cordial and constructive. Even so, it wasn't until the small hours of the morning, when Arsène appeared to be tiring and on the point of walking away, that we finally struck a deal. In fact, it was the desire to work together shared by all three of us that eventually paved the way to reaching a compromise.' Conte also admitted: 'Of course, inevitably, no one left entirely satisfied. Arsène accepted less than he had hoped for, and we ended up paying more than we'd envisaged. They were still modest terms.'

The organisation paid Wenger a decent wage of around £300 per week and contributed towards his living expenses. It was hardly a lucrative deal but it offered Arsène a start in coaching. Money had not yet come flooding into football and so he had to settle for what he was given. As he admitted years later when he was on a handsome salary at Arsenal: 'I don't have any particular attachment to money as this aspect has truly never occupied me. What I'm paid now is a result of finding myself in the financial explosion of this sport. But if I didn't earn as much, I would still be the same coach.'

It did not take long for Wenger to make his mark. As a fledgling coach, he was eager to implement his ideas and led by example in the pursuit for perfection. He installed discipline in the ranks whilst encouraging pure dedication to the team cause. As coach, he would spend hours upon hours examining the opposition's flaws and was always fascinated by inventive fitness techniques that might give his players an advantage in matches. With his flawless planning, Wenger was years ahead of his time.

Under Arsène's command, the Cannes players gained a valuable education, especially the youngsters. Those who know him best tell stories of his relentless hard work in which his behaviour seems to border on obsessive. As Guillou told Rivoire, Wenger had little time for anything else in his life: 'He didn't have any furniture. He had only strictly what he needed. He didn't care about comfort. The only important item of furniture was a good bed. If you have to spend an amount of time looking for nice furniture, that's time you're using up when you could be studying videos of games.'

In hindsight, the players were probably forced to work too hard and the preparation may have been excessive. The big aim for the season had been to earn promotion to the French top flight but Cannes had fallen short. A good cup run was some consolation as the team reached the quarter-finals but it was still a disappointing campaign. Wenger's input, though, seemed to improve the standard of the squad.

It was only a matter of time before the promise that Arsène had shown attracted a string of suitors and this would prove to be Wenger's one and only season at Cannes. The Frenchman was destined to be a top flight manager and earn recognition for the vigour with which he approached his job.

The opportunity to test himself as a first team manager arrived in 1984 when Arsène was offered the chance to take charge at AS Nancy. Jean-Claude Cloet recommended Wenger to the club president as the man to push the club forward. There was not unanimous support for the appointment of Arsène but nonetheless he was unveiled as the new Nancy manager. It did not take long for the doubters to be silenced, though. Director of Football Aldo Platini, father of the great Michel, met with Wenger to agree a three-year contract.

It was a big challenge for a manager new to the job and his squad was not really of First Division quality. He was given limited money for transfers and so was forced to make the most of the resources at his disposal. Wenger relished the prospect of searching the transfer market for bargain signings as it allowed him to spend more hours watching videos of matches! His recruits had mixed fortunes. Some were inspired, others were hopeless. The familiar face of Arribart, Wenger's friend from the French university side, was one of the arrivals.

The experience of that first season at Nancy was one that Wenger would never forget: the stress he put himself under when preparing for a game, the pain he felt when things were not going well and the joy of victory. The student that Arribart had known was now a more serious, committed character. In Rivoire's biography of Wenger, there is a fascinating insight from Arribart, who explains: 'We lost one game at Lens, conceding three or four goals, and back then it really got to him. He'd get so worked up by disappointments like that. On the way back from that match, he actually had to stop the team bus to vomit a few hundred metres from the stadium. He threw up in a ditch. The defeat had literally turned his stomach and made him physically ill.'

Now that Arsène had total control of a team, he was able to test out all the theories and strategies that he had read about along the way. Wenger had his sights set on a lengthy managerial career and so his spell at Nancy represented a chance to develop a winning formula. It is unlikely that any other boss in the French league could compete with the amount of effort that Wenger put in behind the scenes, ensuring that he knew everything possible about any player at the club. Even during the winter break – when the season shuts down for an extended Christmas period in most European leagues – Arsène did not ease off.

His first season – in France 1984/85 – was very promising as Wenger defied the odds on the way to a 12th place finish. It was a fine achievement considering the lack of funding and the tinkering that Arsène had to do to field a decent line-up. Players often found themselves out of position yet rose to the challenge. It was a great effort but it perhaps obscured the fact that the squad was still rather threadbare and, when the talented members of the squad were snapped up by the top sides one-by-one, Wenger was left with few options. He no longer stood a chance of avoiding a relegation scrap.

The success of the first season proved to be a false dawn. With no money being invested, the team found life much tougher in the following two seasons. The mid-table finish of the 1984/85 season looked a better effort with every passing week as Nancy stuttered badly. When the club finished 18th in 1985/86, Wenger and his players faced a relegation playoff to decide their destiny. As fate would have it, Mulhouse were Nancy's opponents in this playoff. Fortunately for Arsène, his side prevailed by a slender 3-2 aggregate margin and retained their top flight status. However, it was simply a case of delaying the inevitable. Relegation was imminent.

In his third season, Wenger was again given no funds and, with a team that had been poor in 1985/86, he was unable to stop Nancy slipping into the relegation zone and dropping to the Second Division in 1986/87. It was a bitterly disappointing moment for the Frenchman but, in truth, there was little more that he or his players could have done to salvage the situation. He had reached the end of his patience at Nancy.

Such was Arsène's frustration, he had actually already begun the search for a new challenge. Behind the scenes, negotiations with AS Monaco had been taking place and Wenger had been very excited about the prospect of a move to such a famous club. Conte, who he knew well, had moved to Monaco and no doubt played a part in securing Arsène's signature. This deal, though, had to wait as Nancy refused to release Arsène from his contract and Monaco were reluctant to pay a compensation package.

So he was aware that the Monaco job was waiting for him as he fought to save Nancy from the Second Division. Nothing was reported at the time about the situation and Wenger kept his cards close to his chest. With some managers, perhaps there could have been an accusation that his off-field distractions had affected the team's chances of survival. But not with Arsène. Nobody could have worked harder to turn things around.

Although Nancy had finished 18th and 19th respectively in the past two campaigns, Arsène had established himself as a respected manager in France and the lowly league positions had not been blamed on him. Wenger's calmness and tactical knowledge made him popular with the players and coaching staff alike. When he brought an end to his tenure at the club, he had ensured that there would be offers for his services.

The move to Monaco soon became official and Arsène had to prepare for his new surroundings. He could have been forgiven for feeling rather nervous as he set off for the French principality as he was now in charge of a major club which expected success from the team. At Nancy, he had had the advantage of low expectations, meaning that he was generally safe from criticism. This would not be the case at Monaco.

His new squad was mostly comprised of French players but there were a few foreigners, including two Englishmen, Glenn Hoddle and Mark Hateley. Liberian striker George Weah was another new face during Arsène's first season and the team's attack certainly looked very strong. It appeared that Wenger had had some input behind the scenes in securing several signings. It was a fresh, exciting challenge and Wenger quickly set about putting his stamp on the side. He immediately realised that things were in place to compete for top honours domestically and in Europe. But there were other talented sides in the French top division, including Marseille, who would be Monaco's biggest rivals over the next few years. It was a duel that Arsène relished.

Despite being in the company of some top players, Wenger never adopted the celebrity lifestyle. He continued to drive to the training ground in his little Renault, which looked rather ridiculous in the car park amongst a fleet of top of the range models. But then he would not have it any other way. He was too busy with all his studious planning. His latest interest was in monitoring what his players were eating and he spoke regularly with Yann Rougier, the club dietician, finding out what he recommended and then instating it as compulsory for all of the squad before games.

All Arsène's grafting paid dividends as he immediately brought silverware to Monaco's trophy cabinet. In his first season at the club – 1987/88 – Wenger and his players captured the league title – one of Arsène's proudest days to date. It was Monaco's first championship triumph for six years and it made all the toil and the sleepless nights worth it when he had the trophy in his hands and could bask in the glory of the moment. The team had been well prepared and there appeared to be an excellent relationship between Arsène and his squad, based on mutual trust and respect. Wenger quickly grew attached to the feeling of winning.

After a couple of barren years, Monaco had reason to celebrate again at the end of the 1990/91 campaign as Wenger and his players lifted the French Cup. In the league, though, Marseille held the edge over Arsène's side and it became a big frustration for him as his side struggled to emulate the 1988 title triumph.

A strong run in the European Cup Winners' Cup led Wenger's team to the final in 1992, only to lose out to Germans Werder Bremen on a heart-breaking night in Lisbon. The day before the final, a terrible tragedy occurred in Corsica as two stands collapsed in a French Cup semi-final, killing 18 spectators. It left everyone in the Monaco camp in a daze, including Arsène. The Cup Winners' Cup final was allowed to go ahead but nobody had the stomach for a big occasion. Wenger's side had progressed to the French Cup final but it was cancelled out of respect to those who died.

As Rivoire points out, the more success that Wenger had in Monaco, the more he began to notice how detached the principality was from mainland France. A lot of French people disregarded the region altogether and, as a result, made their unhappiness known when Monaco started winning trophies.

There was a definite sense from some parts of the country that there was France and then there was Monaco – they were seen as two separate entities.

News of the Marseille match-fixing scandal broke in 1993. The Monaco boss had long suspected that there was something underhand in the manner with which Marseille were winning titles and found the issue hard to bear. Bernard Tapie, the Marseille president, was the man behind the scandal and it was his actions that had destroyed the credibility of the game in France. Automatically, Wenger cast his mind back over the league campaigns in which Monaco had lost out to Marseille and he thought about the extra trophies that his players might have won. The whole matter was an utter disgrace.

Arsène did not have enough concrete proof to make accusations against his biggest rivals and so sensibly bided his time before speaking on the topic.

When he did comment on the issue, the Monaco boss said: 'If Marseille have cheated, their exclusion is logical. Not severe enough. Marseille should be stripped of their French title if corruption is proved. If people like me don't defend football's credibility, we might as well pack up. We have to come down hard on cheats, whether they are called Marseille, Monaco, Paris or Nantes.'

As part of their punishment, Marseille were stripped of the French title but were allowed to keep the European Cup that they had won in 1993. Strangely, UEFA did not take the trophy away from Tapie's team amid all the controversy. Arsène and his players benefited from the ban on Marseille participating in the European Cup because, after Paris St. Germain turned down the offer, it would be Monaco who represented France in the competition and it gave Wenger a taste of the highest level of club football.

He took Monaco to the European Cup semi-finals that season. Arsène's side went out to eventual winners AC Milan but it spoke volumes for the Frenchman's ability to get the most out of his players. Having the likes of Weah and Jürgen Klinsmann was of course a massive boost but the success was based on teamwork. The attack was drilled in the simple system of pass and move but it was performed at pace. Arsène's desire to win whilst playing entertaining football was a part of his philosophy even in his days in the French league.

He would have loved to have won the league more than once but nonetheless Arsène had been successful at Monaco. He had certainly earned the trophies with all his graft. Reports suggest that his flat in Monaco was just as untidy and unfurnished as his home in Strasbourg and that he spent far more of his time in his office at the training ground than anywhere else. It was almost as though Wenger was afraid to slow down and relax for fear of not knowing how to unwind. Some worried that his excessive attention to detail and the long hours that he worked would have an effect on his health.

The season after the European Cup run, Arsène's tenure at the club came to an end. He had been approached by Bayern Munich but Monaco rejected the bid. This incident had further marred Wenger's already-strained relationship with the board. A ninth-place finish in 1994 was well below par and, after a disappointing start to the 1994/95 season, Arsène was dismissed. It was a bitter blow for him to step away from a club where he had enjoyed some magical moments but the board had spoken and Wenger had to go.

Nonetheless, he had come as far as he could in France and a fresh challenge beckoned. The bad ending to his Monaco adventure burned away inside him and he took some time to refocus on his future. His stature in the game had risen to such a level that he could now choose between the various offers that were landing on his desk.

A move to another top European league seemed the most natural option but Wenger has always been a hard man to second guess. Much to the surprise of everyone in football, Arsène instead accepted an offer to join Japanese J-League side Nagoya Grampus Eight. Toyota, owners of Grampus Eight, head hunted Arsène and made him an offer he could not refuse. After all the controversy and media frenzy over the Tapie saga, Japan appeared to be the perfect place for Wenger to return to doing what he does best – getting the most out of players and winning trophies.

Typically, Arsène took his time in weighing up his options before agreeing the deal with Grampus Eight. He spoke to contacts and thought long and hard about the move. The matter occupied him for months while those in Japan were left wondering whether he would become the new manager. When he signed the contract, Wenger was 100% sure that he was doing the right thing.

Yet the decision left pundits bemused. Wenger was now recognised as a top manager – so what was the attraction of the job in Nagoya? What did the J-League have to offer someone like Arsène? To many, it did not make sense. But Wenger never lost his focus. Nagoya Grampus Eight were hardly a top side in the J-

League, though, and there was a mountain of work ahead of the Frenchman if he was going to turn around the team's fortunes.

Wenger would earn 75 million yen (roughly £330,000) a year in his new job but it was not the money that interested him. The switch to Japan was all about experiencing another culture and broadening his knowledge of international football. It would give his CV a unique look. However, sightseeing was not high on his list of priorities upon arrival in Nagoya. Typically, Wenger immediately set about his work, familiarising himself with the teams and players that he would now be facing.

The J-League was fanatically supported in Japan and there would be no shortage of interest in the performance of the new Grampus Eight manager. He inherited a group of players who had been formed by English manager Gordon Milne. This squad had finished bottom of the J-League the previous season – resulting in the exit of Milne and the pursuit of Wenger. Arsène recalls this phase of his life with great satisfaction, telling the *Independent* (2 August 1998): 'People in France thought that I was mad to be fleeing the country but Japan gave me back my love for the game. The players gave me more effort than I could possibly have expected.'

As he looked ahead to the start of the season, Arsène brought in an assistant in whom he placed great trust – Boro Primorac. Primorac had been a witness in the Marseille match-fixing storm. Having given evidence against Tapie, Primorac was probably glad of the invitation given to him by Arsène. Between them, the duo spent hours analysing video footage of matches and discussing tactics. They were united by their passion for perfect football, and the pair would go on to work together for years.

Nothing could have fully prepared Wenger for the transitional phase of his move to Japan. It was a bit of a culture shock and he took time to settle. The first three months were especially testing as he suffered with loneliness and homesickness and began to wonder whether he had made the right decision. The task facing him at Grampus Eight was tricky enough without the added complications of adjusting to his new surroundings.

The Japanese language proved difficult to get to grips with, despite Arsène's linguistic background. It made giving instructions much harder and he could not organise his players as effectively as he would have liked. Other elements of the Japanese culture were also far from easy for Wenger to adopt – he had not expected such teething problems. But he persisted and overcame an anticlimactic start.

His difficulties in settling in Japan were only half the issue. The Wenger era began disastrously, with the team losing eight of their first ten matches and putting Arsène's performance under intense scrutiny. The new manager and his players had not gelled and morale was low. The results reflected the need for better communication at the club but the language barrier continued to hinder Wenger's plans.

As the Frenchman explains, he was faced with a lot of scepticism in Japan after the poor beginning to the season: 'They thought I knew nothing. I lost all my credibility in one month. Then I realised that the players wanted clear orders. Once they had the confidence to take the initiative, we improved dramatically.'

In fact, this is an understatement. The way that Arsène transformed the Grampus Eight squad was nothing short of sensational. The players had been written off as lacking in talent after the first few months and some predicted an abysmal league finish. Yet, slowly but surely, Wenger made his mark and converted his squad to his football philosophies. This had spectacular results as Grampus Eight soared up the table in Arsène's first season in Japanese football. He soon had a cult following.

Arsène turned to talismanic Yugoslav Dragan Stojkovic for inspiration. He was a truly special footballer. Wenger immediately realised that he had been handed a gift of a player and Stojkovic blossomed under Arsène's command. The new boss had signed a couple of French midfielders, Gerald Passi and Franck Durix, 30 and 29 respectively, to give the squad a European flavour. They could carry out Wenger's instructions more easily than the home-grown players and, as a result, held a crucial role in organising the team during matches.

After the woeful start, Grampus Eight won seven of their next nine matches as Wenger's style of play started to pay dividends. He had given his players the confidence to perform and had got his side into tremendous shape physically with his various approaches to dieting and conditioning. Nobody was questioning him now.

His players had huge respect for him and admired his ability to get the most out of every single one of them. The Japanese players were amazed at the detail of Arsène's preparation and the amount of time he spent helping members of the squad on an individual basis. He always knew the best way to lift a player and became a father figure of sorts.

Arsène was in the thick of the action on the touchline and his enthusiasm occasionally boiled over. In rather uncharacteristic fashion, he received a two-match ban after he was adjudged to have harassed an assistant referee. Wenger was a little repentant when addressing the media post match: 'I was so absorbed that I didn't notice that I got out of the technical area. But it was a small incident. It is the third time I have been sent off as a manager.'

His blend of home-grown and European talent took the club to three notable successes during his 20 months in charge. First, Arsène took the club to unexpected heights during the 1995 season, culminating in a second place finish in the J-League table. It was a mightily impressive effort but Wenger wanted silverware. He did not have to wait long.

After a thumping 5-1 win against Kashima Antlers in the Emperor's Cup semi-final, Grampus Eight advanced to face Hiroshima in the showpiece final on 1 January 1996. Beating Kashima, whose side included Brazilian World Cup winners Leonardo and Jorginho, was superb but Arsène's side went one better. In front of a large crowd, Wenger watched his players win 3-0 against Hiroshima and lift the trophy. The fans went wild and Arsène knew that by collecting the club's first ever piece of silverware, he would never be forgotten in Nagoya. Few could have predicted such success after the disastrous start to Wenger's time in Japan.

The third proud achievement for Arsène came when Grampus Eight again defeated Kashima – this time to win the Japanese Super Cup. These trophies really raised the spirits of the club's supporters, who had been so used to failure before Wenger took charge. He was a legend in their eyes.

It is worth remembering that though Japan have since appeared at World Cup competitions, the country was not a strong football nation when Arsène arrived. His influence made a big impression and played no small part in Japan's presence at the 1998, 2002 (as co-hosts) and 2006 World Cups. He seemed to have transferred his love for the game to the Japanese population. Certainly, it is hard to imagine the frenzied mood that swept the nation in 2002 without Arsène's involvement in the J-League.

His progress attracted plenty of suitors. Both Arsenal and Tottenham were rumoured to be interested in acquiring the Frenchman's services as well as Arsène's old club Strasbourg. However, for Wenger, it was the impact of Gunners vice-chairman David Dein that sealed the decision. There was an instant connection between the pair and Dein has since admitted: 'I was convinced Arsène would become our manager from the first day I met him. He was not only charming and highly intelligent, but clearly able to adapt as well.' Dein and Wenger would go on to form a strong partnership and in more recent times Dein told BBC Radio: 'I call Arsène Wenger the miracle worker because he has achieved miracles. He has got a job for life, simple as that.'

Arsène agreed an amicable split with Grampus Eight and brought down the curtain on an eventful and successful period of his life, promising to return at some stage in the future. The club released Wenger four months before the end of his deal and allowed him to begin his customary in-depth research on the Arsenal players he was set to link up with. After some frustrating delays, the deal was done in September 1996.

The Gunners had won the race for Wenger and he would begin a new phase of his life in North London with huge expectations on his shoulders and plenty of sceptical fans to win over. But Arsène's experiences in Japan had ensured that he was now prepared for any challenge that he faced.

ARRIVING AT ARSENAL

With his time in Japan now behind him, Wenger turned his attention to the task ahead of him at Arsenal, where he would not have the luxury of a preseason with his new squad since the league season was already underway. He had not been short of offers when he decided to end his spell at Nagoya Grampus Eight but managing the Gunners was an opportunity that was too good to turn down. Arsène admired English football and the success of the Premiership had raised the profile of the game in England. For the Frenchman, it seemed the logical next step in his managerial career.

However, despite the success that he had achieved with Nagoya, Arsène was an unknown quantity for most in English football and, as he would discover, the Arsenal fans had expected a bigger name to be appointed as the new boss. Compared to others who had been linked with the vacancy at

Highbury, Wenger had little experience of working in Europe and had only a few honours to his name.

One man who was well aware of Wenger's ability was Glenn Hoddle. Hoddle, who played under Arsène at Monaco, was the England manager at the time and had offered his former boss a role in his backroom staff. The *Daily Mirror* reported on 8 August 1996 that Hoddle had approached Arsène while he was managing Nagoya Grampus Eight and Wenger himself told the newspaper: 'I was contacted directly by Glenn. But I have to think it over.' Ultimately, he would turn down the opportunity to link up with Hoddle again but it was an indication that Arsène was held in high regard by those who knew him well. It was just a case of winning over those who had never heard of him!

When Bruce Rioch resigned as Arsenal manager early in the new English season, the Gunners board reportedly looked at bringing in Dutch legend Johan Cruyff to manage the team. He was the type of big name that supporters were anticipating and it was hoped that he could succeed where Rioch had failed. When Cruyff declared that he was not interested in the position, it was then decided that Wenger was the ideal replacement for Rioch. But Arsenal fans were bemused by the appointment. It was a difficult atmosphere for the Frenchman to enter. Club chairman Peter Hill-Wood seemed confident enough about Wenger's pedigree and told the *Daily Mirror*: 'If he's good enough for Glenn Hoddle, he's good enough for us. I'm not remotely concerned about the rantings of people who set out to criticise us for criticism's sake.'

Rumours had spread about Arsène's pending arrival prior to his official appointment and Hill-Wood had not helped matters with an embarrassing blunder in front of the media. Hill-Wood refused to reveal the identity of the new manager but, when asked to whom he had promised this secrecy, the chairman announced: 'To Arsène Wenger and his club.' Stunned faces absorbed the information and Hill-Wood was left red-faced. He had confirmed Wenger as Rioch's replacement.

There was certainly some scepticism over selecting a foreign manager. Supporters questioned why Wenger was preferred to an Englishman and whether he would be able to bridge the culture gap. At the time, there had not been a great influx of overseas coaches and managers and this was an additional pressure that Arsène faced when he accepted the job. There were plenty of people willing him to fail. Bookmakers William Hill certainly were not showing much faith in Wenger. The new Gunners boss received odds of 5-1 to be out of his job before the end of the campaign.

One of those who spoke favourably of Wenger was fellow Frenchman David Ginola, then of Newcastle. He insisted that the Gunners would reap the benefits of their new manager's wisdom and saw no problem with the club choosing a foreigner for the position: 'He is a great guy and, perhaps more importantly, he has a very good feel for football. His appointment should give everyone at Highbury a boost. It's important to bring some foreign coaches to England. Overseas players have been successful and there's no reason why coaches should be any different.' It was a very positive endorsement.

Arsène was not popular with everyone, however. German striker Jürgen Klinsmann, who had played for Wenger at Monaco, had grown frustrated by the Frenchman's approach.

Klinsmann, so prolific when he moved to Tottenham, scored just ten goals in thirty games during his second and final season at the French club. The striker claimed: 'I did not enjoy my time there as much as I had hoped. I found the tactics so frustrating. They were negative and defensive. I couldn't be expected to battle everywhere and still have the freshness to score goals.' According to the *Sunday Mirror*, a friend of Klinsmann admitted: 'He tried very hard to get Wenger to change the system so he could have more support up front. But Wenger refused.' In fairness, the German is one of the few players who has a bad word to say about Arsène's tactics.

Wenger, being a student of the game, was already aware of Arsenal's history and the expectations of the club when he arrived in England. He was familiar with the players and had made a number of trips to see games at Highbury. Arsenal fans might not have heard much about Wenger, but the Frenchman knew all about them and their club. The doubters would soon realise that the new boss meant business and was ready to take the Gunners back to the glory days. Still, no one could have guessed that he would still be in charge 18 years later.

Ironically, Arsène had not always been full of praise for English football. Back in his Monaco days, he had criticised the methods of Premiership managers, telling the media: 'That [England] is where training is the most backward, the least evolved. The teams play every three days and between matches the coach chooses to rest his lads rather than incite them to work.' It was safe to say that Arsène would not be letting his players shirk their responsibilities on the training ground.

Manchester United's domination of the Premiership had

raised the bar in English football and Wenger inherited an Arsenal squad that was not in the habit of winning silverware in recent years. There were plenty of experienced figures who had enjoyed success at the club but the past few years had been barren for the Gunners.

Arsène had little time to shape the team for the 1996/97 season but made some crucial decisions that would affect the team's future. None could be seen to be more important than his role in bringing Patrick Vieira to Highbury – allegedly Arsène was behind the transfer deal, even though he had not begun his tenure as manager. The transfers of Vieira and fellow Frenchman Remi Garde were rushed through before the UEFA deadline, seemingly at Wenger's request. Vieira would go on to make the fee of around £3.5 million look like one of the bargains of the decade.

It was hard not to feel sorry for Rioch, Arsène's predecessor. He had inherited an average squad following the break-up of George Graham's team at the end of the 1994/95 campaign and it was unrealistic to expect him to restore the side to winning ways immediately. Also, he had reportedly been limited in terms of his influence over transfers and had not always been allowed to negotiate deals. It was an impossible position for Rioch.

But Arsène would not stand for anything short of total control. As he explained: 'For me the basics of the job was to have the freedom to run the club as I chose – to make the important decisions about what was to happen inside the club, to buy the players, to sell them and decide on things such as contracts and even a new training ground. It would have been very difficult for me to accept anything different.'

There was so much to do in such little time when Wenger

signed his contract at Highbury. Firstly, he needed to find somewhere to live. Initially, he stayed in a hotel before finding somewhere more permanent. Travelling in London proved a massive shock for him and he even admitted taking the tube to cut time off his journey. As he explained, it was a crazy introduction to life in England: 'I have to look if I can find new players. I have to adapt to a new environment. I have to look if I can find somewhere to live. I have to adjust to the media and TV here. I have no time for anything else.'

Wenger quickly clamped down on some of the excesses at the club. Midfielder Paul Merson had admitted his battle with alcohol prior to Arsène's arrival in London and it was a situation that Wenger tackled head-on, making it clear that nights of heavy drinking would not be tolerated.

Such nights had become a feature of life at many top flight clubs and it took Wenger by surprise in the early weeks. After the dedicated approach of his players at Nagoya, the culture at Arsenal could not have been more different. He inherited a group of players with a reputation for enjoying the excesses in life. Merson, Tony Adams and Ray Parlour, to name just three, had landed themselves in trouble with the law in the previous few years; alcohol was at the root of most of the problems.

Arsène did not take long to understand the gravity of the situation. The list of arrests and charges did not make pretty reading for the new boss but at least he was clear about what he was facing. It was a mess and it was affecting the team's performances. With the talent in the squad, the Gunners should have been challenging Manchester United at the top. Yet, rather than being disciplined internally, the Arsenal players had seemingly received lenient treatment from the board. As a result, the problems continued to mount. Other clubs had similar problems but Wenger's players appeared to be in more danger than most.

The new boss quickly made his mark by outlawing such behaviour. Immediately, Wenger was faced with the fallout from Merson's split with his wife and the Frenchman reacted sympathetically, though he made it clear that the midfielder had to continue to win his fight against addictions if he hoped to be offered a new contract at the club. Arsène told the media: 'I think Paul was concerned about the situation. We have confidence in Paul to solve his personal problems, but if the club can help then we will do it. He's always been at Arsenal and I don't think he would like to leave.'

In Wenger's eyes, heavy drinking was a very serious matter. Growing up around La Croix d'Or – his parents' restaurant-cum-bar – he had frequently watched the antics of customers who drank themselves into a bad state and it had taught him valuable lessons. He knew how lives could be torn apart by alcohol and his philosophy was simple: football and alcohol should not be mixed. He conveyed this message to his stunned squad who realised that things were about to change around Highbury.

The childhood experiences at his parents' bar served Arsène well. As Jasper Rees remarked in his biography of Wenger, *The Making of a Legend*: 'It must have been difficult for a non-drinker to spend so much time in a place like this which revolves around beer. If your parents work in a bar every night, it's difficult to avoid the sight of *demis* being downed, and to avoid downing them yourself. It demands a strong personal discipline to resist.' This would have seemed a major sacrifice for most yet the Frenchman now expected his Arsenal players to follow his example.

The past eighteen months had been a nightmare at Highbury. Since the acrimonious departure of former boss George Graham – in a bribery allegation storm – there had been few highlights to dwell on. Wenger had been entrusted with the task of restoring the club to former glories and chairman Hill-Wood was convinced of Arsène's quality. He told the media: 'This signals a new era for us. I believe Arsène Wenger is going to be a great success and drag football in this country into the twentieth century. We need to catch up with the continentals and we think Arsène is the man to help us.'

But major changes would not happen overnight. Wenger wanted to assess the players currently at his disposal before he explored the transfer market. He had his own ideas about the way in which Arsenal would line-up, based on all the knowledge he had gained in France and Japan, and he was certain that his football philosophies would be suited to the English league.

The Frenchman made a positive impression in his early encounters with the press, showing he was shrewd and intelligent as well as funny on occasion. It was impossible to miss the steely resolve that he possessed and the confidence with which he spoke. Arsène's English course in Cambridge had been money well spent! It was proving very useful. However, Wenger was well aware that a few bad results would see the media immediately breathing down his neck.

His job was made no easier by the sudden departure of Stewart Houston, who Wenger had planned to name as his assistant. Houston accepted the manager's job as QPR, much to Arsène's surprise as the Frenchman recalled in the *Daily Mirror*: 'If he had stayed, Stewart would have been my No.2. The day before the story came out, I spoke to him on the phone and he never mentioned anything about it. Maybe it was a difficult position, but he didn't tell me and I was surprised to hear he had gone.' So Arsène turned to Pat Rice, who had been recommended to him as 'an honest guy who loves the club', to take on the role of assistant manager. Wenger has since reflected: 'Pat helped me such a lot. I would not have lasted without him. A good assistant is vital, and Pat was probably born in a red shirt with white sleeves.' Rice and other backroom staff such as Damien Comolli played key roles in helping Arsène establish himself at Highbury.

At first, the Frenchman just observed. He did not try to impose himself on the squad immediately. Rice took temporary charge while Arsène learned more and more about the strengths and weaknesses of his players. The Frenchman travelled with the team for the second leg of the UEFA Cup tie with Borussia Monchengladbach – coincidentally the club which a young Arsène had so admired. The Gunners were unable to overturn a 3-2 first leg defeat but winning the Premiership was of course the main objective.

As well as improving the team's form, Wenger focused on giving his squad guidelines to follow regarding their behaviour. It all came as a culture shock for some of the players who found Arsène's techniques and philosophies very unusual. In his autobiography *Safe Hands*, David Seaman explains that the team was given a detailed message. The former Arsenal and

England goalkeeper writes: 'Arsène made it clear that there would be total change straight away. There was no messing about. He told us, "This is how I run training and this is how I expect you to eat and look after yourselves." He said we could not carry on eating what we had been used to stuffing down ourselves, as it was no good for us as professional athletes.'

The players, though, were initially reluctant to adopt the new ideas. Wenger suggested an afternoon training session to complement the morning slot – but this notion was dismissed. The severe restrictions on diets brought more complaints. Senior players found Arsène's techniques difficult to understand and there was some friction in the first few weeks. Seaman, Adams and Lee Dixon, for instance, had been educated to play in the George Graham style and these fresh ideas clashed with much of what they were accustomed to. Adams, in particular, voiced his disapproval of Wenger's methods and remained sceptical over some of his foreign signings. There were lengthy discussions between Arsène and his captain, during which the Frenchman listened carefully to Adams' comments and took his complaints on board.

There were certain points, though, on which Wenger would not compromise. For instance, the pre-match meal at Highbury had to be drastically altered. Chips, burgers and other excesses were banned: 'It's silly to work hard the whole week and then spoil it by not preparing properly just before the game. As a coach you can influence the diet of your players. You can point out what is wrong. Some are wrong because they are not strong enough to fight temptation and some are wrong because they do not know.'

Not only was the make up of the meal changed to chicken, fish, mashed potato and vegetables but eating times were also modified, meaning that the players now ate at around 11 o'clock in the morning on match days.

Prior to Wenger's first league match in charge away at Blackburn, the Frenchman stunned his players further by arranging an aerobics session in the hotel ballroom as a part of the preparation. One can only imagine the reaction of Merson, Adams, Ian Wright and co. when the news spread. This was not their idea of pre-match build-up but they went along with their manager's orders and actually found plenty of merit in Wenger's approach. As Wright explains, he could hardly believe his ears: 'We were all thinking, "What the f*** is going on here?" and it took some time to get used to it because you are talking about a complete left-turn when you have been used to straight lines.'

The fact that the Frenchman's methods went on to prove so successful won over most of the squad. The players learned not to doubt their manager. Dixon recalls one occasion when he and Adams approached Arsène during one pre-season and revealed their concerns that the team was not fit enough. The full-back reveals: 'Our feeling was that we had not done enough running. The manager calmly explained to us that it was all scientific and that the team would be fine. Have faith, he said. Sure enough, 10 days later we flew out of the traps full of energy and raring to go. That man knows what he's talking about.'

Arsène was bringing innovative techniques to the team that no other English club possessed. He assembled a team of backroom staff who focused on the fitness side of training and kept a close eye on the players' diets. Wenger emphasised the importance of sleep and relaxation in a player's life and sought to ensure that time away from football was used as effectively as the hours on the training pitch. Seaman admits in his autobiography that the fresh regime paid dividends as the team felt stronger in the closing minutes of games. Less alcohol and a carefully regulated diet had given the Gunners an edge over their league rivals.

Another interesting concept that the Frenchman introduced was the use of supplements. As an Arsenal insider put it: 'There were a few sceptics at the outset but it did seem that the tablets and drinks had an effect. Before long all the players talked about feeling the benefit.'

Wenger made some initial judgements on the state of his squad, telling the media: 'We will buy new players, but maybe not just now. Maybe it will be in the spring. It depends how our results are going and what players become available. I'm happy with the players I have inherited. They have a strong collective mentality. But I need more of them.' Wenger also added a spookily accurate warning about the state of English football: 'The basic education of young players in France is better. The Football Association here [in England] have to look at the system of producing young players.'

Wenger was unbeaten in his first four matches but fell to a 1-0 defeat away to Manchester United. A disappointing own goal from Nigel Winterburn, after a mistake by Seaman, proved to be the difference between the two sides. With his detailed analysis of players, it was taking time for Arsène to learn all about his squad. He still had major decisions to make regarding his transfer policies. The results had been good though and the Gunners sat third despite the loss at Old Trafford.

He got his first taste of a North London derby as the Gunners beat Tottenham 3-1. The passion of the match appealed to Wenger and he quickly realised that he would relish such a fixture. Little did he know at this stage just how good a record he would enjoy against his nearby neighbours. The pace of the game in England also intrigued the Frenchman and convinced him that the Premiership was the place for him to implement his attacking plans. Quick one touch passing would be perfect for exploiting opposition sides.

A 2-1 win over Newcastle at St. James' Park allowed the Gunners to replace the Magpies at the top of the table. Adams was dismissed in the first half but Wenger's side rallied and goals from Dixon and Wright sealed the victory. Such a spirited display on their travels was a real sign of progress for Arsène and the team was taking shape sooner than he could have imagined.

December, though, proved a difficult month for Wenger's team. A victory over Southampton was followed by a blip – a run of matches where Arsenal were well below par. A home draw with Derby maintained the Gunners' breathing space at the top of the table but two weeks later Arsène's side stumbled to a 2-1 defeat away to Nottingham Forest. With Vieira and Adams suspended, the Gunners were heavily weakened and overpowered by a determined Forest team. Wright was harshly sent off with the score at 1-1 and the home side went on to seal the victory. A 0-0 draw with Sheffield Wednesday brought more disappointment as Manchester United ominously began to find their best form.

Vieira was proving a dominant force in midfield and Dennis

Bergkamp and Wright had developed a good understanding in attack yet the Gunners failed to put together good team performances. A 2-2 draw with Aston Villa on 28 December illustrated this point as Wenger's side played well, scored a fine goal involving Vieira, Bergkamp and lastly Wright but could not take the three points.

With every match, Arsène was learning more about the reinforcements that he would require to make a stronger challenge during the next season. The defence was aging but the experience of Adams, Dixon and co. was invaluable. It was across the midfield that Wenger noticed some deficiencies as the players failed to keep possession consistently enough and did not move the ball as quickly as the Frenchman expected. Arsène's favoured style of play required slick, speedy passing and intelligent movement off the ball. Fortunately, Wenger already spoke good English when he arrived in London and, despite having an accent that was hard to understand at times, he was able to get his ideas across to the players without too much difficulty.

His new squad were still coming to terms with Wenger's demands but there was no doubt that they respected Arsène. For many, he had brought the enjoyment back into their football. Wright, who was benefiting from Wenger's wisdom in a big way, admitted in the *Daily Mirror*: 'When he first arrived, we didn't know too much about him and one or two of the boys were asking "Who is this French guy?" But Arsène has taught me so much about myself as a player, and how to look after myself off the pitch, that I feel like he's already added two or three years to my shelf life.'

With his calm demeanour and deep thinking, Wenger was turning the club's fortunes around. He had developed a good bond with his players and knew how to get the best out of each of them. Without yelling at his squad or publicly criticising members of the first team, he established control of the set-up and the results were starting to speak for themselves. Observing his calm approach, it was easy to see why Wenger earned the nickname 'The Professor'.

Arsenal collected nine points out of a possible twelve in the Premiership in January. A solid 2-0 win over Middlesbrough boosted the team's confidence and Wenger was quick to praise his players. Wright and Bergkamp got on the scoresheet. A 1-0 loss away to Sunderland saw Bergkamp sent off and Adams score an own goal – hardly the most memorable of games for Arsène. Two wins in their next two games, though, reminded any doubters that the Gunners were serious about challenging for the title. The 3-1 home victory over Everton was Adams' 500th appearance for the club and Wenger was thrilled with the way his side played in the second half as they scored three quality goals, with Bergkamp, Vieira and Merson finding the net. Bergkamp was suspended for the trip to face West Ham but Merson took centre stage for the second consecutive match while Parlour and Wright scored the goals in a 2-1 win.

February, though, hindered the Gunners' pursuit of the Premiership trophy. Goalless draws on their travels against George Graham's Leeds and Tottenham were frustrating for Wenger but he remained confident of the team's title chances. Despite missing the chance to go top of the table in the league stalemate with Tottenham, he told the media: 'Mathematically, we are in a good position. We are there with twelve games to go. We play seven at home, five away. So it's not so bad.' He found losing to Leeds in the FA Cup fourth round a bigger blow.

Unfortunately for Arsène, the two league draws were followed by consecutive home defeats to title rivals Manchester United and neighbours Wimbledon. The loss to United was particularly disappointing for Wenger because he had hoped that Highbury would become a fortress; a place that opposition sides feared. Yet United waltzed in and outplayed the Gunners. Late on, Wright and United goalkeeper Peter Schmeichel were involved in an ugly confrontation after the striker had lunged in wildly on the Danish stopper. The row escalated as Wright accused Schmeichel of a racial insult and the police became involved.

Arsène tried to defend his striker in front of the press: 'Do you want me to give him sleeping pills? Ian is 33 now. You cannot expect me to change his temperament. I think he is goaded. When you are as efficient as he is at scoring goals, defenders pull your shirt, use their elbows, do everything.' This was one of many times that Arsène jumped to the defence of his players when some felt he should have been dishing out punishments.

The Gunners' performance against Wimbledon was worse still, even if Arsène was without several first team players, and Vinnie Jones smashed in the winner for the visitors. Wenger made it clear after the game that Arsenal would miss out on European football altogether unless they sorted themselves out. The Gunners boss also complained that it was unfair that some teams had longer to prepare for matches than others. In truth, though, Arsenal had simply had a few off days.

An improved league record in March cheered Arsène. 2-0 wins

over Everton and Nottingham Forest were welcome for the six points and the two clean sheets. Another 2-0 victory followed away to Southampton as Stephen Hughes scored his first Premiership goal and Paul Shaw added the second. The month ended with a 2-1 defeat at home to Liverpool. The visitors' second goal defied belief as referee Gerald Ashby awarded a penalty that Seaman and Robbie Fowler were equally astonished by. Fowler even tried to tell the official that it should not be a spot-kick. The striker duly missed the penalty but Jason McAteer scored from the rebound.

Wenger's side managed to achieve an unbeaten league record in April with two wins and two draws. An excellent 3-0 victory away to Chelsea reminded everyone of just how exciting Arsenal could be on their day. Bergkamp produced a world-class performance, creating two goals and scoring the third. The three points also gave Gunners fans the bragging rights over their neighbours again. While United seemed on course to win the Premiership, the Gunners had not given up hope yet. Wenger's players kept up the pressure with a win over Leicester a week later through goals from Adams and David Platt but Bergkamp was yet again the star man.

Amidst all the action, Wenger and Manchester United boss Alex Ferguson launched into a bitter row. Ferguson, employing his usual title run-in mind games, had called for an extension to the Premiership season owing to his team's Champions League commitments but Arsène disagreed, saying: 'If you extend the season it's ridiculous because it will take away all the credibility of the league and people will just laugh at you.'

So accustomed to dominating such mind games, especially

those with Kevin Keegan the previous season, Ferguson was enraged and retorted: 'He (Wenger) has had a go at us a few times this season – he must have a problem with us. He has no experience of English football – he's come from Japan – and now he is telling everyone how to organise our football. Unless you have been in the situation and had the experience, then he should keep his mouth shut – firmly shut.'

It did not end there as Wenger went back for another dig at United. The Frenchman suggested that Ferguson should stop looking for excuses and concentrate on the run-in: 'I have the right to defend my opinion and I still say the best team will win the league because an endurance test is also about motivation, quality and not making stupid mistakes in important games. All those things together are the quality test. And that is the same in every sport.'

It was hardly a warm welcome but this was just the beginning of the explosive Wenger-Ferguson rivalry. The Scot had finally met his match in Arsène, who refused to be intimidated by his counterpart. Even in these early moments, the Frenchman did not take a backward step and claimed: 'He [Ferguson] doesn't bother me. Perhaps the most sensitive can be affected. That is not to say that I am insensitive but that I have more important things to be concerned about other than words or mind games before a match. Alex is an excellent manager but I understand his passion and if I get under his skin then that is good.'

Wenger was very different from anyone Ferguson had faced before. He had a serene calm that would not be shattered by rows or mind games and yet his team was clearly as focused and driven as Ferguson's side. At the moment, the Gunners were not ready to push United all the way but it was only a matter of time before the man behind the glasses had the champions in his sights.

Draws against Blackburn and Coventry killed off any hope of catching Manchester United at the top. They were the types of games that Arsenal would have to start winning if the Gunners were to have any chance of lifting the Premiership trophy in future years. The Blackburn game was especially disappointing because it meant more dropped points at Highbury.

Going into the final few matches, Arsène's side had clinched a place in the UEFA Cup for next season but had their sights set on qualifying for the Champions League by finishing in second place. Wenger told the media: 'Naturally I'm delighted and we're looking forward to Europe next season. However, our campaign is not yet over. I won't rest because I've set my sights on [the] Champions Cup.' Left-back Winterburn added: 'It's nice that one hurdle has been overcome but we really want bigger fish. We want to finish second and that means we must beat Newcastle in our final home game.'

But it was not to be. The Gunners suffered a 1-0 defeat at home to Newcastle that proved extremely costly for their Champions League hopes. A 3-1 win away to Derby courtesy of Wright (2) and Bergkamp brought the league fixtures to an end. But it would be the Magpies who would take the second qualifying spot for the Champions League and this setback came as a great disappointment to Arsène. The win at Derby allowed the squad to end on a high note but Wenger had plenty to ponder during the close season.

So Manchester United were crowned as champions, seven points ahead of the rest of the pack, but with the lowest points total for fifteen years. Then Newcastle, Arsenal and Liverpool ended on the same number of points. The trio finished in that order on goal difference, meaning that Newcastle, not Arsenal, clinched the second qualifying spot for the Champions League. Incredibly, the Magpies' goal difference was just three goals better than Arsenal's and it left everyone at Highbury ruing a collection of missed chances. The Gunners would have to make do with playing in the UEFA Cup. A special mention should also go to relegated Middlesbrough who suffered one of the cruellest Premiership seasons in history. Boro were deducted three points for failing to field a team against Blackburn due to injuries – three points that would have kept them out of the relegation zone – and were losing finalists in both the FA Cup and League Cup.

Finishing third was not the way that Wenger had envisioned ending his first season in English football, especially as he felt that Manchester United could have been caught at the top. Arsène reflected in the closing moments of the season that the Gunners and the other contenders had handed the trophy to Ferguson's side on a silver platter. He told the press: 'It's been said that United have not won the league but that Liverpool, Newcastle and ourselves have lost it. And I would agree with that. I am surprised how close we have come but, like the other teams challenging for runners-up, we have not been consistent enough.'

The Frenchman added in early May: 'When I consider the achievements of my first year in English football, perhaps the biggest is that I've already survived four or five months longer than many people imagined. The biggest bet when I arrived was that I wouldn't last beyond Christmas.' Instead, Wenger had proved that foreign coaches could be successful in England and, in the process, had made life easier for overseas bosses to move to the Premiership in future years.

Losing key matches against their rivals was an area Arsène was determined to address. The Gunners had lost home and away to United and Liverpool and had also lost at home to Newcastle. This was not good enough. Yet he was pleased with the progress that the squad had made since he had taken over in September. There was plenty of potential which, combined with a few important signings, would carry Arsenal into the next few seasons.

It would be a critical summer for Wenger as he plotted ways to strengthen the squad. Up front, Wright had enjoyed a prolific season but Arsène wanted more goals from other positions. The wide players needed to be getting into double figures for their goal tallies and even Bergkamp had room to improve his finishing. Relying too heavily on Wright meant that when the striker had an off day, the Gunners struggled to find a plan B. The hope was that youngster Nicolas Anelka, signed for £500,000 in February, would develop into a quality forward.

The Gunners supporters, who had made their displeasure clear when Wenger was appointed as manager, had since warmed to their French boss and were enjoying his style of football. Certainly, there was no longer anyone asking 'Arsène who?'

DOING THE DOUBLE AND LIVING IN THE SHADOW OF THE TREBLE WINNERS

With his first campaign at Highbury under his belt, Arsène focused on continuing his plans for the squad. He liked what he had seen so far but there were also areas that concerned him. These areas would need to be addressed during the close season as he hoped to better the club's third place finish and really challenge the champions, Manchester United. It would be a busy time for Wenger. On top of his work at Arsenal, he had become a father for the first time and now had a daughter, Lea, who was just months old.

Arsène used the summer transfer market to strengthen the team. Incredibly, though, he did so without spending huge sums of money. Wenger turned to Dutchman Marc Overmars and Frenchman Emmanuel Petit in deals worth £5.5 million and £3.5 million, respectively. Overmars in particular would offer a good supply line to the strikers with his pace and ability to cut inside. Wright, for one, would benefit from improved wing play.

As Wenger explained to the media: 'We wanted players who are used to winning, used to the pressure in the big clubs, and who are winner-types. I think Emmanuel Petit and Marc Overmars have proved before that they are used to being in clubs where you have to win, and that's very important to us. They play in positions where we wanted to sign some players.' The Gunners boss also bought Portuguese attacker Luis Boa Morte, German Alberto Mendez and French defender Gilles Grimandi.

Both Petit and Grimandi had played in defence during their careers and when the transfers were announced, some felt saddened that Wenger appeared to be replacing the famous Arsenal back four that had enjoyed such a great run together. But Arsène, having worked with both at Monaco, knew that the duo were very versatile and saw Petit, in particular, as a man capable of stepping into a midfield role for the club.

While Petit was relatively unknown, Overmars was more of a household name and had been a star for Ajax. Wenger had identified him as the man to break through stubborn defences home and away – something his team had failed to do at times in 1996/97. Arsène referred to the Dutchman as 'a winger-type who can go into the space' and 'a good dribbler' but it was Overmars' pace that appeared most impressive and guaranteed a season of hard graft for full-backs nationwide.

However, in order to fund the arrivals of players such as Overmars, Wenger had to raise some money by selling a few members of his squad. Most notably, midfielder Merson made a surprise exit from the club. He had recovered impressively under Arsène's management and had overcome his problems with alcohol, drugs and gambling. Yet the books had to be balanced and, in truth, Merson was not really the type of player that Wenger had in mind for the new look side. After little interest from Premiership suitors, First Division Middlesbrough stepped forward and met the asking price of around £5 million. It was a sad day for Merson who had enjoyed plenty of ups to go with the downs during his time at Highbury. When in the right frame of mind, his dribbling was top class and his bubbly character would be missed around the club.

Not for the last time, Wenger was asked about his transfer policy and the absence of young English talent. He did not shirk the issue and gave a frank, honest response, telling the press: 'We had no choice, in this age category, but to go abroad. The best players between twenty and twenty-eight are at Manchester United, Newcastle and Liverpool. We are ambitious. When you are ambitious you always want the best quality. If we had equal quality in England we wouldn't go abroad. If the spirit of the players is right and the ambition is right, then you don't say, "I won't take these players because they're not English."' Why should he sign expensive English players when he could find better, cheaper transfer targets abroad?

Spirits were high in the Arsenal dressing room as everyone looked forward to the start of a new campaign. The difference this year would be that Wenger had enjoyed the benefit of a pre-season with his squad and had been able to complete his meticulous preparation, which involved watching countless hours of video on opposition teams and studying pages and pages of tactical notes.

A 6-2 pre-season victory over Norwich City gave the first signs of the menace within the new look Arsenal team. Wright bagged a hat-trick while Grimandi scored twice before going off with an ankle injury. The work that Wenger had done with fitness and dieting was also very evident as the Gunners appeared fresher than at the start of previous seasons. Arsène hoped that his side would be competing in several competitions and so wanted his squad in peak condition.

Most pundits felt that Manchester United still held the edge domestically, despite the loss of Eric Cantona to retirement. Ferguson signed Teddy Sheringham during the summer to play in Cantona's role, allowing the team to play the same formation. The youngsters that had been viewed sceptically at the beginning of the 1995/96 campaign were now confident, established members of the team and Ferguson had held onto his other big name players, rebuffing interest from abroad. For the neutrals, at least, it looked as though there would be more of a title race this season.

The Gunners began their league campaign away to Leeds. Wright continued his pursuit of Cliff Bastin's Arsenal goalscoring record by giving his side the lead but a Jimmy Floyd Hasselbaink goal earned Leeds a point. Though his team collected just a point, Wenger was pleased with the way that they had played. Both Overmars and Petit had demonstrated enough to suggest that they would be very shrewd signings.

Wins over Coventry and Southampton moved the Gunners up the table. Wright was again the star man as he struck twice against Coventry, moving one goal away from equalling Bastin's record. Wenger knew that his striker would soon be entering the record books and delivered a fitting tribute, telling the media: 'I have worked with many strikers in my time, but Ian is like no other I've ever seen. He's a little bit crazier than any other player. I don't see why he could not go on to get 200 (goals). It is his love of the game which keeps him going. He is a great example to everybody. Sometimes too much concentration is put on the bad things he does, but we don't speak enough of all the positive things he does.' Arsène even admitted that he thought Wright was a better goalscorer than the great George Weah, who Wenger had managed while at Monaco.

Against Southampton, it was Bergkamp's turn to take centre stage as he grabbed two fine goals while Overmars got his first for the club in a 3-1 away win. Pundits were taking note of Arsenal's good start and some felt that Wenger's side would be strong title challengers. Arsène had called for more goals from his midfielders to lighten the load on the front two and Overmars had responded.

Bergkamp continued his fantastic start by bagging a hat-trick in a 3-3 draw away to Leicester. Though pleased with the Dutchman's contribution, Wenger was furious that his players had squandered a 2-0 lead and then, after Bergkamp made it 3-2 with seconds left, had conceded again. Such defensive frailty concerned Arsène, though he preferred to focus on Bergkamp's flawless display. A 0-0 draw with Tottenham brought August to a frustrating end but nine points from five games was not too bad at all.

One of the few disappointments of the early months of the campaign came in the UEFA Cup against PAOK Salonika in September. The Gunners lost the first leg 1-0 in Greece and could only manage a 1-1 draw at home as the Greeks scored an 86th minute equaliser to progress 2-1 on aggregate. It was a shame for the club but Wenger had bigger priorities to think about. Otherwise, it was a strong month for the club as they continued their unbeaten domestic run.

On 4 September, Bolton were hammered 4-1 at Highbury as Wright finally broke Bastin's record. The front man scored a fine hat-trick and got a great reception from the Arsenal fans. Wenger decided to withdraw Wright before the end so that the crowd could give him a special standing ovation. The Gunners number 8 would certainly not be forgotten when he ended his career.

A late goal from Winterburn, the unlikeliest of scorers, earned Arsenal a dramatic 3-2 win against Chelsea at Stamford Bridge. Wenger was delighted as the Blues appeared to be possible title contenders. Bergkamp scored the other two goals to help Arsenal maintain their momentum. Frank Leboeuf's red card after 67 minutes – for two nasty fouls on the elusive Bergkamp – proved costly for the home side. Overmars got in on the act at home to West Ham as he, Bergkamp and Wright once again proved unstoppable. The pace of Overmars and the vision of Bergkamp gave Wright no end of scoring chances. The Hammers were out of their depth and fell to a 4-0 defeat.

All four goals came before the half-time whistle and the win put Arsenal top of the table, ahead of Manchester United on goal difference. Wenger was understandably elated after the match but refused to get too carried away. He told reporters: 'After just eight games we must not draw too much from our position but it looks as though we are enjoying our game. When you keep winning it gives you confidence and without that you cannot perform. We still have a lot of work to do but I was pleased that we had greater fluency than we have had before this season.'

Ever the perfectionist, Arsène picked on the team's set pieces and passing in the final third as key areas for improvement.

Everton held the Gunners to a 2-2 draw at Goodison Park on 27 September but could not stop Wright and Overmars adding to their goal tallies. The foreign flair in the side was gelling nicely and neutrals were beginning to take note of this new look Arsenal team. Gone were the days of 'boring, boring Arsenal' and the 1-0 wins. The Wenger era promised waves of attacking football and buckets of goals.

Discipline was proving to be another talking point. Arsenal were fast earning a reputation as an overly aggressive side and Wenger felt referees were discriminating against his players. One report suggested that Arsène's tactic of pressing the opposition all over the field was to blame for the flurry of cards. It led to more tackles and, as a consequence, more fouls.

Earlier in September, one of Wenger's former charges at Monaco, Mark Hateley, suggested that the focus on Arsenal's aggression would be especially painful for the Gunners boss: 'As someone who played for Arsène, I know how much all the attention on disciplinary troubles will be hurting him now. He would never send out a team with instructions to kick the opposition. At Monaco we were aggressive in everything we did – running, tackling, shooting – but were *never* a physical side. He inherited a team which got into a certain mode and played the same way for five or six years under George Graham.'

October began with Arsenal raising the bar even higher. Not content with 4-0 and 4-1 victories, Wenger's players struck five against hapless Barnsley. Bergkamp – player of the month for August and September – scored twice, including a 25-yarder which curled into the top corner. Arsène was full of praise for the Dutchman's performance and hoped he would keep up this form. Bergkamp and many other first team players sat out of the League Cup extra-time win over Birmingham but returned for two disappointing goalless draws as the goals suddenly dried up.

Five Gunners received yellow cards in the 0-0 scoreline at Selhurst Park against Crystal Palace while Petit saw red at home to Aston Villa for putting his hands on referee Paul Durkin in an aggressive way. It was not what Wenger needed as the Frenchman would have to serve a three-match ban. Petit and Bergkamp, suspended after five yellow cards, would now miss the big game with Manchester United on 9 November. The fixture would be the acid test for Arsène's side and would show the Frenchman just how far his team had come since his appointment. Having identified defeats against other top clubs as one of Arsenal's downfalls in the 1996/97 season, Wenger wanted to see progress.

Before that, though, the Arsenal train was finally derailed away to Derby on 1 November as the Gunners were beaten 3-0 in an uncharacteristically poor display without the suspended Bergkamp. Wenger was not happy with the performance and was angered at the nature of the team's first league defeat of the campaign – there was no fight in the side. The Gunners would have to play much better next weekend against champions Manchester United as they pitted their wits against a strong team that would surely fight them all the way for the title.

Wenger cranked up the pressure on Ferguson and his players in the build up to the clash, telling the media that he was not buying into all the hype surrounding United. The Frenchman explained: 'I resent, at the moment, that everyone seems to think Manchester United are the only team in the country. Of course, Manchester United are doing very well but there are several other teams capable of fighting them for the championship. I certainly believe we are equipped to do so. The most important thing is to show what we can do. We have that chance on Sunday.'

To Arsène's delight, his players did indeed show their class and responded well in the wake of the defeat to Derby. United arrived at Highbury full of confidence but left pointless as Platt's header earned the Gunners a dramatic 3-2 victory. Platt's late winner rescued Arsenal from the embarrassment of surrendering a 2-0 lead and made Wenger's post-match team talk a lot easier. Anelka and Vieira had given Arsenal an early lead but United had fought back well and two goals from Sheringham, the ex-Tottenham man, restored parity before the interval. The euphoria around Highbury after Platt's winner, though, showed that the Arsenal fans felt that the squad was good enough to win the Premiership. This result left United just one point ahead of Arsenal, who moved into second.

The strangest incident in the month of November came just prior to the United fixture. Despite Arsenal's powerful opening to the season, rumours began to circulate that Wenger was leaving the club. The Gunners boss was furious, telling the press: 'There are three things that you should know. Number one is that I am very happy at Arsenal, two is that we're doing well, and three is that I have nothing to be afraid of.' The speculation soon disappeared, though – with the win over United taking centre stage.

Whether beating United went to the players' heads or whether there were other reasons involved, Arsenal's form dipped over the next month. November was certainly a bleak time for the club and this would become a disappointing trend in future years. Coventry were defeated in the League Cup but in the Premiership the Gunners lost to Sheffield Wednesday and Liverpool in successive weekends, failing to score in either game. Having scored just four goals in their last seven matches in all competitions, the team's attack was proving a headache for Wenger. He rued the suspensions of Bergkamp and Petit. Neither had been available for the Sheffield Wednesday defeat and, though both returned at home to Liverpool on 30 November, the team's fluent early season passing was strangely lacking.

November was also the month when rumours circulated about the possibility of Wenger signing a French attacker from Monaco called Thierry Henry. Henry had won the 1998 World Cup with the French national team but was now pining for a move to the Premiership. He allegedly told the media: 'Arsenal are the club of my dreams – everything about the set-up makes my head spin.' It was a clear 'come and get me' plea and Arsène was listening.

Other reports suggested that Arsène had tried to sign Henry prior to the World Cup only for the forward's strong displays at the tournament to raise the fee considerably. The pair knew each other from Wenger's Monaco days and Thierry told the press of his admiration for the Arsenal boss: 'Arsène Wenger is the coach who gave me my debut. The only time I have mentioned another club was in August, when I wanted to join Arsenal, and that is still the case.' Wenger's valuation of Henry was closer to £4 million yet Monaco were demanding double that price.

Things gradually improved. Arsenal won away at Newcastle thanks to a goal from Wright, who looked a relieved man after ending his goal drought. The Gunners then surprisingly lost 3-1 at home to Blackburn as Adams had a nightmare afternoon, gifting Rovers two of their goals. With a packed fixture list ahead and the team still playing in three competitions, Wenger had to get the Gunners back on track quickly.

With the team performing erratically, many doubted their title credentials. Michael Hart, writing for *The Evening Standard* in mid-December, claimed: 'It is possible Arsenal will still win the Premiership title but the prospects of that happening this season grow more remote by the week. Three defeats in their last four matches have demoted Arsenal from authentic title contenders to a place among the outsiders, all of whom know that any realistic hope they have is dependent to some degree on Manchester United surrendering their grip on the trophy.'

Arsenal desperately needed to put together a good run of results to claw themselves back into the title race. With a fully fit squad again at Wenger's disposal, Arsenal responded with excellent results. Starting with a 2-1 win on Boxing Day against Leicester, the team showed they had the character to mount a challenge. A strike from Platt and an own goal from Leicester skipper Steve Walsh handed Arsenal the points.

A 1-1 draw away to Tottenham showed the spirit in Wenger's side. Their rivals, still smarting from Christian Gross' nightmare stint as manager, were boosted by Jürgen Klinsmann's presence in the starting line-up. The German, who played for Wenger at Monaco, had come back to Tottenham to help their dire situation. His return lifted the crowd but the Gunners were equal to the hostile atmosphere as Ray Parlour equalised Allan Nielsen's first half goal. Wenger felt his team had more to offer but was impressed with their character. He was less pleased, though, when his players failed to break through against Port Vale in the FA Cup on 3 January.

Early January also brought a bizarre statement from the Frenchman, who said: 'We are a good side. We will show it. I will go home if we don't win something this season.' It left many fans confused. Was Wenger talking about throwing in the towel already? Meanwhile, the media claimed it would take a miracle for Manchester United to surrender the twelve-point lead that they held over Arsenal.

A place in the League Cup semi-finals was sealed with a 2-1 win over West Ham on 6 January as Wright and Overmars found the net. That night, the Gunners attack looked to be gelling again and it boded well for the rest of the season. When games became tight, Arsenal began to find the cutting edge. On 10 January, Leeds were beaten 2-1 and two weeks later the Gunners overcame Middlesbrough by the same score in the FA Cup. Another 2-1 victory – this time against Chelsea in the League Cup semi-final first leg – maintained the strong run of results. The win over the Blues came courtesy of goals from Overmars and young Stephen Hughes. But former Manchester United striker Mark Hughes pulled a goal back for Chelsea to set things up beautifully for the return match at Stamford Bridge.

Wenger kept his composure at all times, even in the face of the pressure of chasing trophies. He told the media: 'There is a history of success here that makes you feel obliged to work to be successful. Wherever you go in football you can never escape the history of a club.' As the Gunners' storming progress continued, it was clear that Arsène was handling the burden of expectation very well.

In late January, reports circulated claiming that Wenger had snubbed a top club, thought to be Real Madrid, in favour of continuing his work at Highbury. The Frenchman admitted: 'I had an approach this season from another club but they asked me to keep it confidential. There are always people who ask you if you would like to manage them. But I just said no. I am not thinking of moving.' Gunners fans everywhere heaved a big sigh of relief after hearing these assurances, especially after some of his recent comments.

There were plenty of reasons for the Frenchman to stay at Highbury. The experience of the likes of Adams and Seaman made the Gunners very hard to break down and the team had a group of attackers that were always ready to pounce on an opportunity to push forward. Overmars' pace was the source of so many goals and he provided much needed width on the left wing. Naturally right footed, the Dutchman looked comfortable on the left, from where he could cut inside and shoot with his right foot. On the opposite flank, Parlour – not popular with all Arsenal supporters – was very hard-working and gave a good balance to the midfield.

As for Bergkamp, his great form showed no signs of stopping. Wenger gave him the freedom to drift around slightly deeper than his strike partner and it was proving a masterstroke as the Dutchman used his incredible vision to lay on chances for his team-mates and his link-up play with Overmars and Wright was particularly good. Bergkamp also contributed a hatful of goals himself as he had one of his most productive scoring seasons.

Wenger's smile showed no signs of disappearing as Arsenal won their next two league games, scoring five and keeping two clean sheets. A 3-0 victory over Southampton was achieved through three goals in quick succession just after the hour mark. Chelsea fared only slightly better, losing 2-0 with Hughes bagging both goals. The result put Arsenal a point behind the second-placed Blues with leaders Manchester United in their sights.

When Wenger first arrived at Arsenal, he had anticipated needing to totally rebuild his defence shortly but was 'astonished' to see the likes of Adams and Dixon defying their ages. He told reporters: 'I expected that I would have to make changes in that defensive area, but they did so well that I just had to ignore how old they were. Even when we were playing badly in November and December, Bould and Winterburn were just great. As a manager I cannot just say because a player is getting old I will not give him a contract.' Arsène's back line were playing out of their skin, limiting opposition teams to few shots on goal and stacking up the clean sheets. This was especially noticeable over the next couple of months.

But a disappointing week arrived first as the Gunners could only draw at home to Crystal Palace in the FA Cup and were beaten 3-1 at Stamford Bridge in the League Cup second leg on 18 February. The defeat meant Chelsea advanced to the final at Wembley with a 4-3 aggregate scoreline at the Gunners' expense, denying Wenger his first trip to England's most famous stadium as Arsenal boss.

Arsène hit out at the Chelsea players for their unsporting

behaviour during the match. He refused to fine Vieira, who was sent off, because Wenger alleged that Vialli had dived for the Frenchman's first yellow card and Wenger added: 'They [Chelsea] have much more experience. They dived a lot, many players made a meal of our fouls and that made a difference. It is said that Patrick [Vieira] is always on at the referee but do you know who was talking to him most? It was Wise, talking in his ear.'

This elimination seemed to anger Arsenal into better performances. Their focus was unshakable as the Gunners beat Palace twice in a week (once in a cup replay) and took seven points from a possible nine in their next three league matches. A 0-0 stalemate against West Ham at Upton Park in the Premiership was followed by another draw against the Hammers in the FA Cup quarter-final. With a tough fixture list ahead, Wenger could have done without adding a replay to the schedule.

A goal from Liberian striker Christopher Wreh was enough to clinch a 1-0 win away to Wimbledon and cut Manchester United's lead at the top to nine points. Furthermore, the Gunners had three games in hand and a league clash against the champions was the next fixture for Arsène's players. The match, on March 14, represented a chance to blow the title race wide open as well as score some psychological points for the run-in. Arsène ensured that his side were ready for the challenge and knew that the momentum was with the Gunners. Wenger spoke pre-match and gave Ferguson a taste of his own medicine with some 'kidology' of his own: 'For once, everyone will be supporting us. Mentally, of course, they [United] have the worry of trying to win the European Cup. And if we get a positive result at Old Trafford, we will never have a better chance of becoming champions.'

United were suffering with injuries to key players and Arsenal arrived in Manchester full of confidence – not to fight for a point but to dominate and take all three. Alex Ferguson, without Gary Pallister, Roy Keane and Ryan Giggs, still sent out a strong side but Wenger's players were in no mood for sympathy. It was a tight contest but the Gunners always had the upper hand with Bergkamp and Overmars a constant threat and Vieira and Petit overwhelming United's makeshift midfield. The deciding moment arrived eleven minutes from time as Overmars raced onto an Anelka pass and slotted the ball past Peter Schmeichel. In this moment, the advantage in the title race switched emphatically to Wenger's side and the Frenchman knew it.

Arsène told the press: 'I believed all along we could catch them and now I think my players believe it. United are in the best position, but it is up to us now. It's in our hands for the first time. We have three games in hand – it's really up to how we perform.' Ferguson opted to blame his injury crisis for the defeat and was distraught to see Schmeichel limp off with a hamstring injury. The Danish goalkeeper would be a major loss.

In midweek, having recovered from the disappointment of the defeat, the United boss was more upbeat. He told the media: 'We're in a situation now that we're used to, so it's not as if we're unaccustomed to it. Over the past six years we've had to battle hard for the championship. Arsenal have not been under any pressure. Now they've come with a run and they're in a position now that every mistake they make will cost them. They'll find out now how difficult it is.'

But the Gunners refused to let the initiative slip or be distracted by Ferguson's jibes. They were playing well, without hammering sides, and there were plenty of reminders of the old days as Arsène's side ground out some priceless 1-0 wins. A penalty shootout victory at Upton Park put Arsenal into the FA Cup semi-finals and put Wenger one step away from his first Wembley final. 1-0 victories over Sheffield Wednesday and Bolton, courtesy of goals from Bergkamp and Wreh, respectively, kept the Gunners' title quest on course.

The three points against Bolton had shown once again the tremendous spirit in the dressing room as Wenger's side had to play with ten men for the final twenty-five minutes after Martin Keown's red card. In late March, Ferguson claimed that Arsenal were 'in the driving seat' due to their strong run. Arsène opted to ignore the comment, which may well have been the latest attempt from Ferguson to unsettle the Gunners.

The FA Cup semi-final draw had paired Arsenal with First Division Wolves and most experts felt the Gunners would achieve an easy victory. Wenger took no chances, however, and his players did not let him down. Bergkamp was suspended but Wreh pounced on his chance to impress by grabbing the winner in a 1-0 victory. Arsenal had scored just once for the seventh successive match but, such was the protection received by Seaman, this streak had resulted in four wins and three draws (four wins out of four in the league). Arsène reserved special praise for Wreh, another player that he had plucked from his former club Monaco: 'When you think that Wreh was unknown two months ago it shows you how well he's done. He was a bargain.'

As the season ticked on, Wenger got his wish as the plans for a new training ground at London Colney were revealed. It would provide the squad with some of the best facilities of any club in

Europe. Writing for *The Guardian*, Nick Callow explained: 'Arsenal's proposed new training centre promises to be one of the most advanced sporting fitness facilities in the country. It is intended to be ready for the 1999/2000 season and will underline Arsenal's holistic philosophy under Arsène Wenger.' The indoor plans included a hydrotherapy pool, treatment areas and gymnasiums while outdoors boasted eight practice pitches. The set-up had been prepared down to the finest details.

On 11 April, back in Premiership action, Newcastle travelled to Highbury hoping to end the Gunners' unbeaten run but an Anelka brace and a stunner from Vieira clinched a 3-1 win. Manchester United were beginning to panic as Arsenal showed no signs of choking on the finishing stretch. A 4-1 victory at Blackburn proved that the Gunners had the class to hammer sides on their day. Wenger's side made a magnificent start and sealed the game within the first fifteen minutes. Bergkamp grabbed the first and Parlour struck twice to put Arsenal 3-0 up after fourteen minutes. The game finished 4-1 and Arsène happily reflected on his team's attacking masterclass. On this evidence, the run-in looked a formality.

But there was more to come. Wimbledon were thrashed 5-0 at Highbury as Arsenal turned on the style. With five different scorers, the Gunners almost taunted Manchester United as they passed and moved their way past the Crazy Gang. United stumbled at home to Newcastle, drawing 1-1, and the mood in the Arsenal dressing room could not have been better. The club's supporters really felt that the title was now within touching distance.

There were some tricky matches at the very end of the season but Wenger set out to complete the job as soon as possible. Manchester United were faltering badly and Arsenal were cashing in. Another solid display brought another three points as goals from Bergkamp and Overmars decided a trip to Barnsley on 25 April.

With the title firmly within sight for the Gunners, Arsène urged his players to stay focused. He said: 'We must be ruthless, professional and concentrated. It is always difficult to finish something off but we are in the last 100 yards of the title race and I'm positive, concentrated and relaxed. The players must be, too.' He got the response that he wanted. A 1-0 win at home to Derby gave Arsenal the chance to seal the title at home to Everton at the weekend, though they lost Bergkamp to injury after half an hour.

Since the United-Arsenal clash at Old Trafford, Wenger's side had collected maximum points in the Premiership while Ferguson's men had drawn twice. These dropped points would come back to haunt United. With three games remaining, it was Arsenal's title to lose. Arsène demanded that his players should keep their composure and not waste a season of hard work. The team responded by clinching the 1997/98 Premiership title with an emphatic 4-0 win over Everton. The manner of the victory – and the fact that the Gunners collected a clean sheet – summed up the style with which Arsenal had played all season, especially since Christmas. It was fitting that captain Adams scored the fourth goal. Adams had been a colossal influence throughout the campaign.

Wenger took the applause of the Arsenal fans as he celebrated with the squad at the end of the match. His joy as the trophy was lifted told the story of a man who had put his heart and soul into a successful project. His team had played some of the most exciting football in Premiership history and this style of play pleased Arsène almost as much as the trophy itself. The Gunners lost both of their remaining matches – 4-0 at Liverpool and 1-0 at Aston Villa – but of course it did not matter. Wenger's squad were already champions.

The last objective for Arsène was the FA Cup final. He had taken the opportunity to rest members of the squad during the meaningless defeats to Liverpool and Villa and so his players were ready to complete a fantastic Double. Bergkamp was still out with the hamstring injury he picked up against Derby and Wenger somewhat controversially chose to replace him with Wreh rather than Wright. Newcastle were the opponents in Arsène's first cup final in England and, having lost twice to the Gunners already during the season, things did not bode well for the Magpies.

Newcastle's worst fears were confirmed as Arsenal proved far too good on the day. Goals from Overmars and Anelka sealed a 2-0 win and a very impressive double for Wenger and his squad. A huge crowd of 79,183 witnessed a composed Arsenal performance that denied their opponents any chance to impose themselves on proceedings. When Anelka fired in the team's second goal, Wenger, usually so calm, could not hold back from showing his emotions as he celebrated the strike that left Newcastle with a mountain to climb. It was a special afternoon for everyone associated with the club and one that Arsène would never forget. It was a happy first trip to Wembley as a manager.

Wenger also took time out during the celebrations to heap

praise on the quality of Overmars, who had been superb in the final. The Frenchman claimed: 'I know Marc had his critics when he first arrived but he showed just why he is a world class player today. Look at his record – it's as thick as a phone book because he has won so many things. You don't play like that if you are not a great player.' Overmars himself was also jubilant, telling the media: 'This is all so amazing, especially to win so much in my first year. Is it the best day of my life? Well, I hope there will be a few more like this.'

Manchester United had won their final two league matches but the mood around Old Trafford was as mellow as it was ecstatic at Highbury. Ferguson rued the injuries that he felt had cost his team in the last few months of the season. He was gracious in defeat and congratulated Wenger's achievement but vowed that United would come back stronger. He was not wrong.

Prior to the FA Cup final, Wenger's excellent campaign was recognised at the end of season awards night as he was named Carling Manager of the Year. It was well deserved considering the powerful manner in which the Gunners had dominated domestic football since Christmas. Arsène spoke proudly after collecting the award: 'In England every game is such a battle and it makes the Championship so hard to win. My staff have worked so hard for me and, like the players, they have been exceptional and magnificent. All we are thinking about at the moment is the FA Cup final and it will probably only be after the season is over that we realise just what we have achieved.'

Bergkamp received the end of season honours for his incredible performances along the way to the Double. The

Dutchman scooped the top award from both his fellow professionals and from the media, taking home an impressive double of his own. His inspiring displays had been such a vital part of the Gunners' title success.

For the meantime, the Premiership was residing in North London and Arsène was a very contented man. It was his first full season in England and he had collected two pieces of silverware. He was now hailed as a genius by the Arsenal fans who had been totally won over after the club's return to the glory days.

As former international Jamie Redknapp later claimed in the *Daily Mail*, Wenger's influence in England was proving a massive success. Writing in 2006, Redknapp said: 'Arsène Wenger has had a greater impact on English football than any other foreigner. Only Gianfranco Zola, a magnificent influence as a player, can compare. The Chelsea lads, especially John Terry, will tell you that Zola changed their attitudes to football. It wasn't as simple for Wenger. A limited playing pedigree would not have impressed his new team.' But the Frenchman had surpassed all expectations.

As a result of the club's fantastic season, the board worked desperately to tie Arsène down to a new contract. The terms were rumoured to be about £5 million over five years. David Dein told the media how highly regarded Wenger was within the set-up and sought to fight off interest in the Frenchman from other top European clubs. Arsène, though, admitted that he had no intention of leaving: 'I am happy at Arsenal at the moment. Money didn't make me come to Highbury, it was not my inspiration nor my target. The important target was to win trophies. I just love what I do. I will sign a new deal so long as I have the freedom to work as I want.'

Dein naturally dwelt on the improvements made by Wenger at the club and recalled the outcry when the Frenchman was announced as Rioch's successor: 'The knives were out for us and we needed a change of direction. We had to have the courage of our convictions and bring in new methods. It was a brave decision to take. We described his appointment as a judgement call, not a gamble, but of course it could have gone either way.' Chairman Hill-Wood added: 'He will sign, I'm sure he will. He didn't want to talk about it before the [FA Cup] final but we will talk this week.' With only one year left on Wenger's contract, it could have been a nervy close season had Arsène not assured everyone of his intention to stay at the club.

It should have been a summer off for the Gunners boss but for Arsène there is no such thing. Unable to ever switch off completely from the game, Wenger immediately began his preparations for next season, knowing that the challengers would be desperate to take revenge on his side.

***

Having won the title the previous season, Wenger knew that retaining it would be even harder. His players had produced an astonishing run at the end of the campaign to which Manchester United had no answer. Yet repeating such an effort would require another special year. Arsène remained optimistic, though, despite the impressive additions that Alex Ferguson had made to his squad after finishing 1997/98 empty-handed.

Petit and Vieira returned to pre-season training as World Cup winners after France shocked the world of football by beating Brazil 3-0 in the showpiece final. Petit even got his name on the scoresheet, grabbing the last of the three goals. Although saddened by England's premature exit, many Gunners fans were pleased that there were some Arsenal representatives lifting the trophy. Predictably, Petit and Vieira returned to Highbury on cloud nine, with the former having been particularly prominent in the tournament.

Wenger had watched the tournament with keen interest and loved the hype surrounding every match. He was happy to see his players performing well at the World Cup – the biggest stage of all. It was much more satisfying for him than the meaningless international friendlies for which he was forced to release his players.

The Arsenal boss ensured that none of his heroes from the Double-winning success departed during the summer but made no great strides in the transfer market. One new face was Swedish midfielder Freddie Ljungberg who joined the Gunners from Halmstad for a fee of £3 million. Wenger knew that Ljungberg had a reputation as a goalscoring midfielder who made intelligent runs behind opposition defences.

Ferguson, on the other hand, spent heavily to lift the gloom around Old Trafford. In came striker Dwight Yorke from Aston Villa for £12.6 million, Dutch centre-back Jaap Stam from PSV Eindhoven for £10.5 million and Swedish winger Jesper Blomqvist for £4.4 million. It was enough to leave most fearing United's new capabilities but Wenger would not be forced into panic buying. He was happy with the squad that he had assembled.

The Charity Shield suggested that Arsène might have been right to stick with his current group of players. United were outclassed in a 3-0 victory for the Gunners as Anelka and Overmars took centre stage. David Beckham, appearing in his first competitive game since his red card against Argentina at the 1998 World Cup, was predictably subjected to an afternoon of boos and abuse as United were humbled by a strong, energetic Arsenal line-up. For all the new faces that Ferguson had brought in, Wenger's side still looked the most exciting team in the country.

Anelka had impressed Arsène enough to convince the Gunners boss that he was the man to lead the line. His pace and clinical finishing were the perfect assets for a team that played incisive, attacking football. Particularly away from Highbury, Wenger hoped that Anelka's pace could be utilised on the counter attack. To many the young Frenchman did not always seem the most cheerful member of the squad but his ability on the pitch was unquestionable.

When Arsenal began the new season with a 2-1 home victory over Nottingham Forest, everything looked in order at the club. The defence continued to belie its age and the attackers appeared fresh after a few weeks of rest during the summer. But a worrying patch of results was ahead and Wenger would have some stressful times as the Gunners suffered an uncharacteristic goal drought.

Three consecutive 0-0 draws in the Premiership brought Arsène and his players under intense scrutiny. In fairness, two of those results were achieved away from home at Anfield and Stamford Bridge, but the media began to ask questions about the team's form and whether Wenger should have been busier in the transfer market over the summer. The stalemate at Highbury against Charlton was less excusable.

On a brighter note, Arsène's first taste of the Champions League was just around the corner. The revamped format meant that the opening round was a group stage, rather than the knockout tie that Wenger had been used to at Monaco. The Gunners were drawn in Group E alongside Lens, Panathinaikos and Dynamo Kiev.

Two more draws added to Wenger's frustration. His players were performing well but just could not find the killer blow. A 1-1 scoreline with Leicester was somewhat fortunate as Stephen Hughes grabbed an equaliser in the closing stages. Arsenal collected another 1-1 draw when they began their Champions League campaign away to French club Lens. It was a contest that Wenger's team dominated but the Gunners paid the penalty for missed chances when Lens scored a late goal. Four goals in six games left Arsène with plenty to ponder while Bergkamp, the hero of the previous season, had not yet registered a goal in 1998/99.

Manchester United arrived at Highbury with revenge in the air. Arsenal had been below par thus far during the new campaign and Ferguson's players hoped to exploit some uncertainty within the home dressing room. Instead, Wenger's side produced their best performance of the season to win 3-0 in front of a delirious home crowd. Adams gave the Gunners the lead and Anelka doubled the advantage before half-time. Nicky Butt was sent off for a foul on Vieira and new boy Ljungberg added the third goal to put the icing on the cake.

Arsène was delighted to see his team back on track and the three points were most welcome. Ferguson, meanwhile, was far from happy and he seemed to be justified in raging over the dismissal of Butt. The United midfielder was not the last man when he fouled Vieira yet referee Graham Barber reached for the red card. This was just the first of four meetings between the two clubs over the course of the season as Arsenal again established themselves as United's closest rivals. Ferguson admitted that his team had been outplayed: 'Arsenal were far better than us, wanted to win it far more than we did, and I don't like saying that as manager of Manchester United.'

A loss away to Sheffield Wednesday was a bitterly disappointing result after all the hard graft against United. A late goal from Lee Briscoe was enough to seal a 1-0 win for Wednesday in a stormy contest that saw Martin Keown and Paolo Di Canio sent off just before half-time. Vieira was also involved in the mêlée. As Di Canio left the field he took out his frustrations on referee Paul Alcock, shoving the official. The spotlight on this incident also ensured that discontent over Arsenal's discipline gathered pace again.

Vieira, in particular, had encountered disciplinary problems but his manager jumped to his defence. Arsène explained to the media: 'We should not victimise Patrick. He is a physical player and once you remove that from his game, he is not the player he was. His reputation precedes him and sometimes he has been badly treated by referees.'

The issue refused to go away. After the fixture at Hillsborough against Sheffield Wednesday, Vieira was alleged to have flashed a V sign at Wednesday supporters and then tussled with a policeman as he left the pitch. Wenger rushed to his player's aid only to land himself in trouble too. Arsène spoke briefly on the topic after the game: 'The crowd were very hard on Patrick during the game, but he has got to learn to deal with that.' The Arsenal boss was beginning to grow impatient with all the questions surrounding the discipline within the squad.

As the media attention continued, Wenger twice felt obliged to speak out. On 28 September, Wenger sought to set the record straight. He told the press: 'Good football is all about the physical side – running quickly, jumping high and putting your foot in. When teams play us, like when they play Manchester United, they are all up for it and that means we're exposed to very competitive opponents. We have to resolve the problems they give us. You have to fight, but you also have to respect the rules. I think we do that.' The trouble was that Arsène continually defended his players in the wake of their dismissals with weak excuses, leading many to think that he had no control over his squad's ill-discipline. Wenger just seemed bitter and angry with referees and the FA instead and he created a 'them against us' atmosphere. His frequent response to questions over major flashpoints was along the lines of 'I didn't see it.'

Then just days later, he addressed the press again: 'What is concerning me, more than the red cards themselves, is that the team could be punished if several players are banned at the same time. I don't think we are a bad team and what I still can't master is where we are supposed to be going wrong. There is a line between being competitive and dirty, but that line does not apply only to us.' Arsène also refused to keep quiet over his belief that Vieira, amongst others, was unfairly singled out by referees and that the French midfielder's reputation now preceded him on the pitch. Wenger spent a lot of time helping Vieira to deal with all the negative media coverage and the midfielder has always been grateful for his manager's support.

He would later reveal: 'When everything was going wrong for me, he [Wenger] realised I wasn't perfect and talking to him helped me. His door is always open. He made me realise that you must not walk out in a moment of anger and that I should stay here and I would be a success. I have realised how great he is for me and how fantastic the club is and, for me, that I made the right decision.'

The Gunners hosted Panathinaikos that evening in the Champions League. The Greeks proved tricky opponents but fell to a 2-1 defeat and it was the Arsenal centre-backs that deserved the credit as Adams and Keown popped up with the goals. It kept Arsène's side on course and Wenger was enjoying his first proper Champions League experience.

On 4 October, Newcastle became the latest side to fail to defeat the Gunners as Arsène's players started to play like champions at last. A brace and an assist from Bergkamp helped Arsenal claim a 3-0 win. These were the Dutchman's first goals of the season and he rewarded the faith shown in him by his manager. Wenger had been patient with his star man and now Bergkamp was finding top form again.

A pair of disappointing draws at home with Southampton and Dynamo Kiev dampened the mood a little in the Arsenal dressing room but three consecutive away wins provided the perfect response. The 1-1 draw with Kiev had left Wenger fuming as his side once again conceded a late goal to surrender two points. However, the players offered no such charity on their travels. A 2-1 win away to Blackburn showed the team's clinical edge while a second string Gunners line-up was good enough to beat Derby at Pride Park in the League Cup third round. A 1-0 win at Coventry on 31 October completed a solid week with Anelka grabbing the winner.

November was a heartbreaking month for the Gunners as they moved from one setback to another. A 3-1 defeat away to Dynamo Kiev in the Champions League on 4 November saw Wenger's side slip from group leaders to bottom spot in the table. There was, though, little to separate the four teams. It was still possible for Wenger's side to stage a comeback. The next day, Arsène faced the media with a positive outlook: 'Last night's result puts Kiev in a very good position. But I still believe we have a chance of qualifying.' He added: 'I am not worried because of the attitude of the players. They are able to turn it around. The spirit among the players is right. We are still up there with the leaders.' There were plenty of pluses to take away on the night and the excellence of the Kiev goalkeeper showed that the Gunners had really tested Dynamo's defence. Arsène hoped that a change of fortune was just around the corner.

He had been forced to field a patched up team against Kiev with Adams, Bergkamp, Overmars and most recently Anelka on the sidelines. These were the type of injury problems that had hindered Manchester United's title chances the previous year and now Wenger was experiencing the difficulties of missing star players. Anelka returned to the side on 8 November to score the winner at home to Everton in the Premiership.

A weakened Arsenal side was hammered 5-0 in the League Cup fourth round at home to Chelsea in midweek and then stuttered to a 0-0 draw with rivals Tottenham. This North London derby was significant for ex-Gunners boss George Graham's return to his former club as manager of Tottenham. Boos rang out around Highbury. There was little to choose between the two teams and Wenger was concerned by his side's lack of penetration. Still without Bergkamp, the Arsenal boss at least had Adams and Overmars back in the starting line-up but on this occasion Tottenham held firm.

A truly miserable afternoon at Selhurst Park against Wimbledon was the worst possible preparation for a crucial Champions League clash with Lens in midweek. Wenger looked on in dismay as he lost Vieira and Bergkamp to injury against their London neighbours in a scrappy contest. As if the injuries were not worrying enough, an Efan Ekoku winner with thirteen minutes remaining gave the Dons all three points.

Shorn of several big name players, Wenger remained optimistic ahead of the Lens match but admitted that a victory was essential to their qualification hopes. Bergkamp, Vieira and Petit were unavailable, leaving Arsène with the task of replacing the core of the team. When Adams was substituted at half-time through injury, the team's spine was well and truly weakened. Lens put in a solid display and always looked threatening in the final third while Arsenal struggled yet again to break down a resolute defence.

As the Gunners pushed forward in search of a winner, they were punished as Lens scored a priceless goal. Wenger and all Arsenal fans were furious with the assistant referee who failed to spot a clear offside against the scorer Michael Debeve. The 1-0 defeat left Arsène's side devastated that their Champions League adventure had ended so prematurely. Parlour gave Wenger further reason to be angry as he was sent off in the final minutes for kicking out at Lens player Cyril Rool. The club's exit from the competition left everyone at Wembley feeling down and Arsène must have rued the decision to play their European fixtures there rather than the noisy cauldron of Highbury. Some felt he had paid the price for not strengthening his squad over the summer.

The month ended with more bitter disappointment at home as another visiting side left Highbury with a share of the points. Middlesbrough scored early through Brian Deane and looked set to take all three points until Anelka struck with a last gasp equaliser. The Gunners were winning fixtures such as this by a comfortable margin during the previous season yet injuries and a lack of confidence had left the team with an uphill battle to retain their title. In the draw with Middlesbrough, the Arsenal players were booed by their supporters and Arsène felt the need to answer the critics post-match: 'Maybe we gave the fans too much last season. If you eat caviar every day it is difficult to come back to sausages.'

December was a mixed month but, as Christmas approached, Arsenal began to find top form again. A 0-0 draw away to Derby on 5 December saw the Gunners draw yet another blank while, on a more positive note, a 3-1 win away to Panathinaikos in midweek showed that Wenger's side had the quality to go further in the competition in future years. A 3-2 defeat at Villa Park was a bitter blow as Arsène watched his players squander a 2-0 lead in the second half. A brace from Bergkamp had given Arsenal a comfortable lead at half-time but vulnerability in defence allowed Villa back into the game and goals from Julian Joachim and Dion Dublin (two) completed the home side's comeback. How Wenger must have wished for Adams, Vieira and Petit to be out there protecting the lead.

20 December marked the start of a good run of results for the Gunners – a run that reflected the side's real ability. Leeds travelled to Highbury and were soundly beaten 3-1 with goals from Bergkamp and the returning duo of Vieira and Petit. On Boxing Day, Arsenal made it two wins out of two with a 1-0 victory over West Ham courtesy of Overmars' early strike. Adams had not yet returned to the starting line-up but otherwise the Gunners had few injury worries and this certainly helped their consistent form. An Overmars goal was again the difference on 28 December as Wenger's side beat Charlton at the Valley to end the year on a high.

Victory over Preston in the FA Cup was followed by a 0-0 draw at home to Liverpool and a 1-0 win at the City Ground against Nottingham Forest – Keown proving the match-winner. Crucially, the defence had tightened up and opposition sides were finding it tough to create chances. A 1-0 win over Chelsea was perfect evidence of this. Bergkamp's first half winner put Arsenal just a point behind the second-placed Blues, whose 21-match unbeaten run in the league came to an end. Fortunately for Wenger, the other title challengers had not capitalised on the Gunners' poor spell. Chelsea were just above Arsenal while Manchester United's advantage was also slight. Many in the media now felt that Arsène's side were hitting top form at the best possible time and could still successfully defend their title.

On 6 February, the Gunners produced a masterclass on their travels to beat West Ham 4-0 at Upton Park. Goals from Bergkamp, Overmars, Anelka and Parlour sealed an impressive win. Wenger knew that the performance had sent out a message to Arsenal's rivals. His side were back and were desperate to lift the Premiership trophy again. A week later Arsenal hit the headlines once more after victory over Sheffield United in the FA Cup. But this time Wenger had to deal with a rather awkward situation involving new signing Nwankwo Kanu.

With the score 1-1, Kanu, the Nigerian bought by Arsène to strengthen the club's title surge, chased down a throw-in from Parlour that was intended to give possession back to Sheffield United after one of their players had picked up an injury. Rather than letting the ball roll back to the United goalkeeper, Kanu collected the ball and crossed for Overmars to slot the ball home. Blades boss Steve Bruce and his players were furious and at one stage it looked as though Bruce would take his team off the pitch. Wenger then had the tricky task of answering questions about the incident. Had Kanu deliberately chosen not to give possession back to Sheffield United? Unsurprisingly, Arsène defended his striker and, in the end, it was agreed that the match would be replayed.

In midweek, the Gunners faced Manchester United at Old Trafford in the biggest test of their resurgent form. In heavy rain, the two powerhouses of English football played out an intriguing contest. Dwight Yorke's missed penalty after half an hour spared Arsenal's blushes and the Gunners continued to impose themselves on proceedings. Anelka's goal, just after half-time, gave Wenger hope of a famous win but Andy Cole's leveller on the hour mark ensured that the points were shared. Without Bergkamp, Petit and Keown, the Arsenal boss took great pride from the way that his side had competed. The result kept the title race wide open.

A scintillating performance at home to Leicester was Arsenal's best of the season to date. A hat-trick from Anelka and a brace from Parlour put the Gunners 5-0 up after just 48 minutes. Though they did not score again, Wenger's side looked in stunning form. Bergkamp was pulling the strings and his understanding of Anelka's runs was beginning to cut defences to shreds. Arsène tried to keep his players' feet on the ground as the positive, confident mood around the club grew and grew. A win over Sheffield United in the repeat of their FA Cup fifth round clash and a draw away to Newcastle completed an excellent February for everyone associated with Arsenal Football Club.

Wenger's side booked their place in the FA Cup semi-finals with a 1-0 victory over Derby on 6 March. Kanu was the hero as he struck a late winner. The Nigerian could not stay out of the limelight in the competition, following on from his involvement in the controversial goal against Sheffield United in the previous round. Three consecutive Premiership wins gave Arsenal a 100 per cent record for the month of March.

A 3-0 win over Sheffield Wednesday came courtesy of three late goals, putting the Gunners second in the table and keeping them in contention for the title. Parlour and Bergkamp then sealed a 2-0 win away to Everton in which the home side's Don

Hutchison was dismissed after just eighteen minutes and Petit was sent off in the second half. Sadly, such poor discipline meant that the topic of Arsenal's aggression was never far from discussion for Wenger when he faced the media. A 2-0 victory against Coventry was another confident Gunners display.

A goalless draw at The Dell saw Arsenal drop two important points but a win at home to Blackburn pleased Wenger as the side kept its sixth successive clean sheet. Bergkamp scored the only goal of the game as Arsenal hung on despite Keown's red card with twenty minutes to go. The FA Cup semi-final draw served up a classic by pairing the Gunners with Manchester United and the winner of this titanic clash would surely be favourites to beat Newcastle or Tottenham in the final. It was now the business end of the season and it was time for the top players to step up with key contributions.

One hundred and twenty minutes of football were unable to separate Arsenal and United at Villa Park on 11 April. Although Nelson Vivas became the latest Gunner to receive a red card, Wenger's players showed the type of spirit and togetherness that he had demanded from them. There were some worrying moments for Arsenal, including a goal from Roy Keane that was harshly deemed offside, but honours ended even to set up a mouth-watering replay three days later. Neither side wanted an extra fixture at such a crucial stage of the campaign, particularly United who were still competing in the Champions League too. But for the neutrals, it was an eagerly awaited match.

And it did not disappoint as the two sides produced a contender for best game of the decade. The contest, again at the neutral venue of Villa Park, had absolutely everything. David Beckham's clever strike wrong footed Seaman to give United the lead in the first half but Bergkamp equalised after the interval via a Jaap Stam deflection. Everything was poised for an explosive finale. When United captain Roy Keane was sent off five minutes later, the advantage swung firmly in Arsenal's direction. Anelka had a goal disallowed and United were forced to defend desperately. The pressure finally told deep in injury-time when Parlour skipped past Phil Neville and was tripped by the United full-back. Referee David Elleray pointed to the spot. Bergkamp, Arsenal's inspiration for the past two seasons, stepped up and fired the penalty towards the right hand corner. But Schmeichel guessed correctly and beat the ball to safety. Cue jubilant celebrations from Schmeichel and his team-mates. The match would go to extra-time.

On the touchline Wenger could hardly believe that the contest was not over. His team had battered United in the closing stages but now faced a gruelling half hour of extra-time. Arsène urged his players to exploit their numerical advantage. By now, though, it was less about skill and more about mental courage as there were weary bodies all over the pitch. The Gunners pressed forward only to be denied again by the massive frame of Schmeichel. Then came the moment that broke Arsenal hearts. Ryan Giggs, on after 61 minutes, was one of the fresher players and when he received the ball – in the second period of extra-time – there was little support. He set off on a dribble, leaving Vieira trailing, then burst past Dixon and Adams and into the penalty area before firing a ferocious shot into the roof of the net. Wenger was stunned. Giggs wheeled away in celebration and was mobbed by United team-mates. The Gunners remarkably mustered the energy for a couple of chances to equalise but it was not to be.

The contrasting emotions of the two sets of players could not have been starker. A pitch invasion from United fans saw the team's players hoisted high by ecstatic supporters. The Arsenal side made their way slowly down the tunnel. Wenger was understandably drained and devastated but he could not fault the effort of his players. The Frenchman gave one of his usual speeches in the wake of the defeat, seeming to praise the opposition but also insinuating that his team had been hard done by. He told Sky Sports: 'The two teams are very close to each other, it was a smashing game, and in the end the luckiest won. We had the chances to win.' Many believed that, though this was a cup game, it was the most critical moment thus far in the Premiership title race and it gave United a massive psychological advantage for the run-in.

As United prepared to face Juventus in the Champions League semi-final second leg, Wenger focused on his side's league run-in and promised that his players would be ready. When Ferguson's side beat Sheffield Wednesday, the Red Devils stretched their lead at the top to four points. Arsenal closed that to just a point (though United had a game in hand) by thrashing Wimbledon 5-1 at Highbury in a match that they dominated from start to finish. Arsène's players took out their frustrations from their semi-final exit on a poor Dons side who found themselves 5-0 down before the hour mark. It showed immense character that the Gunners had bounced back so impressively after the agonising cup defeat and reminded everyone that Wenger was an expert in getting his players into the right frame of mind.

It got even better for Arsenal the next weekend when they overwhelmed Middlesbrough 6-1 at the Riverside Stadium to go top of the table. The win gave the Gunners a two-point lead over United, who had two games in hand, and really cranked up the pressure on Ferguson's side. Against Boro, the contest was once again over by the hour mark as Kanu's first strike of the afternoon made it 4-0 with thirty minutes still to go. It was the type of football that Arsène had always preached about and if United were watching, they would have been a little shaken by the ease with which Arsenal shrugged off their opponents. The next day, Ferguson's team put in a poor display away at Leeds and needed a colossal performance from captain Keane to snatch a 1-1 draw. It left Wenger's side one point ahead of United, having played a game more. This title race was going right to the wire.

Arsène had done a marvellous job of lifting his players from the misery of the FA Cup defeat to United. He had refused to let the squad feel sorry for themselves and demanded a response. Since that night at Villa Park, the Gunners had taken six points out of six, scoring eleven goals in the process. Arsenal and United both won their home games on the first weekend of May, doing nothing to ease the tension amongst the teams' supporters.

But when United only drew at Anfield, the title race became even more interesting. Ferguson's side had led 2-0 but surrendered that advantage and, after Denis Irwin was sent off, had to settle for a 2-2 draw. That same day, Wenger's Arsenal won 3-1 away to Tottenham through goals from Petit, Anelka and Kanu. The Gunners sat three points clear of United, who could return to the top by beating Middlesbrough in their game in hand.

Ferguson's side did indeed beat Boro and so the top two sides remained locked on the same number of points with two games remaining. The teams' goal differences were even closely matched and it looked as though it might be United's higher tally of goals scored that could decide the title race. Wenger's side were away to Leeds then home to Aston Villa. Ferguson's players faced Blackburn at Ewood Park then Tottenham at home. Incredibly, the Gunners were in a situation where they would be hoping for a favour from their North London rivals, managed by one of their former managers, George Graham.

But Wenger's side crumbled under the pressure and suffered a 1-0 defeat away to Leeds. It was a crushing blow to Arsenal's title hopes. A late goal from Jimmy Floyd Hasselbaink made Manchester United big favourites to lift the trophy and left the Arsenal players distraught as they trudged off at Elland Road, knowing they might have squandered their title chances. The Gunners had failed to reproduce the form that had seen them win their last three matches at a canter and it could have been worse if Ian Harte had not missed a first half penalty. Wenger knew his team had gifted Ferguson's side some breathing space and United would travel to Blackburn without the pressure of needing to win.

Arsène told the press: 'We have given United the chance to win it now. I don't expect them to lose against Blackburn. If

United win, we will have to rely on Spurs, and I don't think they will go there [Old Trafford] and win.' It was now well and truly out of Arsenal's hands.

But Blackburn, fighting desperately against relegation, did give United a nervy night at Ewood Park. The match finished 0-0 which sent Rovers into the First Division and gave Wenger and his players a glimmer of hope going into the final weekend of the season. Arsenal had to win at home to Aston Villa and pray that United failed to pick up three points at Old Trafford against Tottenham.

The odds were still stacked in United's favour and Wenger was adamant that his team was focused solely on beating Villa. Only with victory assured would he be interested in other results. Arsène had a fully fit squad to choose from and the Gunners began strongly against Villa. Meanwhile, at Old Trafford, Les Ferdinand had given Tottenham the lead over United. Beckham equalised before the interval and both Arsenal and United went in level at half-time. With Wenger's side still drawing, United seized the initiative as Andy Cole put them 2-1 up. Back at Highbury, Kanu struck after 66 minutes to keep the Gunners in the hunt.

With both matches on a knife's edge, fans could barely watch. A goal for Tottenham would see Arsenal retain the title. A goal for Villa would leave Arsène's side out of the running. Tottenham searched for an equaliser but United held firm and when the final whistle blew it was Ferguson's side who were celebrating. Wenger and his players had fought so hard and had beaten Villa to keep up their end of the bargain but they had to hand over the Premiership title.

Regardless of this, the club's supporters stayed on to applaud the players as they began a deflated lap of honour. They had given everything for the cause and it was hard not to admire the way that Wenger's side had hauled themselves back into the title race. Had Arsenal won at Elland Road, things could have been so different. The Frenchman could list countless occasions in which his team might have picked up the vital extra points that would have pushed them ahead of United.

The Gunners' form from Christmas onwards had been terrific but their inconsistent form in the opening three months of the season had proved costly. To finish 1998/99 empty-handed was a major blow for Arsène after the ecstasy of the Double success a year earlier. To rub salt into the wounds, Manchester United completed a phenomenal campaign by adding the FA Cup and the Champions League to their Premiership crown for a unique Treble. Whilst there was a lot to admire about United's achievements, it made the pain of missing out on the title even harder to bear for everyone associated with the Gunners. Arsène compared it to 'losing a race by a yard' and it had genuinely been *that* tight.

But, just as United had bounced back strongly after Arsenal won the Double, Wenger promised that his team would give an emphatic response of their own. He and his squad would be back next season, desperate for revenge.

CHASING SIR ALEX'S COAT-TAILS

After Manchester United's Treble winning glory, under-standably Ferguson and his players made all the headlines. It had been a phenomenal season. But Arsenal were rather forgotten in the midst of the praise that was flying from all directions. Wenger was unhappy to lose out to United in the title race but knew that only a poor start had denied his team the trophy. So as United were being lauded as conquerors home and abroad, Arsène had reason to feel slightly shunned. After all, the Gunners had finished one agonising point behind the champions.

The big saga of the summer at Highbury was the exit of striker Anelka in a storm of controversy. Coveted by Real Madrid, Anelka made it clear that unless Arsenal offered him significantly better terms, he would move to the Spanish club. Wenger had improved the striker's game no end and it left a bitter taste in Arsène's mouth and cast a big cloud over the summer months.

While Anelka looked to be leaving Highbury, another speedy Frenchman made his entrance. Wenger had been linked with Thierry Henry in the past and finally got his man during the close season in a £10.5 million deal from Monaco. Henry, who had played much of his football in France as a winger, was a youngster with bags of potential and had been part of the 1998 French World Cup winning squad. Another striker who had shone at the 1998 World Cup followed Henry to Highbury – Davor Suker, the Croatian goal poacher. Manchester United, meanwhile, were preparing for life after Schmeichel, who went out on a high after the Treble celebrations.

Out on the pitch, a solid pre-season gave Wenger reason to believe that his squad was ready to fight for the Premiership crown. On 1 August, the Gunners faced United in the FA Charity Shield at Wembley and, despite going behind to a Beckham free-kick, Arsène's side emerged as 2-1 winners. Although such fixtures never offer a true insight into what lies ahead during the season, the victory pleased Arsène. Anelka, not part of the squad, was far from Arsenal fans' thoughts.

Nigerian international Kanu seemed the man most likely to fill Anelka's role in attack, though Wenger also had Henry to fit into the line-up. Neither Kanu nor Bergkamp offered the electrifying pace of Anelka or the ability to make darting runs behind defences. Perhaps Henry would develop into the central striker role. Elsewhere, Brazilian left-back Silvinho had arrived at Highbury and made a good early impression.

The Gunners opened the new campaign at home to Leicester and almost made an embarrassing start. The Foxes took the lead through Tony Cottee in the second half but Bergkamp equalised soon after. With a draw looking likely, Frank Sinclair headed into his own net after substitute Henry had knocked the ball back across goal. Sinclair had become an own goal specialist during his career and the Gunners were very grateful for his latest gaffe. Highbury breathed a collective sigh of relief but Wenger was not fooled by the result. Arsenal had been lucky.

A flurry of activity just before and after the interval at Pride Park saw the Gunners beat Derby 2-1 as goals from Petit and Bergkamp sealed a win in another tight match. Arsenal were picking up victories but their performances had not been convincing. Henry was operating out on the left flank and showed the ability to link up well with the front two. A 0-0 draw away to Sunderland was disappointing, though not unsurprising, and it meant that Wenger's side went into the crunch clash with champions Manchester United on the back of three shaky league performances.

When the two powerhouses of the past few years lined up at Highbury, there was a feeling in the air that suggested it would be an eventful afternoon. The game certainly lived up to its billing as two sides that respected each other, without showing much friendliness towards one another, squared off. The contest was especially memorable for the wonderful midfield tussle between Vieira and Keane and the image of the two hard men literally going head-to-head. Vieira had dominated proceedings early on and Wenger was delighted when Ljungberg gave Arsenal the lead before half-time from Bergkamp's assist. Ferguson clearly ripped into his players and his demands were met with a positive response in the second half, particularly from Keane. The United skipper grabbed an equaliser before the hour mark to restore parity after a crisp one-two with Andy Cole. The match stayed 1-1 until the final minutes. Giggs surged goalwards – bringing back memories of his FA Cup solo run – and when his shot was deflected it fell kindly for Keane who beat Alex Manninger in the Arsenal goal. Game over for the Gunners.

Wenger found the defeat hard to take. His team had matched United but had been guilty of missing chances and making sloppy errors. This was the crucial difference between being champions and being also-rans. There were still doubts over what Arsène's best eleven was and particularly over who should play up front.

Early goals from Vieira and Kanu settled the next league clash – at home to Bradford on 25 August. The 2-0 win was a welcome relief after the defeat to United and Wenger was impressed with the display.

But a 2-0 defeat to Liverpool at Anfield on 28 August meant that the Gunners had already dropped eight points in the Premiership – hardly the form of title challengers. Substitute Davor Suker missed a penalty in injury time for Arsenal as Wenger had to accept that his side had been second best again. With Overmars fit again, Arsène had an embarrassment of riches in attack but was struggling to find the right combination. He found losing to fellow title contenders all the more irritating but could not claim that Liverpool had been lucky winners.

Strangely, perhaps off the back of recent results, Wenger faced a grilling at the Arsenal AGM as shareholders sought answers on various topics, including the sale of Anelka. It all seemed rather unfair that Arsène was subjected to such questioning but as always he handled himself with dignity. At least he had experience of handling issues at these meetings. Back in 1997, the AGM had erupted into chaos as demands were made for Wenger to axe striker Wright.

Pleased to be able to focus on his job again, the Arsenal manager watched on contentedly as his side recorded a 3-1 win over Aston Villa. It was definitely an improvement, with Suker bagging two goals on his full debut, but the Gunners were doing things the hard way as they let Villa take the lead before mounting their comeback.

There was plenty of excitement around the club as Wenger's side prepared for the start of their Champions League campaign. After the disappointing group stage exit last season, Arsène expected more from his players. However, the Gunners were drawn in a tough group alongside Spanish giants Barcelona, Italian side Fiorentina and minnows AIK Solna. Qualification would be tricky.

Arsène and his squad travelled to Florence for their first fixture, hoping to subdue a Fiorentina team boasting the likes of goal machine Gabriel Batistuta and clever playmaker Rui Costa. The tactical work that Wenger had put in prior to the game paid dividends as Arsenal more than matched their opponents, earning a 0-0 draw on Italian soil. Yet it could have been even better for the Gunners if Kanu had not missed a penalty with twelve minutes remaining. Nonetheless, the point represented a good start and gave the players confidence that they could collect points away from home.

Arsenal carried the resilience from Florence into their next three games, winning all of them. Thierry Henry's first goal for the club was enough to earn a victory away to Southampton. It was a classy finish from a player who had looked dangerous throughout the match. Next, the Gunners took their Champions League tally to four points by beating AIK Solna 3-1 in their first home game in the group stage.

This season, it had been decided that Wenger's team would again play their home European fixtures at Wembley, allowing more people through the gates to watch. Last year, the Gunners had struggled there in Europe but a new season meant a fresh start. It was an interesting idea but it did not please everyone and it deprived the team of the noisy atmosphere that Highbury – a considerably smaller stadium – offered. Arsenal left it late to clinch the three points against Solna, requiring stoppage time strikes from Henry and Suker to give the scoreline a comfortable look. A 1-0 triumph at Watford in the Premiership completed an excellent week as the Gunners again scored late, with Kanu grabbing an 86th minute winner.

Next, Wenger faced his toughest challenge of the season as he took his side to the Nou Camp to face Barcelona. The Catalan side included Brazilian star Rivaldo, Portuguese winger Luis Figo and Spaniard Luis Enrique. But Arsène felt his team had big names of their own. Things did not begin well as Enrique opened the scoring after just sixteen minutes yet although Barcelona's domination in the first half was total, they managed just the one goal. When Grimandi was red carded in the last ten minutes, it looked like an uphill battle for the Gunners but remarkably they scored instantly. Suker's shot was parried out and Kanu did the rest. The Arsenal performance had been below par in general but the spirit and never-say-die attitude had carried the team to a valuable point. With Fiorentina and Solna drawing, Wenger's side were well placed in the group after the first three games.

The euphoria at getting the point in Barcelona and the physical exertions of the game made it slightly less surprising that the Gunners suffered a European hangover when they returned to Premiership action. A 2-1 defeat away to West Ham on 3 October was a blow as they were undone by a Paolo Di Canio brace. Suker pulled a goal back but the Hammers held on. Vieira let his frustrations get the better of him as he picked up a second yellow card and was then involved in an unsavoury incident involving Neil Ruddock, spitting at the defender. There would be repercussions for the fiery Frenchman in the form of a costly eight-match suspension. A win in the League Cup was followed by a much improved league display as Everton were hammered 4-1 at Highbury. Suker was again amongst the goals, scoring twice.

A home game against Barcelona presented Wembley with a fixture befitting of the famous stadium. It was the game everyone was waiting to see. Arsenal had made a solid start to the group stage but Wenger knew his team had to collect points in their remaining home games – against Barcelona and then Fiorentina. Arsène opted for the unpredictable Kanu to partner Bergkamp, leaving Suker and Henry amongst the substitutes. The Spanish giants sent out a line-up packed with flair and the front three of Figo, Rivaldo and Patrick Kluivert presented plenty of problems. The Gunners made the worst possible start as Barcelona found themselves 2-0 up after just fifteen minutes. Skipper Adams conceded a dubious penalty and then gifted Luis Enrique a second moments later. Bergkamp pulled a goal back but Barcelona stretched their lead to 4-1 with twenty minutes remaining. The 4-2 final score reflected the fact that Arsenal had been outclassed by a superior side and, with Fiorentina winning against AIK Solna, the Gunners fell to third in the group. The Arsenal-Fiorentina clash had just become a must-win game for Wenger's players.

At the weekend, the Gunners hit back with a 3-2 win over Chelsea at Stamford Bridge. Arsène summoned all of his side's character and was rewarded as a sensational Kanu hat-trick earned an unexpected three points. Trailing 2-0 early in the second half, few would have given the Gunners much chance. Wenger introduced Henry just after the hour mark to add penetration and then Kanu stepped into the limelight. Two clinical finishes on a wet pitch showed the Nigerian's wonderful touch and pulled Arsenal level with seven minutes left. Many Gunners fans would have settled for that point but the team's manager never thought in that manner. He urged his players to keep pressing and remarkably Kanu struck again. This time it was a truly special effort. Tight against the by-line, the striker fooled Chelsea goalkeeper Ed De Goey before curling the ball into the top corner from a seemingly impossible angle. Wenger's delight was obvious as he celebrated in the wet conditions. The victory restored confidence ahead of the massive match with Fiorentina.

With just one win from four Champions League fixtures, Arsenal were in desperate need of a victory when Fiorentina arrived at Wembley. Wenger sent out his team with a positive game plan but it meant that the Gunners were always vulnerable to counter attacking raids. The back four could not switch off with Batistuta lurking. It was a tight contest in which Arsenal shaded the possession and chances yet it was Fiorentina who emerged with the spoils. Batistuta delivered the knockout blow with fifteen minutes to go and left Wenger to pick up the pieces from another failed European campaign. The Gunners had squandered a handful of opportunities and even went agonisingly close to an equaliser in the final minutes. But it was not their night. Wembley would not see any more Champions League football that season. It would be Fiorentina and Barcelona who qualified from the group, leaving Arsenal and AIK Solna to fight for third spot and a place in the UEFA Cup.

It had been one of the most emotional, rollercoaster weeks of Wenger's time at Arsenal. The two defeats in Europe had hit him hard but the win over Chelsea had been a thrilling feeling. Understandably, the squad were distraught after the elimination and it took time for those wounds to heal. The disappointment seemed to still be on the players' minds in a 0-0 draw against a defensive-minded Newcastle side. Arsène had intended to rest Bergkamp and Overmars but had to throw both into the fray as Bobby Robson's Magpies held firm at the back. Wenger got a more positive response when Arsenal travelled to Sweden to face AIK Solna. The Gunners won 3-2 with Overmars scoring twice and clinched a place in the UEFA Cup – a chance to continue their European adventures. It was some consolation but could never compare to the glamour of the Champions League.

A fiery North London derby on 7 November saw Arsenal suffer a rare defeat against their deadly rivals. Wenger was very proud of the success that he had achieved against Tottenham but this was a day to forget. Ljungberg and Keown both received red cards as the Gunners never recovered from a dire start. 2-0 down after twenty minutes, Arsène could barely believe it. Vieira pulled a goal back but, when the contest descended into aggressive confrontations, any chance of a point drifted away. The Arsenal boss promised himself he would do everything he could to avoid future defeats to the club's bitter rivals.

Added to the busy fixture list, there was more excitement for the club. Having decided to leave Highbury in years to come, they broke the news that a site had been selected for the Gunners' new stadium. It would be built at Ashburton Grove. November 1999 also saw Wenger pick up a special accolade as the University of Hertfordshire awarded the Frenchman an honorary PhD. So while the results on the pitch were not going to plan, there were at least some off-field achievements to cherish.

After an emotional night for Dixon's testimonial match against Real Madrid, Wenger and his players put the defeat to Tottenham behind them by thrashing Middlesbrough 5-1 at Highbury. The Dutch duo of Overmars and Bergkamp shared the five goals between them, with the winger grabbing the hat-trick. When Overmars was in this kind of form, there was no defender in the world capable of containing him. His direct running with the ball left defenders backing off furiously and trying in vain to keep pace with him. Boro never seem to fare too well against the Gunners and their hapless back line were exposed far too often.

Wenger was very happy with his players and told the media post-match: 'They played very well, overall it was a very good team performance. We had a good creative game today – good passing, the right concentration for nearly ninety minutes. The challenge is to repeat.' A 3-0 home win over Nantes in the UEFA

Cup third round first leg clash saw Overmars and Bergkamp on the scoresheet again, along with a rare Winterburn effort. Whilst it was clearly second to the Champions League, the UEFA Cup boasted some top class sides including Juventus, Roma and Deportivo La Coruña. It would still be a special achievement if the Gunners could lift the trophy.

On 28 November, Arsenal kept their run going as Derby suffered a narrow 2-1 defeat at Highbury. Wenger gave Henry the chance to impress in a starting role and the Frenchman did not let his manager down as he scored both Arsenal goals. Arsène has always had a knack for selecting the right moments to unleash young players and this fixture proved the perfect stage for Henry. The Frenchman had spent a lot of time playing on the wing for Monaco but Wenger felt Henry was better suited to a central striker role where his scorching pace would be a constant threat. After Arsène's guidance, Thierry never looked back.

A penalty shootout loss to Middlesbrough in the League Cup was hardly a major blow for Arsène and he had reason to be pleased on 4 December as his side overwhelmed Leicester 3-0 at Filbert Street. A 3-3 draw in France against Nantes ensured that the Gunners progressed in the UEFA Cup. Arsène's side had high hopes of reaching the final and seemed to be handling the packed fixture list impressively well. Victory over Blackpool in the FA Cup led Arsenal into a Christmas period that saw mixed results. It began with a 1-1 draw on 18 December against Wimbledon, who were fast becoming one of Wenger's bogey teams. Henry was on the mark again as he equalised Carl Cort's opener.

Boxing Day brought a below-par 3-2 defeat away to Coventry as they fell further behind in the title race. The Sky Blues put in one of their best displays of the season to outfight the Gunners and Robbie Keane impressed everyone with his display up front for the home side. Goals from Ljungberg and Suker were not enough to rescue the situation and Arsenal found themselves eight points behind Premiership leaders Leeds. David O'Leary's young Leeds side had impressed many with their strong run of results but Wenger hoped that their inexperience would offer other teams a chance to capitalise. After all, there was still a very long way to go in the title race.

Arsène did not have long to wait to make inroads into Leeds' lead. O'Leary's team travelled to Highbury for a key contest on 28 December but, with Wenger's players fired up, the Gunners never allowed the visitors to settle. In a physical contest, the likes of Harry Kewell and Lee Bowyer were unable to make their usual impact and goals from Ljungberg and Henry completed an important 2-0 victory for Arsène's side. It sent out a reminder to the other top sides that Arsenal had not given up on the title yet.

After this result, Wenger entered the New Year with renewed hope. A 1-1 draw at Sheffield Wednesday on 3 January was far from ideal; nor was a goalless stalemate in the FA Cup against Leicester which just added to Arsenal's lengthy fixture list. Manchester United were not competing in the competition due to their involvement in the World Club Championship in Brazil and their withdrawal from the FA Cup angered many, including Wenger.

Sunderland felt the force of Arsenal's frustrations on 15

January as they were soundly beaten 4-1. Henry continued to impress with his pace and movement while Suker's predatory instincts were as sharp as ever. They bagged two goals each and kept the Gunners on track.

Losing to Leicester on penalties in their FA Cup replay was a blow for Wenger's side as a good run in the competition had been high on Arsène's list of priorities. But a trip to Old Trafford ensured that there was no time to dwell on what might have been because Ferguson's players would not be showing any sympathy. Just as they had the previous year, Arsenal went to Old Trafford and played very commendably. Ljungberg gave Wenger's men the lead but United substitute Teddy Sheringham hit back after half-time. This draw kept United and Arsenal on level points but Ferguson's side had games in hand over both the Gunners and table-toppers Leeds.

Two consecutive defeats at the start of February put a massive dent in Wenger's title hopes. The first, a 2-1 loss at Bradford, was especially poor. Facing a noisy crowd and a committed Bradford line-up, the Gunners crumbled. Henry quickly equalised Dean Windass' opener but veteran striker Dean Saunders popped up with a goal just before the hour mark which proved to be the winner. Arsène was furious with his team's lacklustre display but noted that Henry had once again made a significant impact.

The defeat to Liverpool at Highbury the next weekend was less surprising as the Merseysiders had a good recent record in the fixture but it upset Wenger just as much as the surrender at Bradford. Titi Camara's eighteenth minute strike was enough to earn the three points for Liverpool as Arsène again watched his side fall short of a convincing performance. The Gunners launched a late assault on the visitors' goal but Gerard Houllier's defence withstood it admirably.

Post-match, Wenger reflected that it had been 'a poor game' but that his side had 'deserved a point, just because we at least tried to play and tried to break Liverpool down.' Perhaps more worrying, though, was the Frenchman's revelation that he thought the title race was only between Manchester United and Leeds now. Admittedly, after these setbacks, Arsenal looked like finishing fourth as Liverpool, Leeds and Manchester United powered on ahead but there was still a good chunk of the season remaining.

Everyone anticipated a backlash from Wenger's players but it never fully materialised. There were signs, though, that Arsenal might put together a series of wins. A 3-1 victory over Southampton preceded a 5-1 demolition of Spanish side Deportivo La Coruña in the UEFA Cup on 2 March. It all but sealed the tie for Wenger's team. A Dixon header gave Arsenal a perfect start and Henry doubled the lead. Deportivo pulled a goal back but any hope they had of salvaging something was dashed when goalscorer Djalminha was sent off. Then the floodgates opened as Henry struck again before Kanu and Bergkamp put the icing on the cake. It was one of the most exciting European nights in the club's recent history and the return to Highbury seemed to have made a difference as the fans created the kind of white hot atmosphere that had been missing during the big games against Barcelona and Fiorentina. Wembley had not been a lucky ground for the Gunners during the Champions League group stage.

A draw with Aston Villa and a loss to Deportivo in a low-key, pretty meaningless second leg followed. The Gunners were beaten 2-1 in Spain but Wenger was happy enough with the 6-3 aggregate score in Arsenal's favour. He looked forward with excitement to the quarter-finals. The team's rocky form continued though as a poor display away to Middlesbrough saw the Gunners lose 2-1 with a makeshift back four that did little to inspire confidence. It seemed an odd time for Arsène to be rotating his squad. There was great frustration for Wenger in the way that his side were performing. He knew that they were capable of so much better.

Arsène's lectures finally seemed to sink in after the defeat at Boro. The players worked harder for each other, particularly in away games, and it led to consistent results. On 16 March, Wenger sent out his team for the home leg of the UEFA Cup quarter-final with German side Werder Bremen hoping for a repeat of the demolition of Deportivo. The Gunners put in a confident team performance and managed to earn a 2-0 victory, giving themselves breathing space in the tie and every chance of finishing the job in Germany. Wenger praised the contribution of an on-song Adams and felt proud of his side's display. Bremen had a few dangerous moments, though, which suggested that the second leg would still be a tricky occasion. Goals from Henry and Ljungberg sealed the win. An even sweeter win came at the weekend as Tottenham were beaten 2-1 at Highbury – revenge for the loss at White Hart Lane in November.

The second leg against Bremen brought a third successive victory as Wenger enjoyed the stylish manner in which his side were playing. A 4-2 win on German soil was a terrific effort as

Parlour bagged a hat-trick. The only negative element on the night was a controversial red card for Henry. Even that, though, could not dampen Arsène's spirits. This cup run was really gathering pace. Consecutive victories number four and five followed as first Coventry then Wimbledon fell to the rampant Gunners. Wenger's players picked up a 3-1 scoreline against the Dons despite having Ukrainian Oleg Luzhny sent off at the end of the first half. Kanu grabbed a brace and Henry added a third from the penalty spot for good measure.

Next for Wenger's on-song outfit was the first leg of the UEFA Cup semi-final against French club Lens. Once more, this first leg would be at Highbury and Arsène was desperate for the Gunners to collect a good result to take to France. Ideally, Arsenal would run riot and put the tie to bed at home. But Lens proved stubborn opponents and dealt well with the attacking threat of Bergkamp, Overmars and Kanu. The Gunners missed Henry who was serving his suspension.

When Bergkamp scored after just two minutes, many expected a massive margin of victory but instead Lens tightened up and returned to France relatively satisfied to have only lost 1-0. They hoped that at home they could turn around this slender deficit. While Wenger would have liked more goals, the clean sheet gave Arsenal the chance to take control of the tie by scoring an away goal in the second leg. Post-match, Arsène admitted his disappointment that his team had not put the tie to bed: 'We became insecure because they closed us down. They played at a high level and we had nothing more to give and lacked presence in the box.' He remained anxious ahead of the second leg.

As Leeds were battered 4-0 in front of their own fans by an unstoppable Arsenal side, Wenger must have questioned why it had taken so long for his players to turn in such irresistible displays. The erratic months earlier in the campaign had been painful yet Arsène had known all along that his squad had the talent to challenge for the title. Leeds had enjoyed an excellent campaign but here, trailing 1-0, Ian Harte was sent off and the Gunners capitalised with three goals in the last twenty minutes. The home side fielded Lee Bowyer and Jonathan Woodgate but the players' off-field controversy coincided with the team's dip in form lately. It made it two wins out of two for Wenger's side against Leeds during the season.

As the Arsenal squad headed for France, Wenger hoped that his players had packed the same scoring boots that they had been wearing at the weekend. It was a massive occasion for the club and a European final was just ninety minutes away. Arsène called for calm from his team and set about plotting Lens' downfall.

The first half went perfectly. The Gunners kept things tight defensively and Henry gave the team breathing space with a precious away goal just before the interval. Now Lens needed to score three times to progress to the final. The home side equalised with seventeen minutes remaining but they had left themselves far too much to do. As Lens threw bodies forward, they left gaps in defence and Arsenal punished them as Kanu sealed a 3-1 aggregate win late on. Wenger and his squad were jubilant. The Frenchman told the media: 'It means a lot for me to take Arsenal to a UEFA Cup final but it was a strange game. I never felt under threat too much because I thought we controlled the match.'

A UEFA Cup final against Galatasaray now awaited the Gunners and it represented a chance to lift some silverware in an otherwise below-par campaign. There was an invincible look about the Arsenal side during their run to the final and their Turkish opponents would have to be on top form to stop Arsène's team. Back in the Premiership, confidence remained high. On April 23, Watford put up a good fight but lost 3-2 to the Gunners at Vicarage Road. A brace from Henry and a third from Parlour had given Arsenal a 3-0 lead but a loss of concentration nearly cost Wenger's side dearly as Watford launched a second half comeback. Arsène was once again indebted to Henry for lifting the team to victory. It was a welcome win but it was a tired performance.

A goal from Overmars, who was rumoured to want a move away from the club at the end of the season, earned Arsenal a 1-0 win at Goodison Park the following weekend and put the Gunners into second place in the league. Wenger's team were on an impressive run but United had long since sealed the title and sat 19 points clear. If only Arsenal had not left it so late. These three points made it six victories in a row in the Premiership.

On 2 May, the Gunners made it seven straight league wins by beating West Ham 2-1 at Highbury. It was a nervy ninety minutes for Arsène as his players laboured against the Hammers, who took the lead through Italian Paolo Di Canio five minutes before half-time. But Arsenal were determined to keep their string of victories alive and staged a strong fightback in the second period. Overmars equalised with just over twenty minutes remaining and Petit smashed home an 89th minute winner that left West Ham fuming – they believed the Frenchman had handled the ball before shooting. With eleven consecutive wins now in all competitions, Wenger was delighted and encouraged his players to maintain this momentum. The response was another win – this time at home to Chelsea. Predictably, Henry was the star man as he scored both goals in the 2-1 victory. His reputation in Europe was growing with every week and he had a big future at Highbury. The Blues had no answer to his pace.

The run of wins came to an end with a 3-3 draw against Sheffield Wednesday. The result relegated the Owls as Arsenal stormed back from 3-1 down. The sloppy defending left Wenger disappointed but in the final third there was plenty to smile about. Left-back Silvinho made it 3-2 with a special strike and that man Henry popped up yet again to save the Gunners a minute later with the equaliser. That was the twelfth goal in ten games for the Frenchman. His clinical finishing was a reminder of just how shrewd Wenger had been in snapping up Henry for a mere £10.5 million – it would prove a bargain in the coming years. There was further reason to be optimistic about the future in midweek as the Arsenal youngsters completed a 5-1 aggregate win over Coventry to lift the FA Cup Youth trophy. The academy was obviously doing a good job of bringing through the next generation of Gunners stars.

With the UEFA Cup final in mind, Arsène decided to rest a number of his first team players for the final Premiership fixture of the season away to Newcastle. It was a memorable day for Alan Shearer as he notched up his 300th career goal but the 4-2 victory was forgettable for Wenger. In fairness, though, the fixture had little relevance apart from giving a few younger players the chance to impress their manager. Arsène was already looking to the big European final and trying to plot Galatasaray's downfall.

As the Gunners side stepped out onto the field for the UEFA Cup final at the Parken Stadium in Copenhagen, Wenger knew that he had done everything possible to prepare his players for the contest. Arsène had the good fortune of being able to select from a fully fit squad and hoped that the strong spine of the team would be too good for Galatasaray. With Adams and Keown at the back, Vieira and Petit in midfield and Bergkamp and Henry up front, Arsenal fans had reason to feel confident. But it quickly became clear that the Turks would be no pushovers. Gheorghe Hagi brought great skill and vision to a Galatasaray team whose defence held out stubbornly.

That is not to say that Arsenal did not have chances. Wenger's frustration grew and grew as the Gunners spurned a number of opportunities and Galatasaray's Brazilian goalkeeper Taffarel made some crucial saves. The game remained goalless after ninety minutes and the contest entered extra-time. The advantage swung firmly Arsenal's way early in the first period of extra-time when Hagi was sent off for lashing out at Adams. Arsène urged his players to capitalise against ten men but it was a tough ask for a weary team and the match would be decided on penalties.

But it all ended in tears. Once again, an English side failed from the penalty spot in a big game. Galatasaray held their nerve impressively to win the shootout 4-1 and leave Wenger to console his devastated troops. It was the cruellest way to lose after all the effort that had gone into the 120 minutes of action. Parlour found the net with his penalty but first Suker and then

Vieira hit the woodwork, allowing ex-Tottenham defender Gheorghe Popescu to slot home the winning penalty. Wenger was heartbroken. Galatasaray lifted the trophy while the Arsenal side were just left with their runners-up medals. It was not the season finale that the Gunners boss had had in mind but, on the positive side, the team had been terrific en route to the final and deserved great credit. After the disappointment of Champions League elimination, the squad and the coaching staff had turned things around admirably.

So Wenger finished the campaign empty-handed again but with more reason to be excited for the future. His younger players were developing well and had been helped by the experience of the likes of Adams, Keown and Bergkamp. Henry, in particular, had stood out as a brilliant buy and Arsène received plenty of credit for opting to play the Frenchman as a striker rather than a winger. The Gunners boss would look at his squad over the summer and think about ways to improve his options. Manchester United had won the Premiership at a canter this year (by 18 points) but Arsenal hoped to put up a stronger challenge in 2000/01. Perhaps the new millennium would be the start of the Gunners' dynasty.

* * *

The summer had been an interesting one in English football. Manchester United had left all challengers in their wake last season but the contenders were expected to raise their game. Ferguson's squad still looked lethal and most pundits tipped United to make it three Premiership titles in a row. Wenger, though, hoped to outlast the Red Devils boss, who was now Sir

Alex after his knighthood, and wrestle the trophy back to London.

The Frenchman used the summer transfer market to make some major changes to his squad. After much speculation, Barcelona came in with bids for Overmars and Petit as the Catalan giants looked to overhaul their midfield. A combined fee of £28 million got Wenger's attention and he took the opportunity to offload the pair and give himself a handsome transfer kitty. Both had been superb players for the Gunners but their form had slipped since the title win in 1998.

Armed with money to spend, Wenger invested wisely. He did not shell out a huge sum for one individual but preferred to buy a handful of players for lower prices. Lauren, the versatile Cameroon international, arrived for £7.2 million from Real Mallorca in Spain while French winger Robert Pires cost £6 million from French club Metz and was expected to fill Overmars' role on the left hand side. Igor Stepanovs was signed to give defensive cover.

While these negotiations were completed with the minimum of fuss, two other deals caused far more problems. First, Edu, the left-footed midfielder, was stopped by customs over passport issues. Wenger had identified the Brazilian as the natural replacement for Petit but had to wait while the player sorted out his documents. Similarly, Arsène's move for Sylvain Wiltord was a stop-start affair. Wenger promised that the deal would go through before the UEFA deadline but was growing frustrated with Bordeaux, Wiltord's club.

Wenger had taken Arsenal from a top five club back to being a title contender. It was a task he had completed effortlessly and with no shortage of style. But while United had been the dominant force in English football for the past two years, Wenger felt his players were ready to regain the Premiership crown. The Gunners had pushed United close in the Treble winning year – taking the title race to the final weekend – yet Ferguson's side had cruised to glory last season by a comfortable margin of eighteen points. It had unsettled Arsène to see his side so far off the pace and he vowed to push United harder in 2000/01. In Henry, Vieira and Bergkamp, he had the resources to fight for the top honours but consistency would be the key factor. United's summer shopping had been limited and the only big signing was goalkeeper Fabien Barthez, who would be the latest to attempt to fill the void left by Schmeichel.

The Gunners made a mixed start to the new season and it certainly did not spread panic in the Manchester area. An opening day defeat to Sunderland was a shock as Niall Quinn's header sealed a 1-0 win for the Black Cats. Wenger's day got even worse when Vieira was harshly sent off in the closing moments. A 2-0 home victory over Liverpool restored order but it was an unpleasant game that saw Vieira sent off again. The midfielder again had reason to feel aggrieved at the decision. Wenger was livid with referee Graham Poll.

Charlton felt the full force of Arsenal's growing assurance as the Gunners registered a second straight win in a 5-3 triumph at Highbury. Henry was in typically dazzling form as he and Vieira scored two each. It was not a straightforward victory, however, as the visitors led 2-1 and 3-2 before Wenger's side mounted comebacks. Arsène was proud of his players and took the opportunity to praise Vieira, who he felt had been victimised by officials lately: 'I'm pleased that we could win this game after such a controversial week, and as well by the performance of Patrick Vieira today because he was outstanding and exceptional. Not only because he's a great player, but mentally his response was great.'

On the same day, Wiltord finally became an Arsenal player, signing for £12.5 million. It was well over what Arsène had hoped to pay for him but Wiltord, who had just won Euro 2000 with France, was a highly rated forward.

Draws in their next two games were far from ideal and Wenger grew irritated that his players were constantly doing things the hard way. At Stamford Bridge against Chelsea, Arsenal gave themselves a mountain to climb, only to score twice in the final fourteen minutes to snatch a point. Silvinho's rocket strike from distance was a special moment and a 2-2 draw represented a decent result. But only collecting a point at Bradford on 9 September was regarded as a missed opportunity to climb the table. Wenger knew that a solid run of wins was required if his team were to sustain their title challenge.

The Gunners did not lose again in the league until 18 November as the players answered their manager's call for consistency. The Champions League first group stage put Arsenal alongside Lazio, Shakhtar Donetsk from the Ukraine and Sparta Prague from the Czech Republic. Wenger's side and Lazio seemed the likely qualifiers on paper but it would not be easy. The campaign began in promising fashion on 12 September with a 1-0 victory away in Prague courtesy of another Silvinho goal.

Further wins against Coventry and Shakhtar Donetsk gave Arsène renewed confidence. He saw his side growing in maturity and felt that silverware was a distinct possibility. Against Shakhtar, though, it was almost another frustrating night in Europe as countless chances were wasted and centre-back Keown had to come to the rescue, scoring twice in the final five minutes to grab a 3-2 victory. Wenger was massively relieved as a draw would have seriously damaged Arsenal's hopes of qualifying. Wins at Highbury in the competition would be priceless.

After a draw at Ipswich, victory over Lazio in Europe was the highlight of September as Arsenal showed their pedigree amongst the elite clubs in the competition. The Italian side arrived at Highbury on 27 September full of confidence and featured plenty of household names including Juan Sebastian Veron, Pavel Nedved and Alessandro Nesta. But Wenger had done his research and the Gunners were too strong. Ljungberg was the hero on the night as he scored both goals in a 2-0 victory.

At the weekend, Arsène had more celebrating to do as his side beat champions Manchester United 1-0 at Highbury. Henry was the match-winner as his spectacular goal proved to be decisive. He received the ball with his back to goal on the edge of the penalty area yet managed to swivel and hook the ball over Barthez and into the net. The goal had come out of the blue and it gave the Gunners something to hold onto as United fought to get a foothold in the game. Wenger's defenders had an excellent afternoon and the visitors found no way through. Arsenal were now level with United, who had made an erratic start to the campaign.

After the game, the Frenchman praised his team's 'character' in one of his now customary post-match speeches. By referring to qualities such as character, intelligence and spirit, Arsène would rarely reveal any significant details about his tactics or team selection. It was almost as if he was hiding behind vague, abstract attributes to protect the secrets of his planning. Clearly, sports figures who receive as much attention as Wenger must adopt a style of question-answering that gives little away to the media. He has perfected this style and has behaved in this manner throughout his time at Arsenal.

A third successive clean sheet at home to Aston Villa on 14 October pleased Wenger. Title challenges were so often build on solid defences so it was important that the Gunners had tightened up at the back. A creditable point at the Stadio Olimpico against Lazio continued the side's unbeaten run. It was testament to the developments that Wenger had orchestrated at Highbury that the team now had no fear on their travels in Europe. The 1-1 draw, courtesy of a Pires goal, put Arsenal into the next round of the competition.

Three more wins saw the momentum increase. A narrow 2-1 victory at Upton Park against West Ham was a spirited team performance from the Gunners and showed that it was not just about their flair in attack. The resilience in the side was just as vital. The Hammers fans created a hostile atmosphere for the visitors but Wenger's team silenced the crowd with an assured display. A 4-2 win at home to Sparta Prague on 25 October sealed qualification for the second group stage and it gave Arsène the luxury of resting players for the final fixture of the first phase against Shakhtar Donetsk.

On 28 October, Manchester City came to Highbury and felt the full force of Arsenal's attacking flair in a 5-0 rout. Cole,

Bergkamp and Wiltord made it 3-0 before Henry scored twice late on. It was no doubt little consolation to City that the Gunners would have beaten any side when playing with such quality. On this type of form, Wenger knew his team could keep pace with United at the top of the league table.

Arsène was delighted to see the flowing football that his team was producing. He had earned a reputation for endorsing a creative style with an emphasis on slick passing and lightning movement. These were the attributes that Wenger demanded from his players, particularly those in forward positions.

A 2-1 defeat at home to Ipswich in the League Cup on 1 November gave Wenger one less competition to focus on. It was not a trophy that Arsène coveted and, frankly, there were bigger prizes to chase. A goal from Henry earned the Gunners a 1-0 win at Middlesbrough in the Premiership as they kept up their good form. The clean sheet was especially welcomed. Losing to Shakhtar in Europe was irrelevant with qualification already assured but Arsène was a little disgruntled to see his side overpowered 3-0 by the Ukrainians.

The defeat to Shakhtar may have had no impact on the first group stage table but it was a precursor for a dismal few weeks for the Gunners. A 0-0 draw at home to Derby on 11 November was the first of the disappointments as Wenger regarded the result as two valuable points dropped. Worse followed as Arsenal lost three games in a row – all away from Highbury. A packed crowd at Everton witnessed a 2-0 win for the Toffees as Wenger's side failed to match the home team's intensity.

The first fixture of the Champions League second group stage was instantly forgettable as the Gunners stumbled to an embarrassing 4-1 loss against Spartak Moscow. The change of climate may have affected the Arsenal players but it was no excuse for the feeble showing in the Russian capital. Drawn in Group C alongside Spartak, Bayern Munich and Lyon, there were tougher fixtures ahead.

Leeds completed a miserable week for Arsène by winning 1-0 at Elland Road thanks to an Olivier Dacourt goal. Wenger took discomfort from the fact that his team had scored just twice in their last six matches. For a group of players that loved to attack and create chances, this was extremely frustrating.

Normal order was restored at home to Southampton on 2 December but the margin of victory was small – 1-0. In previous years, the Saints had endured some awful afternoons at Highbury but faired better on this occasion. Wenger was simply happy to take the three points. With a hectic Christmas fixture list on the horizon, it was all about results rather than the quality of performances at the moment.

The Gunners signed off in Europe for 2000 with a 2-2 draw at home to Bayern Munich. A point against the wily Germans was not, in itself, a poor result but Wenger had watched his side squander a 2-0 lead and could not believe that two crucial points had slipped through his fingers. He feared that they might come back to haunt him in future months.

It left Arsène's side with one point from two games and there was plenty of work ahead. The Champions League would return in February when two group fixtures with Lyon would be vital for the team's chances of reaching the quarter-finals. A 5-0 victory over Newcastle on 9 December was a fine way to enter a busy Christmas schedule, with the Magpies powerless to stop the constant waves of attacks. Parlour bagged a hat-trick as Arsenal swept their opponents aside.

A draw at White Hart Lane in the North London derby was a slight disappointment for Wenger but the 4-0 defeat away to Liverpool on 23 December was utterly humiliating. The Frenchman was stunned by the performance and let the media know that such displays would not be tolerated. Liverpool boss Gerard Houllier was left to reflect on a superb week in which his team beat both Manchester United and Arsenal.

Fortunately, the Gunners only had to wait three days to make amends. Leicester were the unlucky visitors who faced an Arsenal side intent on releasing some frustration. A 6-1 scoreline emphasised the sheer domination of Arsène's players who had responded brilliantly to the criticism at Anfield. A hat-trick from Henry was the highlight of an exciting afternoon.

Sloppy errors let Sunderland escape from Highbury with a 2-2 draw on 30 December. The Black Cats had taken four points from their two meetings with the Gunners during the campaign – not many sides could claim such a tally. The week got worse for Wenger as Arsenal's title pursuit suffered another setback at The Valley against Charlton. The 1-0 defeat meant that Arsène's team had picked up just five points out of the past fifteen. It had proved to be a bleak Christmas in North London and their title quest was going off the rails.

Arsenal's Premiership form continued to wobble but their FA Cup displays were far more successful as they booked a place in the fifth round after wins over Carlisle and QPR – the latter of which was an impressive 6-0 away victory. In the league, though, two more draws for the Gunners gave Manchester

United room to breathe at the top of the table. With Wenger's side dropping points on a weekly basis, a gripping title race seemed unlikely. A 1-1 draw with Chelsea was followed by a 0-0 stalemate at Filbert Street, in which Arsenal played against ten men for almost fifty minutes.

February saw Arsenal gradually finding better form. Was it too late? January had ended with a 2-0 win over Bradford and the new month brought back-to-back 1-0 wins over Coventry and Ipswich. A third 1-0 victory – this time in Europe away to Lyon – raised discussion about a return to the 'boring Arsenal' days when George Graham's team regularly scrapped for narrow wins. By beating their French counterparts, the Gunners had reignited their bid for a quarter-final berth. Chelsea were next to suffer at the hands of Arsène's players as the Blues were knocked out of the FA Cup in a 3-1 Arsenal victory.

Then came one of the most embarrassing weeks of Wenger's tenure at Highbury. A 1-1 draw at home to Lyon on 21 February was a blow as Edmilson snatched a late equaliser for the visitors. Arsène had lost count of the number of times that his team had thrown away leads in the closing minutes of games. But it was not disastrous and still left the Gunners with a good chance of qualification.

Three days later Arsène took his players to Old Trafford to try to cut United's lead at the Premiership summit. It was an afternoon to forget for the Frenchman as his depleted defence crumbled in a 6-1 demolition. He paired Grimandi with Stepanovs at centre-half even though they had never played together and took the rather negative option of picking Silvinho in left midfield to protect Cole from Gary Neville's overlapping runs. All these decisions backfired badly. It was hard to believe that such a student of the game had made a handful of poor selections.

Dwight Yorke ran the Arsenal back four ragged and grabbed a hat-trick in the process but the whole United attack dominated the Gunners defence. With the home fans in full voice, Wenger could only watch on as the horror show unfolded in front of him. It was a long, quiet journey back to London, giving the squad plenty of time to ponder where it all went wrong. He told the media: 'I have had worse experiences but the size of the score makes this a very bad one. Nobody was communicating, we had no leaders, and there were times when we looked like a youth team. We are not into March yet and it hurts me that the title is already over.' His downcast expression said it all. It was later revealed that Wenger had launched into a rare, furious rant at his players after the defeat. Maybe the pressure was finally getting to him as Arsenal slipped out of the title race.

The thrashing in Manchester combined with Arsène's fury sparked the Gunners into life at last. A 3-0 win at home to West Ham was a strong response, with Wiltord scoring all three, and a 1-0 victory over Spartak Moscow put Wenger's side in a decent position for qualifying for the quarter-finals. It would all depend on the last group game away to Bayern Munich. Arsène craved a good run in the Champions League and this season looked like it could deliver a semi-final or even a final. The mood around the club suggested that the United game was now a distant memory.

Blackburn, who would become more and more frequent cup opponents for the Gunners, lost 3-0 at Highbury in an FA Cup quarter-final. The Premiership might be eluding Wenger's side but the Frenchman felt that the FA Cup and Champions League were still realistic targets.

A defeat away to Bayern proved irrelevant in the end as Arsenal qualified despite the 1-0 loss. Everyone at the club awaited the quarter-final draw with baited breath. Valencia would be their opponents, with the first leg to be played in early April. Wenger could not wait.

In the meantime, the Gunners collected four points from two tricky league games. A 0-0 draw at Villa Park brought a fourth clean sheet in five games and the run continued at home to Tottenham as their North London rivals were defeated 2-0. It signalled another season in which Tottenham had failed to register a league victory over Arsenal, much to the delight of Gunners fans worldwide.

Valencia arrived at Highbury on 4 April and entered a loud, tense stadium for a crucial contest. The Spaniards had plenty of experience in European knockout ties but Wenger had studied his opponents carefully and hoped to exploit some weaknesses. On a night full of drama, the Gunners trailed 1-0 at half-time but Arsène turned the match on its head with a tactical switch that caused the visitors all kinds of problems. With Arsenal changing to three up front, Valencia were stretched and first Henry, then Parlour found the net. Wenger's side emerged as 2-1 winners and he was pleased with the strong second half showing.

However, Valencia's away goal troubled him and it would make life tricky for the return leg. A 1-0 win would be enough for the Spanish team to progress and Arsène rued a string of missed chances, telling the press: 'We won the game but it should have been by three or four.'

With an FA Cup semi-final against Tottenham and a handful of league games ahead, the Arsenal players had to quickly switch their attention back to domestic fixtures. A passionate 2-1 semi-final victory over Tottenham showed the Gunners' spirit as much as their class. Again they fell behind and had to recover. Pires popped up with the winner. Liverpool were victorious in the other semi-final, meaning that Wenger and his squad were presented with a chance to avenge the 4-0 defeat that they suffered at Anfield in December. Leading his team out at the Millennium Stadium was a moment that Arsène looked forward to with great pride.

Manchester City felt the full force of the Arsenal attack on 11 April in a comfortable 4-0 home win for the Gunners. It had been a good week for Wenger and he enjoyed the team's display against City. A 3-0 defeat against Middlesbrough was less impressive – Edu and Silvinho both scored own goals – but Wenger had opted to leave a number of key players on the sidelines in order to keep them fresh for the trip to Valencia in midweek. The quarter-final second leg was the fixture that all Arsenal minds were now focused on. The Premiership was out of reach.

Wenger and his players landed in Spain full of hope. Their recent form had been decent and the side was well rested. Arsène and his coaching staff discussed tactics at length, expecting a nervy night in the Mestalla Stadium. As the Frenchman had admitted, his side could not afford to be too cagey: 'The fact that Valencia scored an away goal at Highbury means we have to play and be positive in Spain.'

The match was very edgy and full of tension. Neither side

wanted to make the crucial mistake that could ultimately decide the outcome of the tie. Valencia gradually pushed more and more men forward in search of a goal and Arsène hoped that the likes of Henry would make good use of the extra space. But it was the home team that struck the killer blow as John Carew put Valencia ahead with just fifteen minutes remaining. The Gunners tried to recover but it was too late and the Spaniards defended their advantage with ten men behind the ball. The 1-0 scoreline put Valencia through to the semi-finals but Wenger, as is often the case, was grudging in his praise for his opponents and claimed his team had been unlucky: 'We should still be in this competition because they had hardly any shots on goal and we controlled the second half.' Henry agreed when he spoke to the media.

It was a sad way for the European adventure to end. Arsène's players had performed heroically and the Frenchman could not fault the team's effort. The experience gained during the campaign would serve the Gunners well for the future and Wenger felt proud that his squad had proved equal to such strong Champions League sides as Lazio, Bayern Munich and Valencia. The whole European run had only strengthened the Arsenal manager's desire to lift the trophy one day.

Wenger now worked towards the FA Cup final on 12 May. There were three Premiership matches to play first and he would use those games to make decisions about the starting line-up for the big day in Cardiff. A 4-1 win over Everton was an important result as Arsène was well aware that there were several teams looking to sneak ahead of the Gunners and claim second place. Beating the Toffees meant that Arsenal were closer to ensuring automatic qualification for next year's Champions League but United were out of sight – 13 points ahead.

A 2-1 victory away to Derby was another useful result as Kanu and Pires found the net. Goals from the in-form Ljungberg and Wiltord secured the three points at home to Leeds on 5 May which left Wenger pleased Arsenal were heading into the FA Cup final on top of their game. Confidence was high.

The years of cup finals at Wembley had been very special. Wenger had savoured the atmosphere during his visit in 1998 and was well aware of the history of the stadium. But there was something significant, too, about competing in the first FA Cup final at the Millennium Stadium, while the new Wembley was being built. Liverpool and Arsenal knew each other well and there would be few surprises in personnel for the game. Wenger, going up against his old friend Houllier, drilled his defenders on dealing with the threat of Michael Owen and the midfield energy of Steven Gerrard. Those two had enjoyed excellent seasons but if the Gunners could stop Owen and Gerrard, Liverpool would struggle to impose themselves on the contest.

A capacity crowd filed into the Millennium Stadium with a mouth-watering clash in prospect. It was hard to pick a winner but many felt that Arsenal's experience might just make the difference. Wenger made a big selection decision by leaving the fit again Bergkamp on the bench in favour of Wiltord, thinking that this was not the type of game for the Dutchman to be feeling his way back from injury. It was a strange choice, considering Wiltord wanted to leave the club at the end of the season. The Gunners were by far the livelier side on the day, passing swiftly and forcing Liverpool onto the back foot.

Houllier's Reds were strangely subdued and rode their luck in keeping the game goalless for well over an hour.

Eventually, though, Arsenal broke the deadlock. Having already had numerous close efforts, the Gunners finally made it count as Ljungberg burst onto Pires' pass, rounded Liverpool goalkeeper Sander Westerveld and slotted the ball home. The Swede had been clinical in the past month. The Arsenal fans were on their feet, sensing the silverware would be heading to London. But Houllier's side hit back with seven minutes remaining as Owen found himself in the right place at the right time to equalise with a low strike. Wenger had tried to close the game out by bringing on Parlour but it had back-fired.

The drama of extra-time and even penalties loomed yet the game would not go that far. Boosted by the goal, Liverpool believed that they could capitalise on the Gunners' weary legs. With two minutes left, Owen again found space and, outpacing Dixon, placed a left-footed shot across Seaman and into the far corner. Wenger could scarcely register what he was seeing. After all Arsenal's domination, Liverpool had snatched the cup from under their noses with a five minute burst.

Arsène was gracious in defeat but promised to assess his side's season carefully and strengthen the squad in places. He told the press: 'It's difficult to blame the team. Credit to Liverpool, they defended very well and they found the resources even though when we were 1-0 up they didn't look to be a threat. This is a little bit the image of our season. We always looked like we should win the big games but we can't finish it and we lose concentration.' Looking ahead to next year, he added: 'I have some (players) in mind, but I've been keeping it quiet.' Patrick Vieira, the dejected Arsenal skipper, admitted: 'Maybe we were too confident in ourselves because we were winning 1-0 but that's football sometimes. We always say we will try our best next season, but it is true.'

With the FA Cup final scheduled before the end of the Premiership season, the Arsenal players had to pick themselves up and concentrate on their last two fixtures. It came as little surprise that the Gunners struggled to hit top form in these matches after the disappointment against Liverpool but Wenger had expected more than a solitary point from the games with Newcastle (home) and Southampton (away).

The goalless stalemate against the Magpies at Highbury was hardly a thriller but the trip to Southampton was a special occasion as it marked the end of the Saints' spell at The Dell. It was fitting that the final league game at the stadium was against a team of Arsenal's calibre and, in a fairytale ending, Southampton legend Matt Le Tissier came off the bench to score the winner in the 89th minute. It gave the home side a 3-2 victory and led to huge celebrations inside the ground. Le Tissier had enjoyed so many magnificent afternoons at The Dell, keeping his team in the top flight single-handedly at times, and nobody could have scripted the afternoon better. Even Wenger and his players joined in the applause on an emotional day for the Saints.

The match brought the curtain down on a decent campaign for Arsène's side but ultimately no silverware had been won. Brilliant at times, the Gunners had stumbled at vital moments and Wenger could not dispute the fact that Manchester United were worthy champions. Ferguson's side won the title by ten points, despite losing their last three league games. For Wenger, Arsenal's defeat in the FA Cup final brought added pain but also strengthened his desire to put things right when the new season arrived. Arsène took plenty of positives from his team's performances but knew that top clubs were judged on trophies and, in that regard, Arsenal's end of year report read 'Must do better'.

SUPREMACY REGAINED AND SURRENDERED

Wenger entered the new season desperate to put an end to Manchester United's years of domination. A handful of new signings underlined the club's desire to compete for the top honours. Sol Campbell, the England centre-back, arrived from arch-rivals Tottenham in the most controversial move of the summer. Taking advantage of the Bosman ruling, Campbell jumped at the chance to join Wenger's squad on a free transfer and immediately the Arsenal back four seemed stronger. His partnership with Adams at the heart of the defence looked extremely imposing. It spoke volumes for Campbell's desire to win trophies that he was prepared to make such an unpopular move for the sake of his career. He would not regret it.

Francis Jeffers arrived for £10 million from Everton as Wenger seemingly bowed to the pressure to buy English players. The Frenchman wanted a 'fox in the box' type striker to partner Henry – someone who could get on the end of crosses and score the scrappy goals that the team were missing out on. Continuing his theme of buying British, Arsène signed highly rated Ipswich goalkeeper Richard Wright for £6 million to provide competition for Seaman. Giovanni van Bronkhorst and Junichi Inamoto, on loan, completed Wenger's summer shopping.

However, the real drama of the summer surrounded the future of Vieira. The 26-year-old had established himself as a world class midfielder and now made it known that he wanted to leave Arsenal. Wenger was left with a conundrum. Did he keep an unhappy player on the books or sell him for the best price? Vieira seemed dissatisfied with Arsène's new signings and seemingly had his sights set on a move abroad. The saga dragged on but eventually Wenger and the board convinced the midfielder that it was in his best interests to stay.

Wenger was satisfied that the team was moving in the right direction but he craved a repeat of the 1998 title glory. Europe was another target for Arsène, who hoped his players would gain more experience in the Champions League. The draw for the first group stage pitted Arsenal against Schalke 04, Real Mallorca and Panathinaikos. Qualification seemed more than likely if the team played to their potential and Arsène was hopeful of securing top spot.

Manchester United had flexed their financial muscles during the summer, bringing in Argentine Juan Sebastian Veron and Dutchman Ruud van Nistelrooy for £28 million and £19 million respectively. Ferguson had been frustrated at his side's failings in Europe since the 1999 triumph and hoped these new signings would lift his team to the next level in the Champions League.

Domestically, United looked imposing opponents and Wenger knew they would take some beating.

The campaign started with a mixed opening month for the Gunners. The passing and movement in which Wenger's players had been so well drilled was on show away to Middlesbrough as the Gunners registered a 4-0 victory. It was an exciting way to start the season, even if three of the goals came in the final four minutes. Bergkamp came off the bench to score twice. The Dutchman might have lost some of his pace but his brain was still as razor sharp as when he inspired the 1997/98 Double success. Henry was full of praise for the side's performance: 'I saw something today I never saw last season – we played as a team in attack and in defence.'

This was followed by a rare defeat at home as the team suffered a 2-1 loss to nine-man Leeds, despite producing another free-flowing display. Arsène was frustrated that his players had been unable to break through but the style of play was very much to his liking. He told the media: 'It's a real blow for us to lose a game like this. If you're going to have a good season, you have to be strong at home.'

A 4-0 win in the searing Bank Holiday heat against Leicester showcased more of the fast, one touch passing as four different players got on the scoresheet. It was the first of many breathtaking afternoons for the Arsenal fans at Highbury. The only downside to the match was the red card shown to Vieira for his part in a bust up with Dennis Wise. The French international looked to have carried the ill feeling of the summer into the new season and this distraction was affecting his form.

In September, Arsenal appeared well equipped domestically

but found life tricky in Europe. A 1-1 draw with Chelsea was an adequate result but a 1-0 loss against Mallorca in midweek was disappointing. Coming on the same day as the tragic terrorist attacks on the United States, nobody was really interested in the football.

A 3-1 win over Fulham put the Gunners top of the Premiership table. Ljungberg, Henry and Bergkamp got on the scoresheet as Wenger's side continued their good away form domestically. Arsène told the media after the game: 'I think we can stay at the top of the table. Why not? I believe we have the potential to do that. We look very solid, determined, mentally right.' A narrow, nail biting victory at Highbury against Schalke was a crucial result and put the Champions League campaign back on track. Three days later, though, Wenger felt disheartened to see his players take just a point from a home fixture with Bolton, who had Ricardo Gardner sent off after half an hour.

Their travel sickness in Europe struck again as Arsenal lost 1-0 in Greece against Panathinaikos with scoring woes again glaringly obvious. No goals in two away games was not the way to start the Champions League campaign. But the players made amends at home against the Greeks, winning 2-1. Sandwiched between these European ties were two good Premiership victories away from home. First, at Pride Park, Henry grabbed a brace to seal a 2-0 win and then Southampton were beaten by the same scoreline, courtesy of Pires and Henry, again. On a sad note, that afternoon Wenger received the news that his friend Houllier had suffered chest pains during Liverpool's clash with Leeds and Houllier would require heart surgery to prevent more serious health worries.

The rest of October saw the Gunners take a disappointing two points from a possible six in the league but seal their place in the Champions League second group stage. On 20 October, a 3-3 draw with Blackburn at Highbury saw Arsène again cursing wasted opportunities as David Dunn struck a late equaliser for Rovers. The Gunners then missed the chance to go top of the table when they drew 1-1 away to Sunderland on 27 October.

In Europe, a home win over Real Mallorca was enough to make their away trip to Schalke worry-free and it was just as well as the Gunners crashed to a 3-1 defeat. Wenger knew that the team needed to improve their displays on their travels in Europe. On the plus side, Henry's finishing had been faultless up front and he had already bagged thirteen goals in all competitions as the season moved into November. All Arsène's work in converting Henry into a world-class striker was paying dividends.

Wenger was content but felt that there was plenty more to come from his players. Arsenal were involved in some incredible games in the build-up to Christmas as Arsène stuck to his belief that beautiful, creative football was the best way for the club to return to the summit of English football. Yet it did not always lead to the results that he craved. November, as in previous years, was rather disappointing.

A 4-2 defeat at home to Charlton on 4 November left many fans bemused and Arsène was far from happy, telling the press: 'We should have scored a huge number of goals and there was some really sloppy defending. We conceded two stupid goals. We are all very disappointed.' Victory in the League Cup third round over Sir Alex Ferguson's fledglings was followed by a 1-1 draw with Tottenham at White Hart Lane. Gus Poyet's late strike provided another bitter ending for Arsène on an afternoon when

Campbell was subjected to a noisy reception and a sea of 'Judas' signs as he faced his former club.

On 21 November, Wenger was left in despair as the Gunners made a poor start to the Champions League second group stage in La Coruña against Spanish side Deportivo. The 2-0 defeat made it four losses out of four for Arsenal away from home in the competition. He could not understand the reason for these failures. Placed in Group D alongside Deportivo, Juventus and Bayer Leverkusen, Wenger's side needed to bounce back quickly. Pre-match, Wenger had warned that Deportivo were 'one of the best teams, better than anything we faced in the first group. They are good enough to be European champions.' The Spaniards had shown why they had beaten Manchester United twice in the first stage of the competition.

But the Gunners had the chance to put that result behind them as they entertained United at the weekend. Ferguson had announced that he would be retiring at the end of the season and this news seemed to have affected his side, who were in a bit of a slump. Responding to questions about Sir Alex pre-match, Arsène assured the media that 'it will not be a relief when he [Ferguson] retires.'

United might have been out of form but they took the lead against the run of play as Scholes converted Mikael Silvestre's cross. Wenger stirred his players at half-time and they produced a strong second half display. Ljungberg grabbed the equaliser after a rare mistake by Gary Neville and, from then on, Barthez stole all the headlines. The United goalkeeper passed straight to Henry, who calmly made it 2-1, and then fumbled to allow the Arsenal striker to seal a 3-1 win.

It was a bizarre finale but none of the home fans were complaining. The three points raised the spirits of everyone associated with the club after the disappointment in La Coruña. Post-match Wenger was a much cheerier figure: 'I'm very pleased with the performance and the character of the side,' he told reporters.

After two more wins – one in the league, one in the League Cup – Arsenal hosted Juventus in a vital Champions League contest on 4 December. Good home form had been the reason for the Gunners reaching the second group stage and Wenger urged his players to deliver. With his contract negotiations currently on the agenda, a special European night would be timely for the Arsenal boss. His team performed superbly, winning 3-1 and putting themselves back into contention for qualification. Ljungberg and Henry put the Gunners 2-0 up, a Stuart Taylor own goal gave Juventus hope before Ljungberg settled the game with his second goal. Arsène reflected after the game: 'It was a tremendous collective performance. They wanted it so much and they got it.' In the Premiership, though, it was Liverpool who had set the pace in the league with Manchester United, the champions, struggling to keep up.

Days after the victory over Juventus, a press conference was held to announce that Wenger had agreed a new contract to stay at Highbury until 2005. Chairman Peter Hill-Wood told the assembled media: 'It's marvellous news. He's done an absolutely fantastic job since his arrival in 1996 and our future could not be in better hands.' Arsène was equally happy to have resolved the matter: 'I've decided to stay because I believe I have a group of players that I respect and admire and have a lot of potential to bring this club to where I want them to be. This means at the top level in Europe and in the world.'

Overall, Arsène was happy with the standard of the Gunners' performances in December. The defence may have been conceding goals but in possession Arsenal were tearing teams apart. And it was not just Henry finding the net. Ljungberg, Pires and Wiltord all added to their tallies as Wenger's side began to establish themselves as strong title contenders. Elimination from the League Cup against Blackburn was disappointing for Arsène's second string line-up but days earlier the Gunners had recovered superbly from a 2-0 deficit to win 3-2 against Aston Villa. Highbury was rocking as Henry scored the winner in the last minute with his second goal of the game.

A draw away to West Ham was followed by a 3-1 defeat at home to Newcastle. The Gunners took the lead but Sir Bobby Robson's side responded well and equalised on the hour mark. Parlour had been red carded just before half-time and Craig Bellamy received his marching orders with just under twenty minutes to play. So it was ten-a-side. Then came the dramatic finale. Campbell was adjudged to have fouled Laurent Robert, a penalty was awarded to Newcastle and, as the last defender, Campbell was dismissed. Shearer scored from the spot and Robert rubbed salt into the wound by grabbing a third. The Magpies moved to the top of the Premiership table.

Arsène was livid but apparently not as angry as Henry, who insisted on shadowing referee Graham Poll after the final whistle and berating the official over the penalty decision. It took several players and coaches from both teams to convince the Frenchman to head back to the changing room. Looking at the replays, yes, Poll had been wrong to penalise Campbell but harassing the referee would make little difference to the decision. It made Henry look petulant and did not look good for Arsenal's sportsmanship. Wenger's bitterness was evident when he told the media: 'If it had been eleven v eleven we would have won this game comfortably. We lost a lot of energy when we were playing with ten men.' Robson was far from sympathetic to the Gunners and was rightly irritated by Arsenal's lengthy protests: 'Some people round here don't know how to lose,' he said.

A key win away to Liverpool at Anfield on 23 December showed a better side of the Gunners' character as Arsène's side pulled together to overcome the odds. When Giovanni van Bronkhorst was sent off for a second bookable offence after just thrty-five minutes, Wenger called on his players to display their collective spirit. The response was overwhelming as the ten-man Gunners overpowered Liverpool and hung on for a 2-1 victory. As Arsène would later acknowledge himself, this game turned Arsenal's season around. The belief had returned to the dressing room.

Another 2-1 win, this time at home to Chelsea three days later, summed up the confidence with which the team was playing. Wiltord was the hero on this occasion. Arsène's squad was still competing on three fronts and were certainly most neutrals' favourite side to watch. When the front line hit form, the counter attacking raids were a joy to behold and opposition teams became extremely fearful of pushing too many players forward. The third win of the busy Christmas week was achieved at Middlesbrough with the game again finishing 2-1 in Arsenal's favour.

The New Year did nothing to dampen the enthusiasm around

the club. Arsenal blasted four goals past Watford in the FA Cup and then collected two creditable draws. Liverpool came to Highbury and, despite being on the back foot for the majority of the match, collected a 1-1 draw. Arsène was frustrated that his players failed to hold onto the lead. Ljungberg had put Arsenal ahead after sixty-one minutes but John Arne Riise levelled just six minutes later. Wenger told the press: 'We feel disappointed and should have won' while Ljungberg also revealed his unhappiness, explaining: 'When we went 1-0 up we knew they were difficult to break down, that's why we were so disappointed when they equalised.' A trip to Elland Road also ended 1-1 as Pires equalised Robbie Fowler's opener. These results were far from worrying but they put the Gunners further from the Premiership summit.

Wenger got the right reaction to the dropped points as Arsenal beat Leicester 3-1 at Filbert Street. The three points lifted the Gunners to second in the table, one point behind Manchester United and with a game in hand over the champions. It was the type of performance that Arsène wanted to see on a more regular basis as his side were clinical on the day.

On 27 January, a first half goal from Bergkamp was enough to seal a 1-0 victory over Liverpool in a fiery FA Cup fourth round clash. The Dutchman would later be one of three players red carded as referee Mike Riley also decided to dismiss Keown and Jamie Carragher. The media relished the chance to re-open the debate over Arsenal's indiscipline. Though Wenger stood firm in his support for his players, the facts did not lie. In the five-and-a-half years that Arsène had been in charge at Highbury, his team had received forty-two red cards. Neutrals felt it was about time Wenger took some action against his players but the Frenchman brushed it off, saying: 'It was a real cup tie, but not a dirty game.'

This victory sparked a good run for the Gunners – at home and abroad. With Vieira still causing speculation over his future by being spotted at an airport in Madrid, it was fellow midfielder Pires who took centre stage. He played a part in all three goals away to Blackburn in an entertaining contest that the visitors shaded 3-2. The way that Pires linked up with Henry was as good as anything on show in Europe. Bergkamp, too, was turning in some vintage displays.

A 1-1 draw at home to Southampton was not ideal but a 1-0 victory at Goodison Park was an excellent result. Everton are always a tough, physical side and the Gunners matched their work rate stride for stride, despite not playing at their best. Wenger was less than happy to see his team pick up five yellow cards yet he was jubilant when Wiltord grabbed the only goal of the game just after the hour mark. It might have been a bit of a miss-hit but Arsène did not mind. The longer that the season progressed, the more emphatic Arsenal's displays became. Wenger could not fault his team's style of play and was pleased to see that his occasional rotation of the squad had kept everyone fit and hungry.

Two results in February stood out as emphasising football being played in the 'Arsène way'. On 23 February, Fulham were hammered 4-1 at Highbury with Henry grabbing a brace. The Gunners were 2-0 up after just fifteen minutes and this fast start characterised the energetic way that the team began every match. So often at home, visiting teams would find themselves on the back foot early on. The hapless Fulham defence had no answer to the movement of Henry, Pires and Wiltord who terrorised them from the first whistle. Wenger was certainly impressed with the way that his side had played: 'It was a great performance, with great moves, mobility, power, technique and team spirit.'

The second big result came just four days later when Bayer Leverkusen were steamrollered in similar fashion, making an even more damaging start than the Cottagers had at the weekend on the way to a 4-1 loss. Four different players took a slice of the goalscoring glory. Wenger was a captivated spectator as his side put on an exhibition of passing and moving at pace. The Gunners boss happily told the media: 'It is down to us now at home and if we can repeat this performance we will go through.' Earlier in the month, the two teams had drawn in Leverkusen so Arsenal now had seven points from four games and were still in contention for a place in the quarter-finals. Performances like this made Arsène hopeful of lifting a handful of trophies when the season ended in May.

It was the month of March that really highlighted Arsenal's title chances. Newcastle, Manchester United and Liverpool were all in contention but it was Wenger's team that had the all important momentum going into the final few months. Rather like the finale to the 1997/98 season, the Gunners were hitting form at the right time. Arsène could feel the belief growing within his squad yet he worked hard to stop any complacency creeping in.

A brilliant Bergkamp goal led the way to a 2-0 victory away to

Newcastle on 2 March. The Dutchman managed to flick the ball around Nikos Dabizas with enough spin to put him one-on-one with Shay Given. There was only going to be one outcome. Campbell added a second as Wenger's side marched on. Henry missed the game due to an abdominal injury but the three points had been claimed nonetheless – a fact that pleased Arsène, who told the media: 'It's important to know we can score without Thierry Henry.' The Frenchman also added his verdict on Bergkamp's sumptuous opener: 'Unbelievable. You're blessed when you come to a stadium and witness something like that. What he does is close to genius. He's a player who gets close to perfection.'

Pires got the winner against a stubborn Derby side in midweek before a 1-1 draw at Newcastle in the FA Cup quarter-final. Wenger controversially took the chance to rest a few players. Nonetheless, Edu gave the Gunners the lead at St. James' Park, only for the Magpies to fight back strongly. Robert, again the scourge of Arsenal, equalised and the home side launched themselves at Wenger's team in the closing stages. Many felt Arsène was fortunate to walk away with a draw. Shearer, the Newcastle captain, certainly agreed: 'We should have won, I really believe that.' Wenger, though, simply bemoaned his team's inability to find their usual tempo.

Perhaps the way that Newcastle overpowered Arsenal was a prelude to the midweek clash with Deportivo. Wenger had appeared very confident pre-match, knowing that his side had the upper hand in the Premiership and expecting to move one step closer to Champions League qualification. Both teams had seven points, making this a monumentally important night in

Arsenal's history. Sadly, the players blew the opportunity against wily opponents. The Spaniards struck twice before half-time to leave Highbury shocked and the Gunners never recovered, with Henry missing a second half penalty. Deportivo had won four out of four against Manchester United and Arsenal in the competition and had established themselves as contenders for the trophy.

Wenger now looked to the away trip to face Juventus as his team's last chance to progress. He tried to put a brave face on the defeat but he was clearly hurting badly. He was so accustomed to seeing his own team outclass opposition sides that Deportivo's dominance had shaken him. Juan Carlos Valerón, excellent on the night, and his team-mates had clinched a quarter-final berth. It was just left for Arsenal and surprise package Bayer Leverkusen to fight over the one remaining spot.

Arsène ensured that his team bounced back at the weekend with a 2-1 win at Villa Park. It was real battle, though. Seaman made a crucial penalty save from Gareth Barry with the score at 1-0 and minutes later Pires sealed the three points with a sublime finish. It underlined why the Gunners were so difficult to beat.

They would need all this spirit as they travelled to Turin for their massive Champions League clash with already eliminated Juventus on 20 March. The Italians fielded a weakened side but Arsenal never got going, falling to a 1-0 defeat. Strangely, in a match of such significance, there were too many below-par displays. Henry missed another penalty and Juve striker Marcelo Zalayeta snatched a winner with less than fifteen minutes to go. Ultimately, though, it did not matter because Leverkusen had won against Deportivo to qualify ahead of the Gunners.

It was a bitter ending to a European campaign full of missed opportunities. Wenger felt his team had been 'unfortunate' but Seaman was closer to the mark when he told the media: 'We are disappointed but we lost it at home against Deportivo – that was the night for us to go through and we lost it.' It was a shame that the Gunners had to rely so heavily on their home form, with their away performances still below par in the competition. There was no mistaking the fact that one point from a possible nine on their travels in Europe was simply not good enough.

However, rather than let this blow ruin their season, the Gunners hit back with everything they had. Wenger knew his team could still come away with a Premiership and FA Cup double – all was not lost yet. The joy of reaching the FA Cup semi-finals with a 3-0 replay win over Newcastle was tinged with sadness over losing Pires to an unfortunate knee injury that would keep him out for the rest of the season. He had suffered ligament damage and could now do nothing more than spectate. It left Arsenal without one of their most creative influences – a player who had been exceptional all season and was a leading candidate for the end of season awards.

Fortunately, other stars stepped forward to fill the breach. Henry kept up his fine form with a brace away to Charlton on 1 April and a 2-1 victory over Tottenham kept the strong run going. Teddy Sheringham's equaliser from the penalty spot after eighty-one minutes seemed to have earned Tottenham a point but then Dean Richards fouled Henry and full-back Lauren scored from the spot.

Somewhere Sir Alex was cursing as the Gunners kept themselves clear of United at the top. A 1-0 win over Middlesbrough in the FA Cup semi-final, courtesy of a Gianluca Festa own goal, meant that the Gunners had booked their place at the Millennium Stadium again - their opponents would be Chelsea.

Ljungberg, who had scored the opener against Tottenham, was in fine form and his performances over the next month or so pushed Arsenal towards the title. A tight match with Ipswich was decided by two second half strikes from the Swede. As others around him seemed to be fading, Ljungberg continued to carry the goalscoring burden. His clever runs off the ball caused big problems for defenders and he had a knack of popping up with a crucial goal to break the deadlock.

He did it again in a 2-0 win over West Ham on 24 April as Arsenal left it late to secure the points. It was Ljungberg's fifteenth goal of the campaign. The Hammers had reason to feel aggrieved, though, as earlier a Freddie Kanoute shot appeared to have crossed the line but a goal was not awarded. Wenger felt his side deserved a bit of luck: 'All season, the luck is balanced – we've had some bad luck with decisions and overall I think you get what you deserve.' The Frenchman was delighted with the win, which put Arsenal four points clear of Liverpool and five ahead of Manchester United. Neither Houllier nor Ferguson could see the Gunners throwing the title away now.

Another 2-0 win, this time at Bolton, put Wenger and his players within touching distance of the Premiership trophy. Ljungberg was on target yet again. He had scored the opening goal in the last four league games and his contributions were proving invaluable. Wiltord netted the second and Arsenal needed just a point from their final two matches, the first of which was against Manchester United at Old Trafford.

Having sat third in the table at the end of March, the Gunners entered May five points clear in first place. The team had won all six matches in April and conceded just one goal – a Sheringham penalty – in the process. These proved to be the decisive weeks. Five points ahead with two games to play, it was going to take a miracle for Wenger and Arsenal to be denied. Yet the Gunners boss refused to take anything for granted. He praised Ljungberg, saying: 'Once again Freddie unlocked the door' and added: 'As confident as I am, we have got to keep our concentration up.'

In the meantime, Arsène turned his thoughts to the FA Cup final against Chelsea. He loved the big occasions and the match had arrived at the perfect time for the Gunners. They were playing effortlessly brilliant football and confidence was at an all-time high. The Arsenal boss needed to do little in the dressing room to raise the spirits. The Blues worked hard and proved stubborn opponents but gradually Wenger's side wore them down. Parlour and Ljungberg were the heroes – both scoring stunning goals from distance. Parlour's drive was particularly special and the player's popularity was evident from the frenzied celebrations. Arsène afforded himself a smile as Ljungberg doubled the lead with just ten minutes to go, making it seven vital goals in seven games. The Swede, more than anyone, had raised his game in the absence of Pires.

There were happy faces galore in the Arsenal camp at the final whistle as the team stepped up to receive their medals and then the FA Cup itself. Memories of the defeat to Liverpool in the final a year ago had been banished and the squad enjoyed celebrating with the fans. But the big party would have to wait because the Premiership title had to be clinched first. Wenger spoke proudly of the goalscorers: 'Both Parlour and Ljungberg were fantastic today and in the end I think we deserved to win. We are delighted – and now we must concentrate for two more games.'

The Gunners arrived at Old Trafford on 8 May knowing that they could afford to lose and still lift the trophy with a point at home to Everton. But Wenger did not even consider such an attitude and prepared his players as if victory was essential. Henry and Adams missed out through injury but the eleven who stepped onto the pitch were focused on clinching the Premiership crown in United's own backyard. Wenger had played down the significance of sealing the title at Old Trafford but everyone knew that the Gunners were itching to do it.

After the frustration of losing their Champions League semi-final on away goals to Bayer Leverkusen, Manchester United had promised to take the title race to the final weekend but Arsenal were simply too good. As United pushed forward in search of goals, the Gunners were ready to launch their trademark counter-attacking bursts. When a goal did come, it was the visitors who got it as Wiltord scored one of the most famous goals in recent club history. The game finished 1-0 and Arsenal were champions again.

For United, it was the ultimate indignity to surrender the title to the Gunners at home. But for Wenger and his squad, the victory was all the sweeter as it came at Old Trafford and it made up for the years of disappointment. The triumphant Arsenal manager celebrated with his players and coaching staff and then told the press: 'We wanted tonight to be a shift of power, and to take the trophy back to Highbury. It's just fantastic to win it here as they are the team who dominated English football for the past three years. Since I arrived at Arsenal, we have won the title twice and United have won it three times. So they are 3-2 ahead and now we want to equalise next season.' Arsène knew that Ferguson's team would recover from this setback but, in the meantime at least, all associated with Arsenal Football Club could rejoice at the completion of a famous and stylishly earned 'Double'.

The 1-0 win at Old Trafford also sealed an incredible away record in the league for the Gunners as they collected fourteen wins and five draws from their travels without suffering a defeat. This spoke volumes for the spirit and character that Arsène had installed in his players. Other statistics were also worthy of note. Arsenal had scored in every Premiership match on the way to lifting the trophy and had held their nerve in the title run-in with an incredible thirteen successive victories in the league – a sequence that dated back to early February. Nobody could argue that the Gunners had not deserved to top the table. Liverpool ended up second with United third. Ferguson was not happy and made the bizarre claim that United were superior to the champions. Wenger bit back with a witty repost, saying: 'Everyone thinks they have the prettiest wife at home.'

In the *Arsenal Official Yearbook 2002*, Wenger looked back contentedly at the successes of the campaign: 'I believe this Double was an even greater achievement than that of 1997/98. This is because we had to bounce back from the frustration at the end of the 2000/01 season, when we missed out on winning any trophies.' Tellingly, Arsène added: 'Most importantly, I felt that we won the Championship in style.' They certainly had and the glory had its roots in Wenger's free-flowing, entertaining approach. The Gunners had ensured that there was plenty of excitement wherever they played on the way to lifting two major trophies.

Adams and Dixon bowed out in style in their final appearances for the club and an emotional Adams admitted that Wenger's role in the triumph had been immense. He told Sky Sports: 'Maybe '98 was the players winning it, but I do believe it's the manager that's won this one. Throughout the season he's been extremely confident, unflappable. I think the man deserves all the credit he can get.'

Henry's record of thirty-two goals in forty-nine appearances in all competitions was truly outstanding and he had been a thorn in the side of defences throughout the campaign. But just as significant was the number of goals provided by the rest of the forward line. Bergkamp only started thirty matches but contributed fourteen goals. Wiltord and Ljungberg both struck seventeen while Pires chipped in with thirteen. It had clearly been a team effort. Pires' displays earlier in the campaign earned him the Football Writers' Footballer of the Year. It was hard to ignore the fact that Arsène had helped so many of the squad develop into world class talents.

The Arsenal manager was reluctant to dwell on the glory for too long, though. There was a new campaign to think about and Wenger's tactical acumen would once more be tested to the limit. But he would be ready. He had rarely been found wanting in his managerial career and his attention to detail was unrivalled. The Gunners would be the team to beat next season and the tag of champions would bring added pressure and expectations.

*   *   *

Manchester United, more than anyone, were impatient to get the 2002/03 season underway. Finishing third was an unfamiliar feeling for the players and the manager – one that they were desperate never to experience again. They wanted to take the Premiership trophy back to Manchester to banish the memories of 2001/02. Ferguson moved to strengthen his squad by signing defender Rio Ferdinand in a monumental £30 million deal. Ferdinand, who had impressed many with his performances at the 2002 World Cup in Japan and South Korea, would be expected to sure up a defence that had struggled at times last season.

Yet Wenger resisted the urge to spend big money during the close season. Obviously, he believed 100 per cent in the nucleus of the Double-winning squad but it still came as a surprise that he did not look to bring in big name re-enforcements. The initial transfer activity had been limited to the purchases of goalkeeper Rami Shaaban, utility player Kolo Toure and centre-back Pascal Cygan – the most expensive of these being Cygan at £2.1 million. Gilberto Silva was then added to the squad in a £4.5 million move. He had been part of the Brazilian World Cup winning side, playing a vital role as the midfield anchor man, and many saw him as a belated replacement for Emmanuel Petit.

As Arsène pointed out, it did not matter that he had not spent big money. This Arsenal side was very special – after all, they had been unbeaten away from home in the Premiership in the last campaign. Keeping Vieira at the club had been a crucial piece of summer business as speculation had once more mounted suggesting he would be heading abroad. The central midfielder committed himself to the Gunners and the starting line-up appeared to be as strong as ever. The only question marks were over the defence and whether the likes of Adams and Dixon would be sorely missed.

Football fans worldwide looked on with excitement as the new season kicked off. It promised to be one of the tightest title races in Premiership history. Winning the title had been hard work but Wenger knew that defending it would be even tougher for him and his players.

Arsenal sent out a statement of intent with their Community Shield performance. Facing Liverpool, who had been rewarded for a strong campaign with a second place finish, the Gunners looked as irresistible as ever. It was a physical contest but Wenger's side came out on top thanks to a goal from new signing Gilberto. Arsène was thrilled to see Silva make an early impact: 'I'm happy for him. He's an intelligent boy, makes things simple and gets into the box at the right time. I believe he will be a very strong player for us.' The Arsenal boss went on to hit out at the reckless tackling of Gerrard in the Liverpool midfield. Gerrard was indeed fortunate to avoid a red card that afternoon.

The Gunners began the Premiership season powerfully, flexing their muscles and scoring goals at will. A 2-0 win on the opening day against Birmingham was followed by a 2-2 draw away to West Ham, in which Arsène's players admittedly rode their luck. A 5-2 thrashing of West Brom at Highbury on 27 August was vintage Arsenal and, as Wenger admitted, the team had played some excellent football. The visitors' defending, though, had been most charitable. Arsène was keen to improve on the three home defeats of the previous campaign and demanded that Highbury became a fortress again – an intimidating arena for opposition sides.

Arsenal's unbeaten run stretched throughout September. A draw at Stamford Bridge against Chelsea was achieved through great team spirit. Trailing 1-0 and down to ten men after Vieira picked up a second yellow card, the Gunners' persistence paid off as Kolo Toure equalised. Wenger commented post-match that Vieira's dismissal 'was very harsh' and on this occasion the Frenchman was spot on.

This draw was followed by six consecutive victories during the month. A 2-1 win over Manchester City saw three French internationals on the scoresheet. Ex-Gunner Anelka for City; Wiltord and Henry for Arsenal. Charlton fared no better and lost 3-0 at home as Wenger purred: 'We look like we are getting better and better.' Vieira was back to his best form and Henry looked razor sharp up front.

Arsène had made no secret of his desire to improve in the Champions League. Drawn in a group alongside Borussia Dortmund, PSV Eindhoven and Auxerre, the opening stage seemed to present relatively few stumbling blocks. The schedule began with a 2-0 home victory over Dortmund on 17 September as second half goals from Bergkamp and Ljungberg gave Wenger a strong start. However, the Gunners' home form had never been an issue – it was their away form that had cost them so often in Europe.

Domestically, the run of wins continued thanks to a late winner from Kanu at home to Bolton. It kept morale high for the important trip to Eindhoven in midweek. Wenger's side literally took instant control of the contest as Gilberto scored after just twenty seconds! It was the fastest ever goal in Champions League history and it set the Gunners on the way to an emphatic 4-0 win. It was a truly mesmerising attacking display that left PSV floored.

It was Arsenal's first away win in Europe for nineteen months and Wenger was understandably thrilled for his players, telling the press: 'It means a lot to them. You could see the reaction in the dressing room. It was a deserved victory and I want to congratulate my team because they were intelligent under pressure.'

Back in the Premiership at the weekend, Leeds were the next to suffer from Arsenal's creativity as the champions slammed home four more goals to leave Elland Road as 4-1 winners. Kanu bagged two with Toure and Henry also on target. Neutrals already feared that Wenger's side would be unstoppable and the Gunners boss gave his team the highest praise: 'This is one of the best performances since I have been at the club, one of the top, top, top performances.' That was praise indeed. September had been a spectacularly successful month and Wenger felt confident enough to claim: 'I am still hopeful we can go through the season unbeaten.' In hindsight, the comment piled unnecessary pressure onto Arsène's players and Ferguson would later remind Wenger of this prediction.

October looked like being another profitable month for Arsenal as they gained a narrow victory away to French side Auxerre to continue their new found confidence on their travels in Europe. A 3-1 win at home against Sunderland on 6 October stretched the team's unbeaten league run to thirty matches and Wenger was impressed: 'The unbeaten record proves that we are consistent and champions are consistent.'

But then the wheels came off to a certain extent as the Gunners had a nightmare few weeks, losing four matches in a row. It all began with the intervention of sixteen-year-old Wayne Rooney who came off the bench for Everton and struck a brilliant long range winner for the Toffees at Goodison Park, ending Arsenal's unbeaten league run. Arsène knew all about Rooney's ability and called the teenager 'the biggest England talent I've seen since I arrived in England.' Everton boss David Moyes was desperately waiting for Rooney's seventeenth birthday – just days after the match – when the youngster would be allowed to sign his first professional contract. One positive for Wenger from the 2-1 loss was that Ljungberg's strike at Goodison Park meant that the team had scored in forty-nine consecutive games.

The nature of the defeat seemed to hurt the Arsenal players and there were hints of a hangover from the result on Merseyside when the Gunners lost their next three games in all competitions. Auxerre and Blackburn left Highbury with three points, both snatching 2-1 wins. The loss to Auxerre was particularly poor but Arsène refused to get carried away: 'There is no basic reason to be alarmist. You have periods like these in a season. It's very important that we bounce back now, that's the biggest thing. We win and lose as a team.'

A trip to Dortmund brought another defeat but the Gunners still qualified for the next stage of the Champions League. Tomas Rosicky, who would later join Arsenal, scored Dortmund's winner from the spot after a penalty decision that left Wenger fuming. In a rare sarcastic outburst, the Frenchman said: 'Like on many occasions, the referee made a difference. All credit to him, he scored a good second goal for them. I was happy for him. He deserves a good mention.' Arsenal's final match against PSV became meaningless and would end goalless. Arsène was relieved to have progressed and remained optimistic after being drawn in a second stage group alongside Roma, Ajax and Valencia.

Wenger was glad to see the back of October and worked hard to get his squad back on track. That process began on 3 November away to Fulham. Arsenal seemed more focused and fought hard for a narrow 1-0 win courtesy of a Steve Marlet own goal. Arsène told the media: 'We had to dig deep for this win. I would have preferred to win this match with a different goal, but I'll take that one.' Perhaps the Gunners' luck was changing.

As only one of their three losses in October had come in the Premiership, Arsenal had not lost much ground domestically. Wins at home against Newcastle and Tottenham boosted morale, especially the latter victory against their North London rivals which put Wenger's side top of the table. Tottenham had no answer to the Gunners' attacking swagger and a red card for midfielder Simon Davies after just twenty-seven minutes did not help their cause. Ljungberg and Wiltord then added to Henry's opener.

Top of the Premiership and with their blip behind them, Arsenal seemed ready to put together another of their famous unbeaten runs. Yet their form remained erratic, much to Wenger's frustration. The Gunners travelled to face Southampton at St Mary's Stadium on 23 November and suffered a 3-2 defeat. Campbell was sent off and James Beattie scored twice as Arsenal surrendered a contest that they had seemed to be dominating.

Just four days later, though, Arsenal visited the Italian capital in the first fixture of the Champions League second group stage and outclassed Roma 3-1 with a dazzling array of counter-attacking raids. Henry was sensational on his way to a top class hat-trick and Wenger's side secured their first away win in Italy for twenty-two years. Arsène called it 'a great team performance' but was clueless as to why the players had failed to play with such style against Southampton. It was something he sought to rectify as his side faced some massive clashes in the coming weeks. Meanwhile, Roma boss Fabio Capello labelled Arsenal 'the strongest team in Europe at the moment.'

After beating Aston Villa at Highbury, the Gunners arrived at Old Trafford on 7 December for the biggest match of the Premiership season so far. Manchester United had made a poor start in the league and, in front of their own fans, desperately needed to start turning things around. Wenger was missing Campbell through suspension yet fielded an impressive array of attackers. But to Arsène's dismay, his side were outfought and outwitted by Ferguson's troops as United claimed a deserved 2-0 win. Vieira, usually so imperious in the centre of the park, was surprisingly dominated by Phil Neville, who typified the difference between the two teams – United were full of passion and hard graft; Arsenal were lethargic and lifeless. Ole Gunnar

Solskjaer revealed the delight in the United dressing room: 'It's hard to explain how happy we are because we're so satisfied. Now we know we're back on track and well into the fight for the title.'

Wenger had seen enough and feared that the victory might spur United into form. He challenged his players to prove themselves on the pitch and show more pride in wearing the Arsenal shirt. Arsène certainly got the response that he was looking for. An unbeaten run followed that would propel the Gunners into pole position in the Premiership.

After draws against Valencia in the Champions League and Tottenham in the Premiership, Arsenal got back to winning ways with a 2-0 win over Middlesbrough on 2 December. This was followed by a 2-1 victory away to West Brom on Boxing Day. Despite going behind, Wenger's side fought back strongly against the Baggies with Jeffers and Henry inspiring the comeback.

A 1-1 draw at home to Liverpool completed a solid Christmas period for the Gunners but the visitors had reason to feel aggrieved that they had not taken all three points. There were two penalties in the contest. The first was rightly awarded to Liverpool for a foul by Campbell on Milan Baros and Danny Murphy scored from the spot. But the second was very harsh as Jeffers tumbled and referee Jeff Winter gave another penalty. Henry made no mistake. Post-match, Liverpool boss Houllier was far from amused and claimed: 'Mr Winter was conned by the dive of Francis Jeffers.'

2003 began well with a thrilling 3-2 win over Claudio Ranieri's Chelsea. A Marcel Desailly own goal was the difference between the teams for eighty minutes before an exhilarating last ten minutes. Van Bronkhorst and Henry extended the lead to 3-0 before Mario Stanic and former Gunner Petit struck to make it 3-2 with four minutes to go. Wenger was satisfied with the points and his side's character but the defence had looked edgy. Nonetheless, Arsenal were still five points clear at the top.

A 2-0 scoreline against Oxford in the FA Cup third round got the cup run off to a positive start. Then came one of the Gunners' most fluent displays of the season away to Birmingham on 12 January. Arsenal's pace was simply irresistible as Henry, Pires and Bergkamp tormented the Blues defenders all afternoon on the way to an emphatic 4-0 victory. The vision and weight of passing was a joy to behold as Wenger sat contentedly at pitchside. The second goal of Henry's double saw the striker reach the milestone of 100 goals for Arsenal. It did little to help the morale of relegation candidates Birmingham.

Two more comfortable wins kept the goals flowing. West Ham fell to a 3-1 defeat, orchestrated by hat-trick hero Henry and made easier by Steve Lomas' harsh dismissal early on. In the FA Cup fourth round, non-league Farnborough also lost a man in the first half and paid the price. Jeffers grabbed a brace in the 5-1 victory but it was still a special day out for the Farnborough players as they pitted their wits against some of the best players in the world. The Gunners, fielding an under-strength side, had been knocked out of the League Cup by Sunderland but looked strong contenders for the three honours that they were really chasing.

A 2-2 draw at Anfield on 29 January was enjoyable for the neutrals but less so for Wenger as his team twice squandered the lead. There was also controversy surrounding Liverpool's second equaliser which stemmed from a corner that was wrongly awarded. Arsène was adamant: 'My players have told me it was never a corner before their equaliser.' A 2-1 win against Fulham brought a welcome three points but a 1-1 draw away to Newcastle was rather disappointing, considering the home team had ten men for more than half an hour. It left the Gunners just three points clear at the top.

Arsenal gained revenge for their league defeat to Manchester United with a win in the FA Cup fifth round at Old Trafford on 15 February. Arsène elected to rest Henry and, after surviving a first half scare when Giggs shot over with the goal gaping, the Gunners took the game by the scruff of the neck, despite the absence of their leading marksman. The United fans were silenced as Wenger's side took a 2-0 lead and progressed to the next round. The Arsenal boss was full of praise for his players after the game: 'I think we controlled the game and the result is a consequence of brilliant spirit and a brilliant performance. It strengthens our belief and confidence – and that's important because we have big games coming up.' Ferguson preferred to focus on the way in which the Arsenal players had treated the referee.

Somehow, though, Arsenal's performance was over-shadowed by the post-match incident involving David Beckham and Ferguson. Back in the dressing room, the United manager allegedly kicked a boot in anger which hit Beckham on the forehead. It drew blood and required stitches, which brought much speculation in the media. It handed Arsenal a bigger advantage and left Beckham's future at United in jeopardy. Things would never be the same again for him at the Theatre of Dreams.

The Champions League was not proving so easy, however. Unfortunately, Arsenal's home form was letting them down as they followed their 0-0 draw against Valencia with a 1-1 scoreline against Ajax. Highbury had been such a fortress in the competition in previous years but this time the Gunners were struggling to break down stubborn opponents. It left Wenger's players with much to do and put pressure on them to improve their patchy away form in the competition. For all Arsène's in-depth preparation and assessments of players' fitness, his team had run out of ideas too often in Europe.

But when the Arsenal players were on-song, they exhibited the kind of football that their manager had drilled them in. Arsène's love for slick, speedy attacks was beautifully matched by the skills of his midfielders and strikers. Manchester City were the next unfortunate team to face such a proposition as they succumbed 5-1 in front of their own fans. There was nothing that City could do except marvel at a vintage Arsenal display.

The build up play at Maine Road was as good as anything that the Gunners had produced all season. Wenger did not get carried away, though, telling the press: 'We got what we wanted. It is up to us to keep performing now, everything is in our hands.' City boss Kevin Keegan was full of admiration for the style of Arsenal's play: 'They are on a different planet to us. I have watched them quite a bit and they are an exceptional side. They have good balance in the side and are blessed with a lot of pace. They have five or six individuals who can work a bit of magic or race past someone and score a goal. That is a tremendous armoury.' Cramming the game's highlights into a *Match of the Day* show was an impossible challenge for the BBC!

On 26 February, Arsenal travelled to Amsterdam for a vital Champions League clash with Ajax. After the disappointing 1-1 draw with the Dutch side at Highbury, Wenger hoped for a better outcome this time. But it proved to be a stalemate as neither team found its best form. The 0-0 scoreline left the Gunners with plenty of work to do to qualify but Arsène remained upbeat: 'I'm still confident this team can go through and can go far in this competition.'

Returning to Premiership action, Arsenal easily beat Alan Curbishley's Charlton side at Highbury on 2 March. Jeffers and Pires grabbed the goals in a 2-0 win. Most importantly, the victory gave the Gunners an eight point advantage at the top of the table.

A riveting 2-2 draw with Chelsea in the FA Cup sixth round on 8 March will be remembered for the special goal that Henry scored. The Frenchman raced onto a through ball before spinning past Blues goalkeeper Carlo Cudicini and slotting the ball home. Chelsea, though, showed plenty of spirit and Frank Lampard's late equaliser earned the Blues a replay. Wenger criticised his team for not pressing home the advantage, telling reporters: 'We played a fantastic first half winning every battle and we should have been more than 2-1 up at half-time. But in the second half we didn't do enough to extend our lead.'

A draw in midweek with Roma left the Gunners needing a point away to Valencia in their final match to be certain of reaching the quarter-finals. Like the home clash with Deportivo a year earlier, it was the night on which Arsenal should have made sure that they were in the quarter-final draw. But they could not seize the chance. Vieira opened the scoring and Roma were reduced to ten men when Francesco Totti was sent off for elbowing Keown after twenty-two minutes. But despite the numerical advantage, the Gunners were unable to build on their lead and Antonio Cassano popped up with a shock equaliser just before half-time. In truth, Roma might even have snatched an improbable three points late on when Vincenzo Montella headed over from six yards out. The result left things delicately poised ahead of the final round of fixtures.

A poor performance from a depleted side away to Blackburn on 15 March saw the Gunners lose 2-0 and ended Arsenal's twenty-one-match unbeaten run. But that sequence of results had pulled Arsène's side into a strong position at the top of the Premiership table and many felt that the challengers had left it too late to dislodge them from the summit. The Frenchman was taking nothing for granted, though, and appeared far from happy with the way his players had surrendered meekly against Blackburn. Rovers had got the better of the Gunners over the course of the season and seemed to know how to get under Arsenal's skin.

Wenger roused his squad for the huge match in Valencia in the Champions League, relieved that the team's fate was still in their own hands. But defeat in Spain ended the Gunners' participation in the competition. Needing a draw to reach the quarter-finals, Arsenal fell just short despite a gritty display and an excellent goal from Henry. The winner for Valencia from John

Carew was a sloppy goal to concede but it was the all important moment in the match.

Wenger could not hide his disappointment because he felt that his side had deserved to qualify. But others, including BBC Five Live pundit Alan Green, felt that the Gunners still lacked the experience to be successful at the highest level in Europe. One only had to look at the styles of Champions League finalists AC Milan and Juventus to realise that teams with plenty of know-how in European competition tended to be the most successful.

But there was no time to dwell on this heartache, however, as there were two other competitions to focus on. Arsenal returned to winning ways with a home victory over Everton – gaining revenge for the loss at Goodison Park in October. It was vital that the team got back on track and so Arsène was very pleased that his players had shown the necessary focus.

Another spirited performance from Wenger's players took them into the FA Cup semi-finals. Chelsea threw everything at the Gunners in the quarter-final replay at Stamford Bridge but, even after Vieira was sent off, Arsenal had too much class and determination. Most teams would have been holding on desperately to their 2-1 lead with ten men but that is not Arsène's way. The champions continued to attack and were rewarded when Lauren sealed the result with a fine left-footed strike. Wenger was immensely proud of the display and saluted all of his players: 'We had eleven leaders tonight – not just Patrick Vieira.' The Gunners had shown that they were capable of much more than just attractive football – there was real substance in this performance.

A hard fought 1-0 win over Sheffield United in the FA Cup semi-final was a good response to a 1-1 draw against Aston Villa in the Premiership. Seaman's heroic save from Paul Peschisolido was the crucial moment and Wenger looked forward to heading back to the Millennium Stadium for another final. Sheffield United boss Neil Warnock was furious about the performance of referee Graham Poll but Arsène preferred to reflect on Seaman's performance: 'It was a great save and I am very happy he made it on his 1000th game. It is a reward for all his hard work in training – he is an example of professionalism and to young goalkeepers.' The win set up an FA Cup final against Southampton.

Unfortunately for Wenger, Manchester United were moving into ominously good form. They had quickly closed the gap at the top and hammered Newcastle 6-2 at St James' Park while Arsenal were on FA Cup duty. Scholes smashed a hat-trick on a day when Ferguson's men sent a clear message to the Gunners: 'We're ready to take back our trophy.'

The buzz around Highbury created by the semi-final victory was mixed with a sense of anxiety ahead of the potentially title-deciding clash with United. Even though Arsenal had another five games after the United clash, it would undoubtedly be a significant day in the race to lift the Premiership trophy. The match itself was typically tense and the momentum swung one way and then the other repeatedly. United drew first blood when Ruud van Nistelrooy skipped away from Campbell and outpaced Keown before slotting the ball home. Suddenly, Wenger looked a little edgy.

His players gave him a boost after the break with two goals in twelve minutes but both were rather fortuitous. First, Ashley Cole's shot was heading off target before deflecting in off Henry.

Then the Frenchman was clearly offside as he raced onto a through ball and slotted past Barthez. Highbury was rocking and Arsenal were back in the ascendancy. If the players could hold onto the lead, United would struggle to recover in the closing weeks. But Ferguson's side stepped up a gear and equalised through Giggs' header from a pinpoint Solskjaer cross. After that, it was impossible to pick a winner. Both teams looked for the killer blow but the game finished 2-2.

However, there was still time for late controversy as Campbell was sent off for an allegedly deliberate elbow on Solskjaer in the closing stages. It seemed a harsh decision and the defender's suspension would rule him out of the last three Premiership games and the FA Cup final. Wenger was frustrated, explaining to the media: 'Sol's destroyed because he cannot understand it. Everybody knows he did not touch him on purpose. He had no intention of touching Solskjaer.' Arsène also disputed the idea that United now held the advantage: 'I cannot say that anybody is in the driving seat. It can all change so quickly. The only way to win it is to give your all for each game.' Kevin McCarra of *The Guardian* believed that United 'were superior for long enough to have merited victory' but it was all still to play for.

The Gunners kept up the pace with a 2-0 win away to Middlesbrough. Wiltord and Henry were on the scoresheet as Wenger's side matched United, who beat Blackburn. There was now so much at stake in every match and no end of pressure on the players at both clubs. One slip up could be enough to decide who would be lifting the Premiership trophy. Arsenal sat three points above United but had played a game more.

SUPREMACY REGAINED AND SURRENDERED

A trip to the Reebok Stadium on 26 April was Arsenal's next assignment. With Manchester United not playing until the Sunday afternoon, it was a chance for Wenger's side to crank up the pressure. They began brightly and overwhelmed Bolton, taking a 2-0 lead and appearing very comfortable. Then the unthinkable happened. The Gunners began to sit back and Bolton took advantage, pouring forward and grabbing a goal through Youri Djorkaeff. Suddenly, Arsène's side faced a tricky task in closing out the match. Sam Allardyce's team were relentless and in the final minutes a ball from the left was flicked on by substitute Keown into his own net. It was the fifteenth draw of the campaign for Arsenal and in this moment, the Gunners surrendered the initiative to United – it was a long, quiet trip back to London.

Ferguson's men needed no second invitation, beating Tottenham 2-0 at White Hart Lane the next day. As was so often the case in the last few months, van Nistelrooy was on the scoresheet. As Danny Fullbrook explained in the *Daily Star*, Arsenal were now trailing: 'Manchester United are odds-on to win the Premiership title after Paul Scholes and Ruud van Nistelrooy fired them to victory over Spurs. United held their nerve to take advantage of Arsenal bottling it in the 2-2 draw at Bolton.'

When United won their next game against Charlton, Wenger and his players found themselves needing to beat Leeds at home on 4 May just to keep their title challenge alive. How had things turned against the Gunners so quickly? It proved to be a nightmare afternoon for the Arsenal manager. Leeds had endured a terrible season but they played with great freedom. From the minute that Harry Kewell smashed an improbable goal from the left touchline, the Gunners were under immense pressure. The game seesawed one way and then the other as Arsenal threw men forward. Wenger became increasingly agitated and then utterly despondent when Mark Viduka struck the knockout blow, giving Leeds a 3-2 win and ending any chance of Arsenal retaining the Premiership trophy. Highbury heaved a collective sigh of disbelief.

The final two league games were now largely insignificant but Wenger was determined to finish on a high note. Southampton were the first to feel the Gunners' wrath as the Saints were thrashed 6-1 at Highbury. Arsène's side played as if they were out to prove a point to United and anyone who doubted their fighting spirit. Pires and Jermaine Pennant, making his full league debut, both scored hat-tricks but Wenger found himself wondering what might have been after this comprehensive win. He explained to the media: 'This does give the players some regrets as they feel that, had they won the game against Leeds, we would be champions on Sunday night. We have done a lot for our goal difference and I'm convinced that had we beaten Leeds, we would have won the championship.' There were such fine margins when chasing the title.

Arsenal continued to take out their frustrations on their opponents when they won 4-0 away to Sunderland on the final day of the season. A hat-trick from Ljungberg powered Arsenal to victory as Wenger spoke proudly of being 'faithful to the football we've shown this season.' Henry finished the campaign with twenty-four league goals, one behind Golden Boot winner van Nistelrooy. But the scenes could not have been more different at the final whistle from those at Goodison

Park where the United players were busy collecting the Premiership trophy and singing 'We've got our trophy back, we've got our trophy back'.

Wenger spoke graciously about the title race and paid compliments to Ferguson and his team. The Gunners still had an FA Cup final to prepare for and Arsène knew that they could take nothing for granted against Southampton, even after the recent 6-1 scoreline. Gordon Strachan's side had impressed many during the season but few had expected them to reach this showpiece final. Wenger named a full strength team – apart from the absent Vieira – but his players were forced to work hard by a dogged Southampton team intent on frustrating their more decorated opponents. Pires gave Arsenal the lead in the first half but the Gunners could not extend their advantage and Southampton threw caution to the wind in the last ten minutes. But there would be no upset this afternoon. Arsenal hung on for the 1-0 victory and, in doing so, gained some consolation for missing out on the title.

Wenger seemed a much happier character when he spoke to the media after the win: 'The team was under pressure and they were scared of finishing without a trophy. The last three weeks have been difficult but the boys have been tremendous and they have responded well to the disappointment. We have got the trophy we wanted.' He also dismissed negative comments about the Gunners' 2002/03 campaign, saying: 'I hope that for the next twenty years we will have seasons as disappointing as this one.'

There had been plenty of ups and downs over the course of the season but the players could be proud of themselves. Yes, the team had thrown away the lead too often in away games. Yes, Europe had again been a failed mission. But there was so much to admire about the Gunners. They had been unlucky to miss out on Premiership glory but could at least be content with the FA Cup success. Wenger had added another trophy to his ever-growing collection and knew that his squad had the necessary character to come back stronger next season. But first he had another honour to collect.

In June, Arsène's fine efforts in English football earned him an honorary OBE. The Queen's Birthday Honours list featured both Wenger and fellow Frenchman Houllier. The two friends received their medals and Foreign Secretary Jack Straw made a touching statement: 'Beyond the entertainment they've offered us on the pitch, what has endeared both Gerard and Arsène to the British public is their obvious passion for the English game. Both have often spoken of their love of the atmosphere in our football stadia, an atmosphere which generates a unique intensity on the pitch.' Wenger was flattered to have been rewarded in this manner and treasured the OBE as highly as anything he had won in the game. Who could have predicted this when Arsène first arrived in the country?

THE INVINCIBLES AND
THE SPECIAL ONE

The 2003/04 campaign will always be remembered by Arsenal fans as the season of the Invincibles. For Wenger, it was one of the most memorable years of his career in football. After the despair around the club at the manner in which the Gunners had surrendered the Premiership title to Manchester United the previous season, a positive response was certainly required. United had put together a storming finish to the previous campaign and Arsène's players had succumbed to the pressure.

From the very start of pre-season training, the Gunners were focused on winning the title back. Other competitions were obviously important too but it was the league crown that meant the most to the players and coaching staff. Wenger felt very confident of adding more silverware during the season, even though he had made few additions to his squad over the summer. The biggest deal saw German goalkeeper Jens Lehmann arrive for £3.5 million from Borussia Dortmund as a replacement for Seaman, who had moved to Manchester City.

Wenger had had great service from Adams and Keown in his early years at Highbury but the time had come for the Arsenal boss to find a new centre-back. Campbell continued to dominate but he needed a younger partner. To the surprise of many, Arsène turned to Kolo Toure, who had played in several different positions for the club without sealing a starting role. It would take time to convert Toure into a centre-half but it would be well worth it. Keown would still be involved, of course – Wenger was just looking to the future. This decision says a lot about Arsène's ability to nurture players and convert them into different roles, knowing their strengths and weaknesses.

Meanwhile, United had lost Beckham, who had moved to Real Madrid in a £24.5 million deal, and the majority of their new signings were inexperienced at Premiership level. Amongst them was Portuguese youngster Cristiano Ronaldo who would go on to be a thorn in Arsenal's side in years to come. The Gunners sensed that they had the edge over their rivals but would be taking nothing for granted. Wenger made sure of that. A tight Community Shield between United and Arsenal ended 1-1 with Arsène's side losing 4-3 in the penalty shoot-out. Jeffers was red carded, adding to the question marks over the striker's future at the club. This curtain raiser offered few indications of how the season would pan out.

While Wenger felt United would be Arsenal's closest rivals, the activity at Chelsea had not escaped his notice. Russian billionaire Roman Abramovich had bought the Blues for close to

£60 million, sparking a massive spending spree. How much involvement manager Claudio Ranieri had was a matter of some speculation. Everyone wondered whether Abramovich had a genuine interest in football or whether owning a club was simply a business opportunity. Chelsea's squad suddenly looked more threatening with the arrivals of Damien Duff, Juan Sebastian Veron and Hernan Crespo amongst several others for a combined total of over £100 million.

Arsenal's league campaign began in impressive fashion and Gunners fans quickly sensed that their team was on a mission to make amends and regain the title. A 2-1 win over Everton on the opening day was earned despite Campbell's red card and this was followed by three more victories. Amongst them was a 4-0 scoreline away to Middlesbrough that showcased the attacking class of Wenger's side. When they played in that manner, they were unstoppable. Henry and company made football look such an easy game when they waltzed past defenders and seemingly passed the ball into the net. It was the flamboyant style that Wenger had preached to his squad for years.

September was a less inspired month for Arsenal. A home draw with Portsmouth was frustrating but a 3-0 defeat to Inter Milan in front of a packed house at Highbury was embarrassing. The Italians simply outclassed the Gunners on the night and showed a killer instinct in the final third of the pitch. It was not the way in which Arsène had hoped to begin this latest Champions League journey and there were an uncharacteristically high number of errors on the night.

But Wenger urged his players not to dwell on the result: 'We can complain and cry the whole night but that will not change the result. The only thing we can do is to respond. Inter played well but they were not unbeatable and the difference between the two teams was not 3-0.' Hector Cuper, the Inter manager, saw things rather differently though when questioned by reporters: 'Arsenal had to face an almost perfect Inter side and they could never find the space they wanted.' Drawn in a group with Inter, Lokomotiv Moscow and Dynamo Kiev, Wenger had expected his team to dominate proceedings. Suddenly, confidence was shaken a little.

A stormy encounter at Old Trafford produced a 0-0 scoreline but there was plenty of action. Vieira was sent off with ten minutes remaining after tangling with van Nistelrooy, earning the Arsenal skipper a second yellow card. The Gunners were even more incensed when United were awarded a dubious penalty in the closing stages for a supposed foul by Keown on Uruguayan Diego Forlan. The usually-reliable van Nistelrooy stepped up and smashed the spot-kick against the crossbar – much to the relief of Wenger and all Arsenal supporters. Their unbeaten start to the season had been preserved – but only just.

What followed was hugely disappointing, though, as the Gunners players marred a solid team performance by the manner in which they taunted van Nistelrooy after the final whistle. Clearly, and understandably, Arsenal felt aggrieved by some of the refereeing decisions but this was not the way to take out their frustrations. Wenger once again refused to criticise his team and fell back on unconvincing explanations: 'We have played ten games of ninety minutes and for five seconds we didn't behave. We did not behave as we want to behave. It was no more than that.'

At least publicly, Arsène decided that the antics of his players warranted little comment, leaving plenty of neutrals stunned that he had not clamped down on his team's bad sportsmanship. But Ferguson was quick to speak his mind on the topic when questioned by reporters: 'They got away with murder. What the Arsenal players did was the worst I have witnessed in sport.' The mind games continued.

The FA *did* act, handing out heavy penalties to those involved in the post-match antics. Keown was banned for three games, Lauren for four and Vieira and Parlour for one each. A series of fines were also dished out to these four offenders as well as to Ashley Cole and to Arsenal Football Club. Giggs and Cristiano Ronaldo were the United players that received fines. The incident further soured Wenger's relationship with Ferguson.

On 26 September, the Gunners got back to winning ways by seeing off Newcastle 3-2 in a tight contest. The fluent attacks had returned and it was a good omen for the midweek trip to Russia to face Lokomotiv Moscow. A win on their travels would certainly help to make up for the dismal display against Inter Milan. But once more, Wenger had to watch as his side struggled to break down a well organised defence. The match ended 0-0 and Arsène noted that it was another European contest in which his team had failed to find the net. Worse was to follow in Europe in October.

Domestically, the Gunners were brilliant in October as they overcame some tough challenges to take seven points from a possible nine in the Premiership. The month began with a trip to face Liverpool at Anfield. The home side took the lead but a spirited Arsenal comeback was completed when Robert Pires found the top corner with a strike which fully deserved to be the winner. Liverpool boss Houllier claimed that the Gunners 'were lucky today' in the wake of the 2-1 scoreline but Wenger was very pleased with the display.

Two weeks later, Arsène was smiling again as the Gunners won 2-1 at home to Claudio Ranieri's ever-improving Chelsea side. But it took a bad error from Blues goalkeeper Carlo Cudicini to separate the sides in a close contest. Wenger was pleased with the three points but noted some areas for concern in the way that his team played. For instance, he told the media: 'We didn't push enough in the first half.' Everyone who saw the game knew that the Gunners had been more than a little fortunate.

Arsenal's European form continued to be a problem. Having looked strong in recent domestic games, few could have predicted a 2-1 defeat away to Dynamo Kiev. Wenger admitted that his players 'gave absolutely everything' but it was little consolation. It was Kiev's second goal – presented to them by Lehmann's poor clearance – that proved to be decisive. Arsène refused to blame his goalkeeper and was more concerned with the prospect of needing to win their last three matches to be sure of qualifying. The Gunners' hopes were hanging by a thread and they still had to travel to the San Siro to face Inter Milan.

A hangover from the defeat to Kiev saw Arsenal draw 1-1 with Charlton to end a bad week. At least the point kept them top of the Premiership table. During the week, some pundits expressed their belief that Wenger's side had blown their European hopes but the Frenchman kept faith in his team. He knew that the Gunners could beat anyone on their day and kept the morale high in the dressing room. The more experienced players in the squad led from the front and could not wait to get out onto the pitch to make amends.

On the bright side, the Gunners were still unbeaten in the Premiership as they entered November. Arsenal arrived at Elland Road and, finding a Leeds team low on confidence, took full advantage. The game was effectively over by half-time and was dead and buried after fifty minutes when Gilberto Silva put Wenger's side 4-0 up. Leeds worked hard but the pace and movement of Henry, Pires et al was unstoppable. The 4-1 final score reflected Arsenal's dominance but, in truth, the Gunners could have scored more. Arsène took the chance to praise his team's strong mentality post-match and this was the first of five crucial wins in a row.

Dynamo Kiev were beaten 1-0 at Highbury thanks to a late Cole header, keeping their qualification hopes alive. On 8 November, back in domestic action, Wenger's side came from behind to win a tight North London derby 2-1 with two rather fortunate goals. The first, scored by Pires, might have been disallowed for offside in the build-up, and the second, credited to Ljungberg, took a huge deflection to beat Kasey Keller in the Tottenham goal. Birmingham, who never seemed to fare well against the Gunners, fell to a 3-0 loss at home on 22 November.

This good form raised Arsenal's morale before the crunch trip to the San Siro on 25 November. Wenger prepared his players for a tight match and hoped that they would provide the much needed cutting edge, even without Vieira and Bergkamp who were unavailable. Pre-match, the Gunners boss was very honest when speaking to the media. He explained: 'I won't be fulfilled if we don't win the Champions League. But I know I'll never be fulfilled no matter what I achieve as a coach. If we go out of the Champions League, I'll beat myself up and feel really upset. Unfortunately, I do that every season.'

Arsène's side did not let him down as they powered past Inter to record an emphatic 5-1 victory. Having been written off in late October, the Gunners had come roaring back. Henry scored twice and Inter never got to grips with the speed of Arsenal's football. Wenger was thrilled but he still kept his composure post-match. He told the media: 'Not in my wildest dreams could we have predicted that sort of result. It just shows you how fragile team sports are and how things can change so quickly. After we'd lost 3-0 at home, who'd have predicted we'd come here and win 5-1?' The Gunners had not qualified yet, but with a home match against Lokomotiv Moscow as their final fixture, the odds looked to be in Arsenal's favour.

Unsurprisingly, the midweek exertions took their toll on the Gunners and a disappointing 0-0 draw against Fulham was not totally unexpected. The players had given everything in Milan and this was one slip up that Wenger could at least tolerate to a certain extent. He simply hoped that the two lost points would not be decisive in mid May. There were plenty of massive fixtures ahead and Arsène hoped that his team would stay injury-free.

December was, as always, a busy month. Wolves were despatched 5-1 in the League Cup fourth round before a 1-1 draw against Leicester. The important match with Lokomotiv Moscow proved to be relatively straightforward as the Gunners won 2-0 and clinched qualification for the second round. Wenger was quick to praise the character of his players when he spoke post-match: 'I am very proud of the way my boys have turned round a situation that no one expected them to turn round. I believe we have turned the corner with our remarkable mental strength.' Arsène also hit out at some of the critics: 'There is a bit of reluctance among some people to give us credit in Europe.' Nevertheless, the mood around Highbury was very positive. Many felt that having overcome the odds to qualify, it would be hard to stop Arsenal now in the knockout stages.

A 1-0 win at home to Blackburn came courtesy of a Bergkamp goal. But post-match, the discussion centred around Wenger's future as reports circulated about interest from Spanish giants Real Madrid and Barcelona. Arsène moved to clarify the situation: 'As long as you feel you can push the club higher, you want to be part of it. As a manager it could be my last job – I don't think I have to move at some stage at any cost.'

Victory over West Brom in the League Cup quarter-final and an away draw with Bolton were followed by three consecutive wins. Wenger was thrilled to see the consistency back in his team's play. On Boxing Day, Wolves suffered a 3-0 defeat at Highbury as the Gunners turned on the style with Henry grabbing a brace. Southampton fared little better three days later as a Pires goal, beautifully crafted by Henry, kept Wenger's side on track.

The New Year saw Arsenal working hard to keep up with their congested fixture list. Still in contention for four trophies, there was little chance for Arsène to rest players. The Gunners thrashed Leeds 4-1 for the second time that season at Elland

Road in the FA Cup third round. Lehmann gifted Mark Viduka the opening goal but from then onwards it was all Arsenal. Wenger was impressed, telling the press: 'The team responded to the mistake very well.' Leeds caretaker boss Eddie Gray agreed: 'They've got too many players that can hurt you.'

Arsène decided to explore the market during the January transfer window as he searched for more firepower in attack. Usually very cautious over spending large sums, he shocked many Arsenal fans by paying a high price for young Sevilla attacker Jose Antonio Reyes. The total fee had the potential to reach well over £15 million but Wenger set up the deal so that the payments were staggered and some of the total depended on appearances. Reyes had lit up La Liga and had received rave reviews. Arsène spoke confidently about his new recruit: 'Reyes is a fantastic signing. He is a very talented young player, who can play in midfield or as a supporting striker. Jose will be a great asset to our squad.'

It takes a lot to persuade Wenger to part with big money but the Gunners boss was delighted to complete the signing of the Spanish wide man. It would certainly offer another option in attack – not that the team were having any problems finding the back of the net. Perhaps Arsène felt that Reyes could provide fresh impetus for the closing months of the campaign when vital matches would be coming thick and fast. Maybe he was seen as a long term replacement for Bergkamp.

A draw with Everton was followed by another 4-1 scoreline – this time at home to Middlesbrough. The win over Boro put the Gunners top of the table again. Arsène heralded the display as 'one of the best performances here this season.' A 2-0 win away to Aston Villa maintained the momentum and kept Arsenal just ahead of United. Henry grabbed both goals but Villa were furious that his first – a quickly taken free-kick – was allowed to stand and David O'Leary, the Villa boss, also claimed that the second goal (from the penalty spot) was an incorrect decision. Wenger, though, defended the referee's performance and focused on continuing the team's run of good results. The Frenchman reminded everyone that the Gunners were still to lose in the league this season: 'We are twenty-two Premiership games unbeaten but we are not looking beyond the next match. We always try to win the next match. That is how we deal with it. There is a long way to go but we have the hunger and the motivation and belief.'

Losing the first leg of their League Cup semi-final against Middlesbrough was a slight disappointment for Arsène but he was a lot happier four days later when his team beat the same opposition 4-1 in the FA Cup. Wenger gave some promising youngsters the chance to impress and spoke favourably to the media about their impact: 'Some of our young players showed great talent,' he said. It was a good way in which to end a solid January.

The Gunners' spurt showed no signs of halting as they overcame Manchester City 2-1 at Highbury. It was a close contest but Wenger's side had just enough class to see off a plucky City outfit. A 2-1 loss to Middlesbrough saw Arsenal dumped out of the League Cup but then, in all honesty, the competition had only ever been fourth on the Frenchman's list of priorities.

Ten straight wins after the League Cup exit suggested that

losing to Boro had only strengthened the desire of Arsène and his players. The run began with a 3-1 win at Wolves, who lost to the Gunners for the third time during the campaign, and continued on 10 February at home to Southampton in a 2-0 victory. Henry scored his 100th Premiership goal as Arsenal went five points clear at the top despite not playing at their best. Wenger acknowledged the fact that the Saints had been rather unlucky.

The Gunners kept up their hold over Chelsea with a 2-1 FA Cup win at Highbury thanks to a double from new boy Reyes. The Blues had taken the lead through Romanian Adrian Mutu but the spirit in the Arsenal dressing room was evident in the second half. Reyes' first goal was particularly special as he lashed a left-footed strike past Cudicini in the Chelsea goal.

A week later, the two teams met again, this time at Stamford Bridge. To the disappointment of Abramovich and Ranieri, the result was identical and it proved a critical weekend in the Premiership. Just as in the FA Cup tie, Chelsea took the lead as Eidur Gudjohnsen scored within thirty seconds. But goals from Vieira – after Bergkamp's pinpoint pass – and Edu allowed Arsenal to leave with the spoils. As Manchester United had drawn 1-1 with Leeds, Wenger was able to enjoy a seven point advantage at the league summit.

However, the Gunners boss refused to get carried away: 'The seven point difference is not enough with the three-point system. It's not a two horse race at all because Chelsea are still in it.' Nonetheless, it was a healthy lead to have as the season entered late February.

Wenger and his squad travelled to Spain in midweek for the

first leg of their Champions League second round tie with Celta Vigo. When the draw was made, Arsène had been relatively pleased, fancying the Gunners' chances against Celta. The first leg proved to be a thrilling, attacking contest which Arsenal shaded 3-2, picking up three important away goals in the process. Edu was the hero, scoring twice. Arsène was delighted and knew deep down that his side should have enough class to finish the job at Highbury and seal a place in the quarter-finals. Wenger claimed: 'Doing well in the league gave us confidence to score goals.' This victory also emphasised the improvements in Arsenal's away form. Kick-started by the win in Milan, Wenger's team now seemed more assured on their travels.

The unbeaten run continued as Arsenal won 2-1 at home to Charlton on 28 February. The streak had reached an incredible length by now and some experts began to wonder whether the Gunners could stretch it until the end of the season. Wenger was less concerned about the record and more interested in his team cementing its place at the top of the table.

Arsène's players had made the most of Manchester United's slip-ups to build a lead over Ferguson's side. Next, the Gunners produced a masterclass in the FA Cup sixth round against Portsmouth at Fratton Park, winning 5-1. Such was the quality of the performance that the Pompey supporters could not help but applaud the opposition. It was one of those rare moments in football when the beauty of the play unites both sets of fans. Henry and Ljungberg grabbed two goals each and Wenger reflected on a job well done: 'The result is wonderful but it is even more enjoyable to see opposition fans cheering our team. Our game was really fluent. Our passing and movement gave Portsmouth many problems.' Reyes had one of his best games for the club and was looking like a promising talent.

Qualification for the Champions League quarter-finals was assured with a 2-0 victory at home to Celta Vigo. The Spaniards tried their best but the Gunners were just too strong. Wenger was thrilled that his team had gone through with the minimum of fuss: 'We controlled the game. The way that we handled the game shows we have matured. It was important to start by scoring goals and then not to put ourselves in trouble by being steady defensively and we did that.'

Back in the Premiership, Arsenal grabbed two more wins to move nearer to regaining the league trophy. On 13 March, Wenger watched his side pick up the three points at Ewood Park in a 2-0 victory. A week later, at Highbury, a 2-1 scoreline against Bolton brought more cheer to everyone associated with the club. The team's supporters were buzzing with excitement.

The Champions League quarter-final draw paired the Gunners with London rivals Chelsea. Arsenal had enjoyed the better of their recent tussles with the Blues and the bookmakers made Arsène's side firm favourites. Remarkably, these would be the fourth and fifth contests between the teams this season. The Gunners had the possible advantage of playing the second leg at home in front of a packed Highbury and Wenger knew that this could hold the key to finally reaching the semi-finals.

The first leg at Stamford Bridge was a typically tense affair with both sides cautious not to surrender the initiative. The match finished 1-1 – a fair result on reflection – and it set everything up nicely for the return leg. Arsenal had scored an 'away goal' across town in London and Wenger was well aware that his side had the psychological edge over the Blues after winning so many of their recent contests. Desailly was dismissed late on and would miss the second leg. It was hard to tell if Arsène was impressed with his team's display but his opposite number Ranieri had kind words to say about the Gunners. He told the press: 'This season Arsenal are playing in another world.'

Next for the Gunners were two matches against rivals Manchester United – one in the Premiership and one in the FA Cup. Normally, this fixture is full of pressure with so much at stake but for once the atmosphere was far from electric as the teams met in the league. United trailed Arsenal by twelve points and both sides knew that the title race was effectively over already. The game was close with Louis Saha's late goal rescuing a point for the visitors in a 1-1 draw. Gunners fans left Highbury bemused at some of Wenger's defensive substitutions which had handed the initiative back to United.

The FA Cup semi-final brought an equally disappointing display from Arsenal. The competition represented United's last chance of silverware and Ferguson's squad was raring to go from the first whistle in contrast to Wenger's shell-shocked, clueless line-up. The Frenchman decided to rest Henry for the match, perhaps with an eye on the big European match in midweek, and left Reyes out too. These moves backfired on the Arsenal boss.

Paul Scholes gave United the lead in the first half and, from then on, the Gunners found a wall of United shirts blocking the route to goal. Arsène made changes, threw Henry into the fray and willed his players forward yet the breakthrough did not come. Frustrated, Wenger had to accept that on the day Ferguson's team had deserved their place in the final. The Gunners had not turned up willing to fight and their meek surrender made painful viewing for their supporters.

With the Champions League second leg against Chelsea ahead, Arsène lifted his players from their disappointment and reminded them of the prizes that were still up for grabs this season. Maybe the team had had one eye on the huge second leg clash when facing United. European glory was the target as the Gunners stepped out at Highbury on 6 April, just ninety minutes from a prestigious Champions League semi-final. Wenger was entering the biggest match of his career to date.

It was all going so well. Arsenal went ahead on the night and on aggregate with a goal from Reyes. The home fans were on their feet, as expectant and delighted as the manager himself. Ranieri's failure to deliver a major trophy thus far meant that his days would be numbered at Chelsea unless the Blues could produce the goods. Abramovich would not tolerate a lack of success. It seemed as though Ranieri's players sensed this in the second half and Wenger could only watch as Chelsea forced their way back into the contest. The equaliser duly arrived courtesy of Frank Lampard and the tie was once again level.

Arsène urged his players to seize the initiative again. The squad had already given so much for the cause this campaign but the Frenchman needed just a little more. Unfortunately for Wenger, it was Chelsea who stepped up for their manager with just a few minutes remaining. A neat move and a clever one-two between Wayne Bridge and Hernan Crespo put Bridge through on goal and the England defender buried his shot in the far corner. This second away goal killed the tie for the Gunners and Highbury was silenced. The European dream was over and it would take some time for Arsène to come to terms with this setback.

The Arsenal boss sloped off solemnly down the tunnel. Ranieri, meanwhile, was understandably on cloud nine, exclaiming: 'I am mad with joy at the result.' The Blues were through to face Wenger's old club Monaco in the semi-finals. A sad – but perhaps unsurprising – aspect of the match was that the majority of neutrals were cheering for Chelsea. The Gunners' domestic dominance had been obtained through scintillating football but the public is so often drawn to support the underdog. Therefore, the late Bridge goal pleased many up and down the country.

One of the most distressing elements of the elimination was that this was a fantastic chance for Arsenal to go all the way and lift the trophy. When Wenger looked at the quarter-final results, he saw without doubt that the Gunners would have been clear favourites to win the competition if they had advanced. After all, Chelsea were joined in the semis by Porto, Deportivo La Coruna and Monaco. Real Madrid and AC Milan had been surprise losers in their quarter-finals and the last four had a somewhat anti-climactic feel to it. Arsène and his squad had missed their best ever opportunity to advance to the showpiece final of the Champions League.

Fortunately for Wenger and his players, the title was well within their grasp. The emotions of the Chelsea defeat might otherwise have had a serious knock-on effect on their chances of lifting the trophy. The way in which Henry dismantled a stubborn Liverpool defence on 9 April suggested that the Gunners were focused on the present as they extended their lead at the top to seven points. The first half had been poor but Wenger's words at half-time inspired a major improvement.

Arsène felt much cheerier after his striker's fine hat-trick in the 4-2 win. The pick of the goals was the Frenchman's second as he collected the ball well outside the area and proceeded to dance past hapless Liverpool tackles before beating Jerzy Dudek. It put the Gunners 3-2 up. Suddenly, in that moment, the midweek misery was forgotten. The unbeaten run continued and, with only seven league games left, a Premiership campaign without defeat was looking more and more possible.

A 0-0 stalemate at St James' Park left the Arsenal attack frustrated and poor Leeds paid the penalty as the Gunners destroyed the confidence-shy side 5-0 on 16 April. Henry struck four of the five goals in a scintillating display. Wenger had masterminded three thrilling wins over the Yorkshire club during the season and Arsenal had scored thirteen goals in the process. A North London derby on 25 April was the toughest remaining test but the Gunners had the added incentive of needing just a draw to clinch the title at White Hart Lane. The challengers had failed to put pressure on Arsène and his players and, with four games remaining, it was just a matter of time before Arsenal were confirmed as champions.

But Tottenham were desperate to be party poopers. Their players and supporters would like nothing better than to be the side to end the unbeaten streak. Arsenal came flying out of the traps and led 2-0 at half-time. The away end of the ground was already starting the celebrations. Tottenham fought back, and even pulled level with a last minute penalty, yet a point was all that the Gunners required. When referee Mark Halsey blew the final whistle, the party began as Wenger and his squad basked in the glory. The agony of losing out in 2002/03 could now be forgotten.

The Premiership title had been sealed but there was still one major target to play for – Arsenal's season-long unbeaten league run. This was enough to keep the players on their toes as they sought a place in the record books. Draws with Birmingham and Portsmouth put the Gunners two games away from completing this mission. The squad was tiring from the exertions of the long campaign but the collective spirit in the camp kept the players going. An error from goalkeeper Edwin van der Sar handed the Gunners a 1-0 victory away to Fulham at Craven Cottage. It was the fourth clean sheet in six matches for Arsène's defence – their ability was often overlooked due to the quality of the attackers. One match to go.

On 15 May, the curtain came down on the 2003/04 season and Wenger made sure his players did not let their standards slip at the final hurdle – not that they needed much motivation. Leicester were the visitors to Highbury and there was an expectant, party atmosphere inside the stadium. The Foxes did their best to spoil the celebrations, taking the lead in the first half through ex-Gunner Paul Dickov, but ultimately Arsenal had the last laugh on their big day. Two second half goals – an Henry penalty and a calm finish from Vieira – handed the points to the Gunners and the entire squad and coaching staff took the plaudits for going an entire Premiership season without defeat. In a thirty-eight-match league campaign, losing three or four games had been the norm but Wenger's team had not even been defeated once.

As Arsène said: 'Everywhere in the world, in any big championship, you would get a lot of respect for going through a season unbeaten. Every week my players refuse to lose.' George Graham had managed a campaign with just one defeat in 1990/91 as Arsenal boss but the unbeaten league season was an elusive statistic until Wenger's Invincibles finally cracked the code.

Henry had been a revelation. His tally of thirty-eight goals underlined his value to the team and he rightly received a string of end of season awards. Few defences in Europe had found an answer to his style of play and Wenger acknowledged that he owed a lot to his striker.

So, the Champions League had again escaped Arsène's clutches and the side had fallen at the semi-final stage in the FA Cup, but their Premiership success had been spectacular. After losing out narrowly to Manchester United in 2002/03, Wenger had vowed to bring the trophy back to Highbury and, with the help of his array of stars, he had kept his promise. The attacking quartet of Henry, Pires, Ljungberg and Bergkamp took most of the plaudits but it was most definitely a team effort. There had been some wonderful highlights for Arsène to reflect on: the clinical 5-1 win in Milan, the classy 5-1 victory at Portsmouth and the resilient 4-2 triumph over Liverpool. Wenger had raised the bar in the Premiership and it was now down to the other top managers to take up the challenge of matching the Gunners' brilliance.

* * *

Wenger entered the new season full of confidence but defending the title would be tougher than ever for the Gunners as Manchester United, Chelsea and Liverpool returned stronger than ever. Chelsea had sacked manager Claudio Ranieri and replaced him with Jose Mourinho, the charismatic Portuguese who had won the 2004 Champions League with unfancied Porto. Mourinho quickly earned the nickname of the 'Special One' after some very self-assured press conferences. As he had with Ranieri, Abramovich made plenty of transfer funds available to Mourinho. The new Blues boss brought Ricardo Carvalho and Paulo Ferreira with him from Porto and his other signings included strikers Didier Drogba and Mateja Kezman, winger Arjen Robben and goalkeeper Petr Cech. As Chelsea continued to pile up debts, Wenger was far from impressed that there had been no sanctions to stop the Blues' spending.

Meanwhile, Manchester United had signalled their intent by signing teenage sensation Wayne Rooney after his impressive displays at Euro 2004 in Portugal. Everton eventually accepted a deal from which they would get £20 million up front and a possible further £7 million depending on Rooney's achievements at Old Trafford.

Arsène was happy with his squad as the start of the season approached. There had been limited activity in the transfer market but the club had kept hold of Vieira again when at one point he seemed destined to join Real Madrid. More would be expected of Reyes this campaign. He had struggled at times to adjust to life in England and needed to improve his understanding with the other attackers, especially with Henry. Clearly, the Spaniard had a ferocious left foot and great pace yet he had wasted good chances too often. As Wenger stressed, though, Reyes was still young and had plenty of time ahead of him to develop. There was no better place to develop than under Arsène's watchful eye. In May, young Dutchman Robin van Persie had become the latest fledgling to join the Gunners and fans were excited to catch their first glimpse of the highly-rated forward.

A Community Shield victory over United was a good omen for the season ahead. Wenger's young players shone, with Reyes in particularly exhilarating form. A comfortable 3-1 win pleased Arsène and his squad appeared to have greater depth than previous years. United had been hit with injury problems and Ferguson must have been concerned to see how easily the youthful Gunners overpowered his side.

On 15 August, Arsenal began their Premiership campaign at Goodison Park. A Rooney-less Everton were no match for the Gunners who ran out easy 4-1 winners. The counter attacks that had characterised the unbeaten run were in evidence again with Bergkamp, Reyes, Ljungberg and Pires grabbing the goals. Wenger was in high spirits: 'We've only played one game, so it's very early but we'll try to do again what we did last season. Last year, we wanted to play good football, go forward all the time. We won't change.'

With Vieira resting a groin strain, Arsène picked young Spaniard Cesc Fabregas for his Premiership debut, aged just seventeen. Fabregas, plucked from Barcelona's youth programme, seemed to embody everything that Wenger preached in terms of passing and close control. Before long, Arsène was recommending the youngster for an international call-up, telling the press: 'A boy of that age can have one good game but he is consistent. It is not stupid to say that he could be in the full Spain squad. They have a lot of midfielders but they shouldn't be scared to bring him in.'

The team's potent finishing rescued a dangerous situation at home to Middlesbrough on 22 August. Trailing 3-1 after some sloppy defending, Wenger's players produced a stirring comeback to triumph 5-3 and extend their unbeaten streak. It was clearly going to take something incredible for the Gunners to surrender that record. Highbury was electric that afternoon as the home side reminded everyone of their class. The Arsenal manager spoke proudly to the media: 'Once again, you saw our mental resources, we never lost our nerve. We were tested mentally and football-wise and we got a fantastic response from the players. When we have a bad defensive day, we can have a great offensive day and that is the way we all pull together.' The win extended the unbeaten streak to forty-two games and equalled Nottingham Forest's top flight record.

Further wins over Blackburn and Norwich completed a flawless August and allowed Arsenal to sit proudly at the top of the table. The success against Blackburn saw the Gunners break Forest's record and take possession of a place in history for the longest run of unbeaten league matches in English football. Wenger took great pride from this achievement but promised that there would be no complacency: 'We won't relax because of this. When it is going well, be humble and rigorous. We have to show we are intelligent people and be more demanding of ourselves.' It sounded like the principles on which Arsène organised his own life. Meanwhile, Manchester United made a very poor start and Arsenal had left them trailing.

After beating Fulham 3-0 at Craven Cottage, the Gunners began their Champions League campaign. Drawn in Group E with PSV Eindhoven, Rosenborg and Panathinaikos, there were few potential banana skins. PSV, from Holland, visited Highbury for the opening fixture and became the latest team to succumb to the home side's dominance, though they only lost 1-0. Remembering the qualification struggles of the previous season, Wenger was determined to reach the second round more comfortably this time.

The string of six wins ended at home to Bolton who fought hard for a 2-2 draw, much to Arsène's frustration. A home match against the Trotters should have represented a likely three points but a little complacency had marred the performance. Wenger gave an honest assessment to the press: 'We didn't find our usual technical level today. Overall you cannot say it was an undeserved result for them. We got caught in the air from their set pieces and showed weaknesses. We looked naïve for their goals.' Bolton had enjoyed success against all the top teams so there was no reason for concern at Highbury.

The Gunners made no mistake a week later at the City of Manchester Stadium, beating City 1-0 and claiming their fourth clean sheet of the campaign. Wenger knew the significance of keeping the strong run alive but urged his team to be more clinical: 'It was a big win to win here. It was a hard-earned victory. We played well in the first half but we didn't get the second goal – and when you don't finish the game off, the other team has a chance.'

A draw in Europe against Rosenborg was followed by an emphatic win at home to Charlton in the Premiership. Henry was the central figure, scoring two – his first was a glorious back-heel through the legs of his marker Jonathan Fortune. Aston Villa fared little better two weeks later as they fell to a 3-1 defeat against the rampant Gunners. The unbeaten run continued.

October brought the announcement that the new Arsenal ground would be called the Emirates Stadium, owing to the sponsorship deal that the club had struck with Emirates Airline. With the process moving along, everyone was eager to see the finished product. But frustration in Europe continued to bother Wenger as his side failed to finish off opponents. A 2-2 draw with Panathinaikos put the Gunners on five points from their first three games – at least it was four more points than at this stage a year ago. Lehmann was the unfortunate villain on this occasion as he made two blunders that cost his side dearly. Wenger, however, refused to point the finger at his goalkeeper, telling the press: 'It's very difficult to make individual judgements straight after a game. We should have got three points but we've got to be satisfied.'

Their biggest test of the season so far came on 24 October at Old Trafford against Manchester United. Arsenal's unbeaten record had stretched to forty-nine games with the win over Villa and the players were desperate to reach the half-century mark against their bitter rivals. Past meetings between the sides guaranteed that it would be a fiery contest.

The Gunners were denied an early chance when Rio Ferdinand appeared to barge Ljungberg to the floor. Ferdinand was the last man and referee Mike Riley would have had to send the defender off. Instead, the official waved play on. The match remained close until the final twenty minutes when Riley was again at the centre of controversy. Rooney and Campbell went for a ball in the area and when the United striker fell to the floor, the referee pointed to the spot. Replays showed that there was little, if any, contact. Van Nistelrooy scored the penalty. The Arsenal players were so incensed by the injustice of the situation that they were unable to recover their composure and Rooney himself added a second late on to seal the result. The Gunners' unbeaten run had come to an end in the most unsatisfactory circumstances and Wenger was furious.

After the game, there was chaos in the tunnel and around the dressing rooms as the two teams continued the hostilities. Amidst all the shouting and scuffling, a slice of pizza – from the post-match buffet – was thrown by an Arsenal player and hit Ferguson in the face. Surely this rivalry had now gone too far. The media quickly dubbed the contest 'The Battle of the Buffet'.

Arsène made his feelings clear about the defeat when speaking to the press: 'Riley decided the game, like we know he can do at Old Trafford. We were robbed. There was no contact at all for the penalty, even Rooney said so. It happened last season [when van Nistelrooy fired his spot-kick against the crossbar] and it's happened again.' Wenger was also angered by a nasty challenge by van Nistelrooy on Cole and the rough treatment dished out to Reyes by the Neville brothers. United fans questioned why Arsène was being such a bad loser and Paul Hince wrote on the *Manchester Evening News* website: 'The mark of a true sportsman, I was taught early in life, is to be humble in victory and generous in defeat. Obviously, Arsène Wenger received a different education. Because if he's generous in defeat, I can knit treacle.' Sir Alex would later refer to this match as evidence that the Gunners were 'the worst losers of all time'.

Meanwhile, Arsène tried to focus on the positives, saying: 'I don't feel it will be a turning point. I think this defeat will make the players stronger because they feel a deep injustice.' Captain Vieira added his opinion: 'You get used to it when you play at Old Trafford, we are used to it. We'll be back and we'll be stronger.'

It was little consolation to Wenger that it had taken such dubious decision-making to finally defeat his team. He would have loved to extend the run to fifty games at Old Trafford. But it was not to be. Though Arsène claimed that the loss would have no impact on his players, the following few months would suggest otherwise. Ferguson, meanwhile, hoped that the result could kick-start his side's season.

Victory over Manchester City in the League Cup was pleasing for Wenger but then three draws in their next three fixtures highlighted the fact that the defeat at Old Trafford had shaken the Gunners. A 2-2 draw at home to Southampton on 30 October showcased some uncharacteristic mistakes and a 1-1 draw in midweek against Panathinaikos provided further reasons for concern. Again, Arsenal were making heavy weather of qualifying. These were matches that the Invincibles were sealing by half-time just weeks earlier. A 1-1 scoreline at Selhurst Park against Crystal Palace completed a miserable seven days. The below-par performances had to stop because Chelsea were proving capable of pushing the Gunners all the way in the Premiership, even if United were still off the pace.

A win over Everton put Arsène's side into the League Cup quarter-finals but the nervy league displays continued in the North London derby at White Hart Lane on 13 November. The attacking verve was still in evidence but defensively the Gunners seemed rattled. Their pace and movement on the day was just enough to seal the victory but Wenger could not have expected a 5-4 scoreline. Leading 3-1, Arsenal almost let Tottenham back into the match as the home side threw everything into attack. It had been a fantastic game of football, full of twists and turns, and the Frenchman was keen to focus on the fact that his team was back to winning ways.

Wenger explained to the media: 'I enjoyed it, but there were some uncomfortable moments. Games like these North London derbies are either 0-0 or completely crazy. You could say this one was definitely completely crazy. I think we showed great character. Our defenders are not as happy as our attackers, but we are happy to win. People are maybe going overboard because we've not won our last two league games, but we have lost one out of fifty-three.'

Two more draws, though, left Gunners fans dismayed by the change in fortunes. Only managing to pick up a point at home to West Brom was not good enough and Wenger knew it. A draw away to PSV in Europe was another missed opportunity to seal qualification for the second round, though it could have been worse considering that Lauren and Vieira were both sent off in the second half. Arsène and his players needed to get a result against Rosenborg in their final fixture to be sure of reaching the next round.

Their second defeat in fifty-five league matches came on 28

November against Liverpool. Considering that Arsenal had been stuttering, the result was not totally unexpected. Gerrard, operating in a free role, had a terrific game but it was youngster Neil Mellor who took the plaudits with a long range winner. Wenger looked dismayed at the final whistle but had composed himself by the time he answered the media's questions and offered an old excuse: 'We gave a lot against Eindhoven and that may have affected us. I don't think we defended particularly badly but at the moment every mistake we make goes in and we don't look as sharp physically as we usually are.' A 1-0 defeat in midweek to Manchester United in the League Cup did little to improve the mood around Highbury.

Mourinho and Chelsea, meanwhile, were continuing their march towards the top of the league table. Few expected the Blues to mount an immediate assault on the title with their new manager but Mourinho had adapted instantly to life in London. Chelsea's form was putting plenty of pressure on Wenger's side – whether the Frenchman was prepared to admit it or not – and the rivalry between Arsène and Mourinho was beginning to develop.

Arsenal responded in the right way to their recent woes. A 3-0 victory over Birmingham at home suggested that the players had rediscovered the form of 2003/04 as they tore into the visitors. Three days later, the Gunners beat Rosenborg 5-1 to clinch qualification for the second round. It was the second emphatic win of the week and the perfect way to prepare for their next league fixture – against Mourinho's Chelsea at Highbury.

There was no end of hype in the build up to the big match.

Arsenal, the champions, facing Chelsea, the challengers. Much was made of the two managers and their different personalities. Arsène: calm and collected. Jose: flamboyant and passionate. Mourinho's side had an array of foreigners, just like Wenger's Arsenal, but the core of the Blues side was English as John Terry and Frank Lampard emerged as two of the country's top players.

The match proved to be thrillingly competitive as the two teams fought out a 2-2 draw in which neither side deserved to lose. The visitors scored twice from set pieces as Mourinho seemed to outwit Wenger tactically. Whereas in the past the Gunners had so often overcome Chelsea at home, Mourinho's arrival had strengthened the Blues' belief.

Arsène regretted missing the chance to beat a fellow title contender: 'It is frustrating because we were twice in the lead but we were pulled back. We had chances to win the game.' Mourinho, though, was irritated by Arsenal's second goal – a quickly taken free-kick by Henry – and felt aggrieved to leave Highbury with just a point: 'We were the better side and we should have won the game.'

Four straight wins gave Arsenal maximum points from the Christmas period. Wenger knew that it would be a critical time and his players did their bit to ease the pressure. A victory away to Portsmouth on 19 December began the sequence and a 2-0 home triumph over Fulham came a week later. On 29 December, the Gunners travelled to St James' Park and grabbed a 1-0 win thanks to a goal from Vieira.

2005 began promisingly with a 3-1 victory away to Charlton on New Year's Day. The Arsenal attackers took advantage of some lapses from the Addicks and gave out a serious education in pace and movement. Chelsea, though, had taken advantage of the slip-ups from the Gunners and United, and Mourinho's side sat comfortably at the top of the table. Wenger tried to crank up the pressure on the Blues by suggesting that it would be stressful for them to keep up the pace.

A 1-0 defeat to Bolton on 15 January brought criticism of Arsenal's ability to handle away fixtures against more physical, aggressive teams. Wenger disagreed with these comments but could not dispute the fact that the loss at Bolton had made catching Chelsea an even tougher proposition. The Blues were suddenly ten points ahead and Wenger appeared to throw in the towel, shortly after claiming that the race was still on: 'Chelsea can only lose it now because they have already won it.' It did not stop Arsène and Mourinho bickering in the press, though. The Gunners were victorious in their final two matches in January, beating Newcastle 1-0 in the Premiership and Wolves 2-0 in the FA Cup.

February began with one of the most eagerly anticipated fixtures of any league season: Arsenal v Manchester United at Highbury. Strangely, this year it was not a clash between the top two teams but between sides chasing the leaders. This, though, did nothing to defuse the intensity of the contest. Wenger told the media pre-match that the losers faced dire consequences – he felt they would be out of the title race.

The two sides had had a stormy relationship over the past few seasons and this had led to some ugly scenes. However, this particular night topped previous matches for its fiery nature. The animosity began earlier than usual as an altercation in the tunnel between Vieira and Roy Keane, the two captains, was captured by Sky Sports cameras. The argument referred to something that Vieira had said to Gary Neville at the end of the warm-up. The finger pointing and angry words ensured that the game would not lack a physical edge. It promised to be a classic and it did not disappoint.

Vieira put the tunnel incident behind him to give Arsenal an early lead with a powerful header from a corner. It got the Highbury crowd going and lifted the intense atmosphere up another notch. United came back strongly and equalised through Giggs, ever a thorn in Wenger's side. Bergkamp put the Gunners back in front before half-time, firing through Roy Carroll's legs, and at the break Arsène felt confident his players could go on to take all three points.

But it was United who came out stronger in the second half with Giggs and Cristiano Ronaldo to the fore. Ronaldo equalised and then Giggs, released by Keane, outpaced Vieira, rounded relatively untried goalkeeper Manuel Almunia and crossed for Ronaldo to grab a second. Almunia had made Giggs' decision for him by charging off his line and it left the goal totally exposed. Suddenly, the game had turned on its head and Wenger looked bemused as to how it had happened. John O'Shea rubbed salt into the wounds by adding a fourth with a clever chip and the Arsenal fans had seen enough. United had just dominated the second period, even though Mikael Silvestre, the French defender, was sent off.

Wenger preferred not to discuss the tunnel fracas but, true to his pre-match verdict, he admitted that the title race was now over for his players: 'We will not give up but now we are too far behind. It is Chelsea's title now. Manchester United still have a slight chance but there is too much for us to do. But we still have our pride and will keep trying to do as well as we can.' Two defeats against United in a season was a statistic that pained Arsène and his squad. Ferguson was understandably brimming with pride and promised to chase Chelsea all the way.

With their title challenge apparently over, the Gunners still had plenty to think about. Wenger told his players that they must attempt to finish as strongly as possible in the Premiership but he also had his mind on two other competitions: the FA Cup and the Champions League. The second round draw in Europe had paired Arsenal with German powerhouse Bayern Munich but the second leg would be at Highbury, giving the Gunners a little boost.

Arsène's side played with great freedom in their next two league games, almost as if Wenger's comment about the title race being over had lifted some of the pressure on them. A 3-1 victory over Aston Villa at Villa Park was slick and stylish – with a 3-0 lead established within half an hour – but the 5-1 win over Crystal Palace was even better. The Gunners boss was certainly in a positive mood after watching his side dismantle their fellow Londoners: 'We have always said that the best answer to anything is to produce on the pitch and we did that.'

This fixture was also noteworthy for the fact that Wenger selected a sixteen-man squad that did not contain a single Englishman – the first time that this had occurred in Arsenal history. He shrugged this off, however, claiming: 'I don't think Arsenal fans mind if they see all-foreign teams. They want to see quality. If you see a fantastic player you don't mind where he is from.' While the Gunners were winning, such an issue could be overlooked but it was a rather damning verdict on the state of English football that Wenger could not find an Englishman suitable for his team.

One of the home-grown players in Arsène's squad, Cole, became the hot topic of conversation in February as Wenger became infuriated by Chelsea's attempts to lure the defender to Stamford Bridge. 'If they don't behave as they should, it's down to the Premier League to start an inquiry and to get them punished,' he told the press. Mourinho told Arsène to call him if he wanted answers. The Cole saga would drag on and on and Arsène would become more and more infuriated with the behaviour of Mourinho and Chelsea.

The next two weeks proved to be another blip for Arsenal. A weary-looking display in the FA Cup at home to Sheffield United ended in a 1-1 draw and then a dismal showing in Munich left the Gunners with a mountain to climb in the second leg. The trip to the Olympic Stadium was always going to be tough but Wenger was disheartened by the way his team performed. The match finished 3-1 to the Germans but could, in truth, have been worse. Kolo Toure's late goal gave Arsenal fans some hope for the return leg. Arsène was downbeat post match as he explained his side's failings. He called it 'our worst performance in the Champions League' and added: 'The players are really down in the dressing room. I feel we really turned in a bad performance.'

The Frenchman admitted that Toure's goal had at least kept the tie alive but it was the Ivorian's defending that was a bigger concern as he played a part in the team's downfall. Vieira, meanwhile, appeared to question Wenger's transfer policy in the wake of the defeat.

All was not lost in their quest for European glory, but the

Gunners would have to produce one of those magical Highbury nights to reach the quarter-finals. Back in Premiership action, Wenger saw the slump continue with a 1-1 home draw against Southampton on 26 February. A penalty shootout victory over a plucky Sheffield United side put Arsenal into the FA Cup sixth round but it would take more than that to raise the morale around the club. With Chelsea and Liverpool prospering in Europe and the Blues still leading the Premiership table, there were few smiles on show in North London.

Wenger demanded an improvement and his words paid dividends as the Gunners upped their game at home to Portsmouth, running out easy 3-0 winners. More of the same would be required in midweek if the Gunners were going to oust Bayern Munich from the Champions League. Arsène's players did their best but ultimately the deficit was just too much to overhaul. Needing to win by at least two goals, Arsenal attacked Bayern but met plenty of resistance. Henry finally broke the deadlock in the second half and the team roared forward in search of a second goal that would put the Gunners through on away goals. To Highbury's despair, the crucial blow would not come and Wenger had to deal with an agonising 3-2 aggregate defeat. Should he have been more aggressive with his tactics? Some fans certainly felt so.

Arsène's agitation boiled over when addressing the media after the match as he revealed his disappointment: 'We lost it in Bayern in the way we gave away the goals away from home. A 1-0 home win is good, but our display in Germany cost us.' The Frenchman refused to criticise his players but also hinted that fresh faces might be arriving in the summer. When questioned on the topic, Wenger replied coyly: 'Will I rebuild the squad this summer? It's difficult to say now.'

The FA Cup run gathered pace with a gutsy 1-0 win over Bolton at the Reebok Stadium. Sam Allardyce's side had caused Wenger problems in past encounters but as soon as El-Hadji Diouf was dismissed, the Gunners seized the advantage. Ljungberg was the match winner with a neat finish from a pinpoint Pires pass. A week later, Blackburn suffered a similar fate as Arsenal kept up their pursuit of Chelsea and sought to pip United to second place.

Wenger's side scored four against Norwich for the second time during the season and a fourth successive league triumph came away to Middlesbrough. With just one goal conceded in their last seven matches, the Gunners were hitting form but, unfortunately, the top prizes had already slipped from their grasp. If only Arsenal had played with such spirit and style against Bayern weeks earlier. Still, the FA Cup was now the big target and it represented a last chance for Arsène to lift silverware in this campaign.

The Arsenal boss and his squad travelled to the Millennium Stadium on 16 April knowing that Blackburn, their opponents, would be desperate to cause an upset. Mark Hughes had overseen big improvements at Ewood Park and Rovers had become a tough team to beat, as Arsenal had found out to their cost. Blackburn's physical style of play was a much-discussed topic and it angered Hughes to hear his side being belittled. Wenger urged his team to avoid provocation and remain composed. A Rovers team containing the intimidating presences of Andy Todd, Robbie Savage and Lucas Neill would certainly be ready for a battle.

The match went according to plan for Arsène. The tactics that he had worked on in the build-up to the game saw the Gunners exploit Blackburn weaknesses, namely a lack of pace in defence. Van Persie had a superb afternoon, scoring twice and overcoming some very rough marking. One particular challenge from Rovers defender Todd brought a storm of controversy and Wenger had plenty of comments for the media post match: 'I don't feel that Andy Todd needed to lift his elbow and he was late to touch him. He could have stopped himself. We responded to some over-the-edge fouls but kept great focus and never lost our nerve. For a young team that was remarkable.' On some occasions, Arsène has been accused of being blinkered over major incidents involving his team but here he seemed absolutely right.

Manchester United won the other semi-final 4-1 against Newcastle to set up a third Arsenal-United clash of the season – this time at the Millennium Stadium in May. After the fireworks in the two league games, everyone looked forward to the showpiece final. For Wenger, it would be a chance to banish the memories of the 2-0 and 4-2 defeats at the hands of Ferguson's team.

A trip to Chelsea in midweek might at one stage have been a dramatic title showdown. Instead, it proved to be an anticlimax as neither side overly exerted themselves in a 0-0 draw. The Blues had enjoyed an excellent season – the Premiership was almost secured and Mourinho's players had already lifted the League Cup. In some respects, a goalless draw was a decent result for the Gunners.

Even with the league season petering out, Arsenal managed to rise to the occasion in the North London derby, beating Tottenham 1-0 at home to clinch a double over their neighbours.

The fans might have grown frustrated at times but a win over Tottenham always cheered the Highbury faithful. A week later, on 2 May, West Brom became the latest team to fall to the Gunners in a 2-0 defeat. Wenger's side had really tightened up their defence in the past few months, keeping clean sheets in ten of their last eleven games in all competitions. It was an impressive record and boded well for next season. Arsenal were holding off United in the race for the second automatic Champions League spot, sitting four points ahead.

With three league games remaining, Arsène encouraged his players to finish strongly. Everyone in the squad was competing for a place in the starting line-up for the FA Cup final and Wenger hoped that this would raise the level of performance in the closing weeks. A 3-1 victory at home to Liverpool on 8 May was exactly what the Frenchman had called for from his team. The defeat condemned Liverpool to a fifth place finish – behind fierce rivals Everton. The red half of Merseyside may have had a Champions League final to look forward to but finishing in fifth was a massive disappointment. The blue half did not hesitate to remind their neighbours of this!

Arsène's delight at the display was evident when he addressed the press after the game but the injury problems within the squad were worrying: 'The injuries are serious. Gilberto has a recurrence of an ankle injury, Patrick Vieira has hurt his knee, while Robert Pires turned his ankle. We will have to see how they are on Monday. What's positive with so many young players is the quality of the game we can reach – it makes me optimistic.'

Things got even better in midweek as the Gunners turned on

the style in an attacking masterclass against Everton. The Toffees were simply blown away by the relentless waves of Arsenal attacks in a comprehensive 7-0 defeat that would live long in the memory. Arsène's smile was as broad as it had been for weeks as he admired the performance. This was more like the Invincibles era again and it was the type of display that the supporters had been crying out for.

Bergkamp had a superb night and it led to questions about his future. The Dutchman was desperate for a new one-year deal at the club but Wenger refused to confirm anything in front of the cameras: 'I've made a decision, but we won't announce it until the end of the season. He is a super-special player. You don't meet a Dennis Bergkamp at the end of every street. He is a great example to the other players and the likes of Robin van Persie have made a huge improvement this season.'

It was an emotional night for the Dutchman as he contemplated the possibility that this would be his last league match at Highbury. Wenger was equally moved, recalling how Bergkamp had masterminded the 1998 'Double' and influenced so many contests with his sublime touch and vision. But his time at Highbury was not over yet. Contract negotiations would be successful and Arsenal would get one more season of Bergkamp magic.

A 2-1 defeat away to Birmingham was a disappointing note on which to end the league campaign. But at least more youngsters were given a chance to gain first-team experience as the Arsenal academy continued to prosper. There had been promising signs in the final few weeks and Gunners fans were much more positive about their prospects for next season.

In the meantime, Arsène and his players cast their minds forward to the FA Cup final in Cardiff where he and Ferguson would once more come head to head. Arsenal and Manchester United would be arriving in the Welsh capital in a bid to salvage some silverware from an otherwise barren year but there could be only one winner. Both teams had suffered an early exit from the Champions League and both had fallen away in the league. It was all set up for an exciting finale to the English season. Many expected a thriller to match the 4-2 scoreline at Highbury in early February.

They would be disappointed, though. A match that had been billed as a classic turned out to be a stalemate. Wenger approached the game cautiously and his players just about managed to contain United's main attacking threats. Ronaldo and Rooney put in brilliant displays but the finishing touch eluded them. Arsenal looked to absorb the pressure and hurt United on the break, yet it was a strangely negative ploy from Wenger, usually an advocate of attacking football.

Having played each other so often, there were few surprises for either manager. After ninety minutes, the game remained goalless and extra-time was also unable to separate the two teams. The FA Cup final would be decided on penalties for the first time ever. In the spot-kick lottery, it was Wenger's Gunners who prevailed. Lehmann, who had made a string of crucial stops during the contest, saved Scholes' penalty and this proved enough as Vieira, not always the most popular player with Arsenal fans in recent times, slotted home the winning kick.

Wenger praised his players for their hunger and joined in the celebrations as his players embarked on a lap of honour. In truth, United had been the better side but it was Arsenal who lifted the trophy and that was all that mattered. Arsène explained to the media: 'We really had to dig deep. I'm very proud because it was a difficult game. There were some times in the second half when we were a bit lucky but we defended very well and to keep a clean sheet is good.'

The Arsenal players were equally jubilant. Ashley Cole enjoyed responding to the boos from the United fans, saying: 'I just wanted to shove it down their mouths.' In contrast, Vieira graciously praised the opposition: 'You have to give credit to Manchester United. They created so many chances but our spirit was fantastic.' The Gunners relished the moment and the chance to give their supporters a special day out.

As United captain Roy Keane explained to the press: 'It's small consolation to say that we had all the chances. We dominated but I'm sure the Arsenal players won't be too bothered about that – they've got the winners' medals and the cup and we haven't.' It summed up proceedings perfectly.

For Sir Alex, a third place finish in the Premiership and a failure in Europe were not good enough and the shootout defeat completed a miserable year for United. Ferguson's side would not give up, though, and Wenger knew that they would be hungrier than ever when the 2005/06 campaign kicked off. Champions Chelsea would have to fight off two driven teams if they wanted to retain the title.

The FA Cup success was a good way for Arsène to kiss goodbye to a forgettable season. After the ecstasy of the unbeaten run in the previous season, 2004/05 could never have matched those heights but Wenger was rightly disappointed with the way his side had faltered at vital moments. It was all part of the learning process, though, and his squad would be stronger for the pain of surrendering the Premiership title. The Gunners had won the league three times but had never retained it and Arsène was keen to rectify this statistic in future years. Had Wenger known how long it would take for Arsenal to win another major trophy, he might have savoured this FA Cup glory even more.

THE REBUILDING PROCESS

There was plenty of excitement prior to the start of another mouth-watering Premiership season. The Gunners had been disappointed to surrender the title to Chelsea and were desperate for revenge. The joy of the unbeaten league campaign of 2003/04 had been replaced by a sense of despair at losing out to the Blues. Certainly, Wenger and his players were not lacking in motivation.

The summer of 2005 saw Vieira finally give in to the lure of a move abroad. But surprisingly he did not join Real Madrid, who had forever been linked with the midfielder, preferring a switch to Italian giants Juventus. He had been a terrific player for Arsenal – one of the best of the Wenger era – and he would be sorely missed. Yet the feeling remained that the fee of £13.75 million that the Gunners received from Juventus made it a good deal considering that Vieira's best days were behind him.

Wenger gave Vieira a fitting send-off: 'I share the sadness

with our supporters that Patrick has left us. But on the other hand I would say to them "trust us and support us". Patrick was a great player for us, one of the greatest in the club's history.'

Arsène used the money from the sale of Vieira to strengthen his squad, signing Belarusian Alexander Hleb from Stuttgart to bolster the competition for places in midfield.

The Gunners boss then announced that Henry would be the new club captain. The striker was more of a focal point now than ever and would be relied upon to carry the goalscoring burden again. He had the respect of all the players and seemed the obvious option to take over from Vieira.

There were plenty of people who questioned the logic of selling Vieira, especially with the other top sides in the Premiership improving their squads. Chelsea's summer shopping included the transfer of powerful Ghanaian midfielder Michael Essien from Lyon while United turned to Dutchman Edwin van der Sar as the answer to their on-going goalkeeping crisis and picked up South Korean Ji-Sung Park from PSV. How would Arsenal respond?

The Gunners' campaign began with a 2-0 win over Newcastle. Jermaine Jenas was sent off for the visitors in the first half but it took the team until the eighty-first minute before they exploited the man advantage. Henry found the net from the penalty spot after Ljungberg had been brought down and van Persie grabbed a second. A week later, though, Arsenal fell to their first defeat of the campaign as champions Chelsea earned a 1-0 win at Stamford Bridge through a second-half strike from Didier Drogba. Mourinho had enjoyed the edge over Wenger again.

This mixed start continued with a 4-1 win over Fulham and

then a 2-1 loss away to Middlesbrough. Henry and centre-back Pascal Cygan scored a brace each against the Cottagers but Arsenal showed none of this clinical finishing on Teesside, much to the frustration of Wenger. The Frenchman fumed when speaking to the press: 'We should never have lost. We missed our chances and we gave them presents for their two goals. We were good enough to win this game.'

A run of five games unbeaten improved Arsène's mood. A last gasp victory in the Champions League over FC Thun was a positive start in a group that also included Ajax and Sparta Prague. Qualification seemed a formality as none of their opponents could match the Gunners' attacking flair. A 2-0 win over Everton at Highbury on 19 September was memorable for two headed goals from Campbell, who was deputising as captain with Henry out injured.

A 0-0 draw away to West Ham and a European win over Ajax kept up the momentum and a dramatic 1-0 victory at home to a stubborn Birmingham side salvaged three points from a frustrating afternoon. A blip away to West Brom gave Wenger an embarrassing afternoon and the Arsenal boss explained: 'We played with a good spirit and showed great potential, but we lacked maturity and with a bit more experience we would have won this game easily.'

After a solid win in the Champions League in Prague, the Gunners picked up another victory at home to Manchester City. Pires grabbed the only goal from the penalty spot but the most bizarre moment arrived late on as Arsenal squandered a second spot kick. In what appeared to be a training ground move, Pires tried to tap the ball forward gently from the spot for Henry to run in from the edge of the D and score. But Pires failed to make contact and the incident ended with red faces all round. Some criticised the Arsenal players for a lack of respect but Wenger defended the penalty fiasco: 'Robert was uncertain and scared to miss the penalty and he made a big mistake and a wrong decision. He was not lacking seriousness or respect – he was lacking confidence.'

This spot-kick routine, clever in theory, was pioneered by Ajax duo Johan Cruyff and Jesper Olsen but Henry and Pires failed to emulate it. Henry, though, admitted that he had hoped to show the crowd something different: 'I take all the blame, it was my idea. Maybe we should not have done it, but football is a game and it is entertainment.' Fortunately for the Gunners, the miss did not prove costly. Arsène would have reacted rather differently if his team had conceded an equaliser moments later.

On 29 October, Wenger took his team to White Hart Lane, bidding to keep up his good record against Tottenham. It was a dire Arsenal display but their resilience enabled them to escape with a draw. Trailing for most of the game, Arsène's players were well below par but Pires pounced on a mistake from Paul Robinson to equalise with thirteen minutes to go. The big concern for Wenger was that his team were still without an away league win and had looked feeble at times on their travels. With Vieira no longer in the midfield, the Gunners struggled at times to impose themselves and were easily out-muscled. On a brighter note, the draw made it just one defeat for Arsenal against Tottenham in their last twenty clashes.

Wenger was proud of the comeback: 'The team realised we needed to do more and if we had not come out with a different attitude, we were in danger. I am delighted with their response. It is great credit to the team.' The Frenchman also had to explain that his decision to leave Pires on the bench had not been related to the penalty incident against Manchester City.

Wenger's tense rivalry with Chelsea boss Mourinho was heightened at this time when the Portuguese hit out at some of Arsène's barbed comments about the Blues. In an astonishing outburst, Mourinho labelled Wenger 'a voyeur' and added: 'He speaks, speaks, speaks about Chelsea. I don't know if he wants my job. He loves Chelsea.' The Chelsea manager also mentioned Arsenal's league woes: 'When you are on game number eleven and you still can't win away from home, and when you are without Thierry Henry and he [Wenger] can't win a game, he should be worried about them.' Clearly, Mourinho had taken exception to some of Arsène's jibes.

Qualification for the Champions League second round was assured after a 3-0 home win over Sparta Prague. With four victories out of four, Wenger's side seemed to be saving their best form for European nights. It meant that Arsène could rest a few players for the final two group games. Two goals from van Persie sealed the comfortable three points. It made a nice change to have qualification wrapped up so early.

The Gunners scored three more goals at home to Sunderland on 5 November. Van Persie continued his promising form by grabbing the opener before Henry, now fit again, weighed in with a brace. A thrilling first half at the JJB Stadium two weeks later saw Arsenal go in at the break 3-2 ahead and Wenger's side held onto that advantage in the second period. Again it was van Persie who scored Arsenal's first goal and Henry who struck the other two. The team were clearly having no problems finding the net and Arsène was impressed with the way that the Henry-van Persie partnership was developing.

An away trip to Switzerland to face FC Thun seemed a perfect chance to rest senior figures but Wenger opted to keep several big names in the line-up. Henry, van Persie, Ljungberg and Campbell all featured but the Gunners made hard work of breaking down a Thun side reduced to ten men after thirty-five minutes. Pires' late penalty clinched a 1-0 win on a very cold and rather forgettable night. Arsène could at least reflect on five wins out of five.

Blackburn were the next to feel the force of an on song Arsenal side. A 3-0 win for Wenger's team came through goals from Fabregas, Henry and van Persie. Fabregas was relishing the chance to fill Vieira's place in the centre of midfield and he played like a seasoned professional, not a teenager. But Bolton lived up to their tag as Arsène's bogey team by beating the Gunners 2-0 at the Reebok Stadium on 3 December. Two first-half goals left Arsenal with a mountain to climb and Wenger was bitterly disappointed to see his team out-muscled on their travels once again. He told the press: 'It was a difficult game but we made it difficult for ourselves. We were shaky on the set-pieces and it was a physical game. Bolton wanted it more and deserved to win. It was just not good enough. But Bolton played well and took advantage of our lack of commitment and desire.'

December quickly got worse as the Gunners stumbled from one poor performance to the next as Wenger despaired. A 1-0 loss to Newcastle on 10 December was hard to take as Gilberto Silva was dismissed with over half an hour remaining. Chelsea then compounded Arsenal's misery by winning 2-0 at Highbury on 18 December. The Blues' good form, combined with the Gunners' woes, had effectively ended Wenger's hopes of winning the title. The three points put Jose Mourinho's side nine points clear of Manchester United and a whopping twenty points ahead of Arsenal. In no time, the Gunners' league challenge had fallen apart but credit had to go to Chelsea for their flawless run of results.

Wenger had plenty of complaints after the loss to the Blues. Firstly, he pointed to van Persie's wrongly disallowed goal when the score was 0-0, saying sourly: 'We scored a regular goal but the referee made a very bad decision. I associate the referee and the linesmen in the same team – the Chelsea team.' Arsène also claimed that Michael Essien should have been sent off for an alleged elbow on full-back Lauren. Blues boss Mourinho, meanwhile, discarded Arsenal's title challenge as something 'we should not worry about' and preferred to focus on United and Liverpool as his biggest threats.

The Portuguese certainly had the bragging rights. In fairness to Mourinho, he had tried to end his feud with Wenger by sending a Christmas card – an act that the Frenchman did not acknowledge. Mourinho's response was to head up the tunnel at full-time rather than shake Arsène's hand. It was the latest episode in the long running row between the two. But like Wenger's rivalry with Ferguson, it was all based on a degree of respect and an absolute obsession with winning.

As Chelsea continued to churn out victories, Arsenal did their best to kick start their season. A 1-0 win at Charlton on Boxing Day was followed by a superb 4-0 result at home to Portsmouth.

All four goals came in the first half as Wenger's side swept Pompey away in emphatic fashion, leaving Harry Redknapp fearing for his team's Premiership status.

A 0-0 draw away to Aston Villa put even more distance between the Gunners and the top sides. Tottenham were sitting in fourth spot and Wenger was facing the worrying possibility of failing to qualify for the Champions League. The visit of Manchester United was usually a spicy affair but when the sides met on 3 January there was little of the customary spark. The match ended goalless and United slipped thirteen points behind Chelsea, widening the smile on Mourinho's face.

January was truly a month of many ups and downs. A 2-1 victory over Cardiff in the FA Cup was a good start but a 1-0 loss to Wigan in the League Cup semi-finals frustrated Wenger, even though he always put out a second string line-up for the competition. There was plenty to do at home in the second leg. The Gunners hit back in spectacular fashion as they beat Middlesbrough 7-0 at Highbury, playing the type of football that Arsène had preached throughout his tenure in North London. Henry cashed in with a hat-trick to cap a fantastic individual display. Wenger was thrilled: 'We played our game and the goals came as a consequence of the quality of our game.'

Things went downhill again with a 1-0 loss at Goodison Park. James Beattie scored for the Toffees in the first half and the Gunners once more showed a soft centre on their travels. To make matters worse, Fabregas received a red card in the closing minutes as frustration took hold of Wenger's players. The Arsenal boss was becoming all too familiar with giving post-match comments after away defeats. He said: 'We lost a difficult game in a frustrating way because it was mainly a physical battle. Away from home we have a problem. We always lose 1-0 and we need to find a response by the end of the season to finish in the top four.'

The next three matches offered no improvement. Seemingly having booked their place in the League Cup final, Arsenal then conceded a late goal against Wigan to ruin their chances. It sent Paul Jewell's side through to the Millennium Stadium on away goals. To make matters worse, Bolton hurt the Gunners once again to make it two cup eliminations in a week with a 1-0 win in the FA Cup fourth round at the Reebok. There would be no successful FA Cup defence for Arsène's players.

Wenger had rested several key players for the Bolton game and paid the price as Stelios Giannakopoulos struck with a late header. The Gunners boss told the media: 'I feel we should have won this game by three goals difference. Bolton didn't create anything the whole game and won with one chance and one goal. Practically, we have lost two trophies this week in the last minute. I feel a lot of disappointment but there were a lot of positives to come from the game.'

Arsenal were seemingly edging from one disaster to the next. A 3-2 defeat at home to West Ham completed one of the most disappointing sequences of Wenger's managerial career. Defensive errors from Campbell contributed to the Gunners' downfall and the centre-back came off at half-time, sparking rumours that Campbell had driven away from the ground immediately. Arsène cast a glum figure when he answered questions after the game and tried to put a positive spin on events: 'We lost and it is difficult to understand how we lost because their keeper was very busy and our keeper was not busy. Overall, commitment was right, the quality of our game was right and we succumbed to basically mistakes that can of course happen in football.'

The month of January had put a massive dent in Arsenal's season. Well adrift in the Premiership and eliminated from both cup competitions, Wenger and his players only had the Champions League left to play for. Real Madrid would be Arsenal's second round opponents and it would be a chance for David Beckham to return to Highbury. Madrid had an array of stars but Arsène hoped his own big name players would step up to the occasion.

A victory arrived at last as Birmingham were beaten 2-0 at St Andrews and the Gunners picked up a much needed clean sheet. Bolton caused yet more problems for Wenger by grabbing a 1-1 draw at Highbury, putting more pressure on Arsenal in their pursuit of fourth place, and Liverpool did the Gunners' fragile confidence little good with a 1-0 win over Arsène's side at Anfield on 14 February. It was hardly the ideal preparation for a trip to the Bernabeu a week later.

But the Champions League was becoming a safe haven for Arsenal. Free from the disappointments of their league form, Wenger's players seemed more committed and relaxed and they displayed greater team spirit. There was a togetherness in the team that had been so badly missing on some of their away trips during the campaign. When the Gunners arrived in Madrid on 21 February, few gave them much chance of avoiding defeat after some of their recent Premiership results. But Arsène and his squad had other ideas as they produced one of those magical European nights that will live long in the memory.

Facing a Real side packed with household names including Raul, Beckham, Zinedine Zidane and Ronaldo, the Gunners chased and harried the Galacticos into making errors. Having reached half-time on level pegging, the belief in the dressing room grew. Wenger urged his side to keep playing positive football on the counter attack. Just after the interval, Henry came up with a moment of pure inspiration.

Picking the ball up near the halfway line, the French striker darted towards goal, leaving defenders wrong footed. He glided past Sergio Ramos, the highly rated Real centre-back, and beat Casillas with a left-footed finish. Madrid was stunned. It was performances such as these from Henry that attracted constant interest from Spain's top clubs.

Arsenal's poor domestic form had indicated that they might be easy pickings for Beckham and company but Wenger's side had risen to the occasion. They now defended their slender lead manfully and stubbornly as Real grew frustrated and ran out of ideas. At the final whistle, the players celebrated an excellent win – the most spirited of the campaign. There was still much work ahead at Highbury in the second leg but the Gunners had proved a lot of people wrong with this mature 1-0 victory.

Wenger was delighted and struggled to contain his excitement. He told the media: 'We needed big nights from Henry, Kolo Toure and Gilberto Silva but the young players did well. There wasn't a single player who wasn't outstanding. I'm happy in every department.' Henry took most of the plaudits but it had been a total team effort. The French striker said: 'You see that as soon as Arsenal is not scared to play, we can play good football.'

Just as Liverpool had done in 2005, Arsenal were saving their best displays for Europe. Adrift in the Premiership, the league games lacked great significance compared to the glamour of the Champions League. Wenger was concerned about his side finishing in the top four, though, and this was looking less and less realistic. It was good to be progressing nicely in Europe but there would be a major inquisition if the club fell short of a place in next year's Champions League.

There was more excitement in January as Arsenal completed the signing of sixteen-year-old Theo Walcott from Southampton for an initial price of £5 million, which could rise to £12 million. Everyone waited with baited breath to see the youngster's impact.

The domestic struggles continued away to Blackburn where the Gunners, conquerers of Real Madrid just days earlier, lost 1-0 to a Morten Gamst Pedersen goal. Wenger could not understand where it was going wrong in the Premiership: 'I'm very sad because I don't think we deserved to lose this game. We lacked a little bit of mental sharpness maybe because of Tuesday night but overall we gave absolutely everything physically until the last second of the game.'

A 4-0 win away to Fulham on 4 March ensured that the Gunners were in scoring form ready for the visit of Real Madrid. After the win in the Bernabeu, Wenger had warned against complacency, telling the media: 'I still think they will turn up and give everything. To sit on our lead at Highbury would be a major mistake.' The Madrid side was packed with quality and it would only take a moment of magic from Beckham or Ronaldo or Zidane to turn the tie on its head.

The match was a very tense affair as Real caused more problems for Arsenal than they had in the first leg. Lehmann was forced to make several vital stops as the Gunners tried to weather the storm. Collectively, the team defended excellently and Real just could not find an opening. When the full-time whistle went, Highbury rejoiced as the 0-0 draw put Arsenal through to the quarter-finals 1-0 on aggregate. Arsène savoured one of his best moments in football: 'To play two games against Real and not concede a goal shows remarkable spirit. Something is happening with this team. They are gelling together. They have shown character, and that is very good. I feel we have grown as a team during these last two months.' The Gunners were now the only English representatives left in the competition after Barcelona eliminated Chelsea and Benfica shocked holders Liverpool. Remarkably, United had crashed out in the group stage.

Finally, Wenger got his team to carry their European form into the Premiership and the Gunners stretched their unbeaten run to seven games over the next month. Victory at home over Liverpool came courtesy of two Henry goals and Charlton were comfortably beaten 3-0 with Pires, Emmanuel Adebayor – signed in the January transfer window – and Alexander Hleb on the scoresheet. Next up for Arsène and his players was a Champions League quarter-final first leg. The draw had been made and Arsenal would face Juventus and former captain Vieira.

Wenger spoke kindly about the return of Vieira, telling the press: 'We'll be 100 per cent up for it and will welcome Patrick back to his favourite ground.' Vieira was also looking forward to the contest: 'At times destiny serves up some surprises. Obviously it will be a special match, seeing that I'll be returning as part of the opposing team.' Arsenal vice-chairman David Dein promised Vieira a 'very warm reception.'

On 28 March, the big night arrived and it was not a match that Vieira will care to remember. Wenger's players came roaring out of the traps and never allowed Juventus to get into their stride. Fabregas overshadowed Vieira in the centre of midfield and it was the Frenchman who made the mistake that led to Arsenal's opening goal. Pires dispossessed Vieira in the Juventus half to start the build up that ended with Fabregas slotting past Gianluigi Buffon. The Italians were rattled and never recovered their composure. In the second half, Henry doubled the advantage after good work from Fabregas, who was emerging as one of the team's key players. The frustration became unbearable for Juventus who had two players sent off late in the game.

Wenger applauded the commitment of his players after the 2-0 first leg win and spoke confidently about reaching the semi-finals: 'I believe we will finish the job in the second leg in Italy but there is still a lot to come. I am very happy with the performance of the team and the togetherness. There was also fluency and speed and the technical quality was very high in patches.'

The high of beating Juventus was carried into the home Premiership clash with Aston Villa. Wenger sent out his side in hope of another ruthless display and he was not to be disappointed as the Gunners hammered Villa 5-0. Henry

Above: Arsène at AS Monaco in 1987 with recent signings Mark Hateley (*left*) and Glenn Hoddle (*right*).

Below: Wenger then moved into Japanese football, managing Nagoya Grampus Eight from 1994 to 1996.

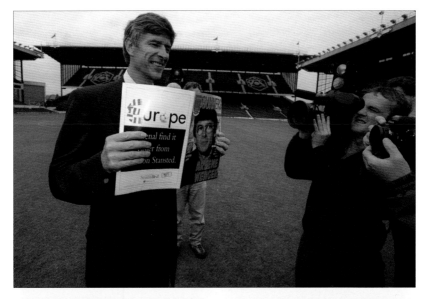

Above: A new era dawns for Arsenal FC. Wenger settles in at his new home of Highbury in September 1996.

Below left: Arsène introduces his new signing Nicolas Anelka to the fans in February 1997.

Below right: Le Prof in his early years at Arsenal.

Above: Wenger and legendary club captain Tony Adams hold the championship trophy after the FA Carling Premiership match against Everton. Arsenal won 4-0 to secure the title with two games in hand.

Below: Thierry Henry joins Arsenal in August 1999 from Juventus. The French international played under Arsène at AS Monaco and was the leading scorer for the French World Cup-winning squad at France '98.

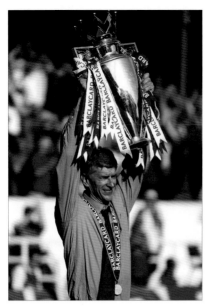

Above left: Arsène holds aloft the Premiership trophy, winning the title after the match between Arsenal and Leicester City at Highbury on 15 May 2004.

Above right: With the Manager of the Year Award during the BBC Sports Personality of the Year in December 2004.

Below: Wenger, Henry and Vieira share a joke before placing a specially-made time capsule containing keepsakes from Arsenal's old stadium underneath the new Emirates Stadium in 2004.

Above: Arsène accepts an honorary OBE from Foreign Secretary Jack Straw in the Queen's Birthday Honours List, along with Liverpool manager Gerard Houllier, in July 2003.

Below: Queen Elizabeth II meets Arsenal chairman Peter Hill-Wood and Arsène in February 2007 in London.

Above: Fabio Capello, Wenger, Franco Baldini and goalkeeping coach Ray Clemence in August 2008.

Below: Zinedine Zidane and Wenger in Geneva, Switzerland in January 2009.

Above: Final whistle for Wenger and Sir Alex after the first leg of the Champions League between their teams at Old Trafford in April 2009.

Below: Arsenal fans show their support for Wenger in late May 2009.

Above: Arsène celebrates victory during the FA Cup final between Arsenal and Hull City at Wembley Stadium on 17 May 2014.

Below: An end to the drought: Arsenal players pour champagne on their manager as they celebrate coming back from two goals down to win the match 3-2.   *All pictures © Getty Images*

grabbed two more goals as Arsène watched his team complete a fantastic week of football. They were now hitting top form but would need more emphatic wins if they were to overtake Tottenham in fourth place.

The crucial trip to Turin was next on the agenda for Wenger. As usual, he spent hours preparing his side tactically for the game and hoped that his players could emulate Manchester United's heroics in 1999 by sealing the tie at the Stadio Delle Alpi. Juventus were expected to throw everything at the Gunners from the first whistle but instead it was Arsenal who looked the brighter side. Arsène's defence coped comfortably with the Italians and the visitors were always menacing on the counter attack. The minutes ticked by with few alarms and Wenger's team celebrated another famous scalp. A semi-final tie – the club's first ever in the competition – with Villarreal was all that separated the Gunners from a place in the Champions League final.

The Frenchman mixed delight with caution in his post-match interviews: 'We must keep our feet on the ground,' he warned. 'Villarreal are a bit like us; no one expected them to be where they are, so it is two outsiders. We are very proud – two months ago no one expected that from our players.' With Barcelona and AC Milan fighting out the other semi-final, though, Wenger must have been thrilled to be facing Villarreal instead.

The Gunners' bubble finally burst at Old Trafford where Manchester United overpowered Wenger's side to win 2-0. The exertions of the team's European adventures seemed to catch up with Arsenal as they struggled to match the intensity of their fresher opponents. United were still chasing leaders Chelsea and this win increased the pressure on the Blues. For Arsène, though, there was the disappointment of losing to bitter rivals in what was Arsenal's ninth away defeat in the league. With Tottenham now five points ahead of the Gunners, clinching the fourth Champions League spot was looking a tricky proposition.

A draw away to Portsmouth and a home win over West Brom gave Wenger's side a reasonable build up to the semi-final first leg against Villarreal at Highbury – the last European match at the famous stadium. It would be vital to gain a lead to take to Spain and not conceding any away goals was also imperative. A packed house welcomed the players onto the pitch. The opening goal on the night came from an unlikely source as centre-back Kolo Toure struck for Arsenal just before half-time. The two sides were well matched and the visitors did not lose their shape after Toure's goal. Highbury remained full of tension as the action unfolded.

The match finished 1-0 and Arsène appeared content to travel to Villarreal with the slender advantage. He explained to the media: 'I think it is a good result but we will know after the second game. We wanted a second goal but sometimes we were too nervous. We faced a good team, very strong in the midfield, and we couldn't impose enough to create more chances. At home you never know what is enough in a semi-final and it is difficult to go forward.'

Looking ahead, Wenger called on his players to find top gear over the next week: 'We have got Spurs on Saturday and then the second leg of the Champions League semi-final – so the next six days will define our season – but we are confident we can do it.' A victory at home to Tottenham would put the Gunners back on track for fourth place. It would be a massive day – the last North London derby at Highbury.

But their North London rivals were in no mood to surrender their league position. Tottenham manager Martin Jol had done a superb job and his team arrived full of confidence, knowing that a victory would give them a lot of breathing space above Arsenal. It was sure to be a nervy afternoon all round.

The game ended 1-1 leaving the Gunners four points behind Tottenham with a game in hand. But the result was overshadowed by the controversy surrounding Tottenham's goal. It led to a showdown between Wenger and his counterpart Jol as Arsène revealed his frustration that there were Arsenal players down injured when Tottenham opened the scoring. Afterwards, Jol claimed not to have seen the incident but Wenger was not convinced. The Frenchman fumed to the media: 'Martin Jol said he didn't see it. Frankly, I don't believe it. It's not necessary that I lie about what I think – I don't believe that he didn't see it.'

Jol, for his part, was furious with Wenger's accusations: 'He called me a liar and irrespective of all the rights and wrongs of the situation, I don't think a manager should behave like that. I'm not a liar. I told him straight after I haven't seen it because I was watching Edgar Davids and you could see it on TV. I said to him [Wenger]: "I didn't even see it so don't blame me."' The player in question, Michael Carrick, was bemused by the whole thing when questioned by the media: 'I didn't realise they were injured or down at the time. If I had, I would have put the ball out. We're not cheats that's for sure.'

The drama of the occasion had been totally enthralling but

Wenger felt bitter that his side had failed to close the gap on their rivals. Now Arsenal needed to win all of their remaining matches and hope that Tottenham dropped points. It was a tall order considering the Gunners' European distractions.

Wenger turned his attention to the massive midweek clash with Villarreal. He was ninety minutes away from leading his side into a Champions League final. The buzz from the UEFA Cup final in 2000 had been tremendous but this would be even better. He yearned to win Europe's premier club competition. Arsène worked hard on plans to limit the influence of Juan Roman Riquelme, the Villarreal playmaker, and urged his players to make a positive start to the contest.

A nail-biting evening was in prospect as the two sides walked out onto pitch. Arsenal began in timid fashion and the home side dominated the first period. Wenger tried to push his players forward but waves of yellow Villarreal shirts continued to peg the Gunners back in their own half. The tension was lifted momentarily by a spectator who ran on and tried to put a Barcelona shirt around the shoulders of Henry – a reference to the on-off saga of the Frenchman's rumoured Arsenal exit.

Villarreal started the brighter again in the second half and the Gunners were living very dangerously, needing last gasp tackles and a string of Lehmann saves to preserve their advantage. The German keeper was having an inspired night. With Arsenal desperately trying to run down the clock, disaster struck. When Jose Mari fell under contact from left back Gael Clichy, referee Ivan Ivanov of Russia pointed to the penalty spot with two minutes remaining. Riquelme placed the penalty towards the bottom right hand corner but Lehmann produced a magnificent stop, guessing correctly and parrying the ball out. He was mobbed by grateful team-mates and the Gunners clung on in the final seconds to seal their place in Paris for the Champions League final.

The jubilant scenes amongst the Arsenal players were in stark contrast to the devastated Villarreal bodies that lay scattered around the pitch. Wenger gave a rare show of emotion as he clenched his fists in celebration. He had done it. The Gunners were in the final. The Frenchman praised Lehmann's heroics when he had composed himself for the media: 'I said to myself that if it is our year, Jens will save it. I knew he had strength of character, and I knew he would not be beaten easily.' Arsène's pride in his young charges was impossible to miss: 'We were lucky, but I'm very proud of the character in that young team and I'm very happy. We just didn't play, whether that was down to physical or psychological reasons I don't know, but we showed great character.' Having reached the final, everyone at the club was desperate to lift the trophy.

· Back in the Premiership, the Gunners had to come down from cloud nine to focus on catching Tottenham. A 3-0 victory away at Sunderland was a crucial result and cranked up the pressure on their North London rivals. Already relegated Sunderland had no answer to Arsenal's classy approach play and Henry was particularly elusive. The Frenchman created the first two goals and then scored the third from a free-kick. His display certainly impressed Wenger: 'We know that Thierry can do these things, he does it so often for us. He took his goal well and set up the other two. That's the thing about him, he can score and provide.' The rumours of Henry's possible Arsenal exit continued to spread, however, much to Arsène's disgust.

A 3-1 win at Manchester City increased the pressure and pushed the race for fourth to the last match of the season. Arsenal would be at home against Wigan while Tottenham travelled to face West Ham. If the Gunners could better Tottenham's result, they would snatch the last Champions League spot. It was a fitting climax to Arsenal's magical time at Highbury. Clinching fourth place would be a good way to say farewell to a stadium that had brought the club some very special days.

The Champions League final was an exciting occasion to look forward to but, right now, the Premiership was the sole focus. Wenger's players had to put the emotions to one side and they did not let their manager down as Henry bagged a hat-trick and Wigan were defeated 4-2. The striker bent to kiss the turf after his third goal. It was that kind of afternoon. Things got even better as news filtered through that Tottenham had lost 2-1 at Upton Park. Arsenal had finished fourth and were guaranteed of Champions League football for the following season. The only low point of the day was the suggestion that a number of the Tottenham players had suffered from food poisoning and this news item took some of the gloss off Arsène's happiness as conspiracy stories spread.

There were emotional scenes at the final whistle as the players said goodbye to Highbury – a stadium that would be sorely missed by fans and footballers alike. The memories from down the years would never be forgotten. The Emirates would be a hugely impressive structure but Arsenal would be hard pressed to match their success at Highbury in their new home. Wenger told the media: 'For the history of the club and for this building here, to finish on a high I am very proud. We would all have felt guilty to have walked out of here on a low after what has happened here for years. There was fantastic excitement, strength of character and quality as well.' Henry, meanwhile, added: 'We are fourth in the league and the table does not lie after thirty-eight games, so we deserve to be in this position. We've missed so many players this season and we did it the hard way. When I kissed the ground after my third goal, I was saying goodbye to this stadium.'

The Gunners had ten days before the Champions League final in which to relax and prepare. Wenger began to work on strategies for stopping the influential and extremely talented Barça trio of Ronaldinho, Lionel Messi and Samuel Eto'o. When the match arrived on 17 May, it promised to be a feast of football with both sides capable of scintillating attacks. Sol Campbell was picked in the centre of defence with Philippe Senderos injured, and the English centre-back would have a busy ninety minutes. Arsène was a very proud man as he led his side out in Paris at the Stade de France – his players had come a long way since the start of 2006. For Wenger, the trip to Paris meant returning to the very place where he had studied for his coaching diploma.

The match did not turn out to be the classic that some experts had predicted. When Lehmann was sent off after just seventeen minutes, the contest died as a spectacle. The Gunners were forced to play more cautiously and Barcelona did not go for the throat of their opponent. Instead, Wenger's side stunned everyone by taking the lead. Eight minutes before the half-time break, Emmanuel Eboue, signed in January, won a dubious free-kick and Campbell met Henry's delivery with a solid header that left Victor Valdes in the Barça goal with no chance. Incredibly, ten-man Arsenal were ahead!

The second half was a similar scrap with Barcelona stringing together neat passes while the Gunners harried and played warily. With fourteen minutes left, the complexion of the tie changed. Henrik Larsson, the Swedish striker, came off the Barça bench to take a role in attack and turned the match on its head. First, Eto'o equalised from a Larsson pass and then full-back Juliano Belletti delivered the 2-1 sucker punch. Suddenly, Arsenal trailed with ten minutes to go. Wenger threw Reyes into the action but it was too little, too late.

As the Barcelona players were receiving their medals and the trophy, Arsène could only reflect on what might have been. The Gunners had missed a couple of gilt-edged chances to extend their lead and this had proved very costly. Henry, a summer target for Barcelona, was one of those who wasted key opportunities.

Post-match, the disappointment in the Arsenal camp was clear for all to see. Wenger talked to the press and referred to a moment of poor officiating in the second half: 'The referee made a big mistake at a crucial moment – their first goal was offside. The way we lost is very difficult to take because we played fantastically, like we have the whole European season. But in the final, people only remember the team that has won.'

Henry, so often linked with a move to Barcelona, added a bitter outburst: 'I was kicked all over the place. I expected the referee to do his job. I don't think he did. In the first half Rafael Marquez and Carles Puyol went right through me and they didn't even get a yellow. Then I got the ball in front of the bench and Mark Van Bommel kicks me and I end up getting a yellow. I'm sorry, some of the refereeing today was horrendous.' The Frenchman also bemoaned the fact that Eto'o had been in an offside position when he pulled Barça level. It all sounded rather like sour grapes from Henry on a night where Arsenal had come so close to a phenomenal achievement. Maybe the striker would stay in North London after all.

After all the build up, the defeat left a sense of underachievement around the club. The Gunners had not picked up any silverware and had finished fourth in the Premiership – a seriously below par effort. The Champions League run had been enthralling but, ultimately, the team had ended the season empty-handed.

Wenger, though, concentrated on the positives. Some exciting youngsters such as Fabregas had emerged on the scene and progressed beyond belief during the campaign while the improvements in the Champions League were there for all to see. There were plenty of seasons ahead for many of Arsène's young charges. A slight silver lining for Gunners fans came in the form of the fact that, having failed to beat Barcelona, Wenger might wish to stay at Arsenal for longer so that he could sample the winning feeling in Europe.

The Gunners boss also remained hopeful that Henry would still be an Arsenal player when the 2006/07 season began. Questioned over whether the striker would be leaving, Wenger replied: 'I don't know. I don't think so. There's not long to wait now and I will try to talk to him because we have to prepare for next season. We have many young players in our team. We have a big future as a big team but we need Thierry Henry to achieve that. He has such an influence on our side and can help us become a major force in the world.' While Henry's future was unclear, Bergkamp's playing career came to an end as he hung up his boots at the end of the season. The Dutchman's contributions over the past ten years would never be forgotten. He would go down as one of the club's finest ever players.

With the Emirates Stadium awaiting the Gunners for the 2006/07 campaign, there was extra reason for anticipation over the summer. Wenger settled in for a summer of World Cup viewing but all the controversy in Italy regarding match-fixing brought back the sad memories of Tapie and Marseille.

* * *

Having reached the Champions League final, Wenger could reflect on some strong development within his squad during the previous season. Finishing fourth, however, was not good enough and Arsène made a better Premiership campaign a top priority. All Gunners supporters were relieved to see Arsène again resist the urge to move to Real Madrid during the summer.

In late June, an associate of Villar Mir, a candidate in the Real Madrid elections, had told a Madrid radio station: 'For some reason, the subject has not been leaked until now. Wenger is not going to admit it and it will be covered up. When Wenger told David Dein, the Highbury vice chairman reacted like a hyena and did not like it at all. Dein was furious but Wenger has a clause in his contract that allows him to leave if a sufficient offer comes in from Real and if Villar Mir is elected Wenger will be the next coach.' Wenger insisted that such rumours were nonsense and that there had been no agreement. The Frenchman suggested that the whole issue was merely 'election talk'. He just focused on the new season in England.

The club had also managed to hold on to Henry, who had seemed destined to join Barcelona. As the striker admitted, it was the chance to continue working with Arsène that had been critical when making his decision. Henry revealed that 'it crossed my mind to leave but I think with my heart and my heart told me to stay.' Wenger had also added several new players to an already impressive squad, including Tomas Rosicky, the Czech international, who arrived from Borussia Dortmund.

Two players who Arsène could not persuade to stay were Campbell and Pires – both great servants of the club. Campbell had gone through a difficult patch in his personal life and told the media that he needed 'a fresh challenge'. Wenger hailed the defender as being 'instrumental to our success over the past five years' and it was with sadness that Arsène watched Campbell leave the club and join Portsmouth. Pires, meanwhile, signed a two-year deal with Villarreal after the Gunners only offered him a one-year extension. Like with Campbell, Wenger heaped praise on the winger, saying: 'He is not only a great footballer but a good man – we are sad to see him go.'

Most intriguingly, this would be Arsenal's first season in their new home, the Emirates Stadium. After all the planning and the waiting, it was now time for a fresh start – hard though it was to leave Highbury behind. The new stadium boasted a capacity of 60,400 and provided state-of-the-art facilities for the players and coaching staff.

A move away from Highbury had long been in Wenger's plans.

Even back in 1997, the Frenchman made it clear that a bigger stadium was essential. As the *Mail on Sunday* reported, Arsène said: 'The real solution would be to move. There is no real choice for us because people don't want the club to extend the stadium. If you want to compete with the biggest clubs, which are getting gates of around 10,000 to 12,000 more, then we have no option. A bigger capacity brings in more money.' Wenger sympathised with the club's supporters who were being kept out by the limited ticket availability and he admitted: 'You cannot keep your fans happy by always refusing to let them buy tickets. You cannot have them asking for a ticket in September for a match in January.'

In 2004, Wenger had welcomed the on-going stadium plans, saying: 'The project meant taking on a risk and gamble but it shows that we move on, get better and compete with the best. We never give up and we never accept defeat.' Most managers would have taken a step back from this type of project but Arsène had thrown himself into it. His travels around the world – to places such as Milanello in Milan – had given him numerous insights and he had had plenty of input into the construction work at Ashburton Grove.

It had been a long journey but, seeing the Emirates on match day, it had been worth the wait – and the reported £357 million cost. Wenger had been right. The club had been crying out for a new venue and the attendance figures would bring in plenty more money. With the Gunners' global reputation as a top team, the 38,000 capacity of Highbury was simply not enough. Fans from all over the world were flocking to North London to see the likes of Henry and Fabregas. A whole host of activities were planned to celebrate the opening of the Emirates Stadium, including the creation of a time capsule full of Arsenal memorabilia with the motto 'The deeper the foundations, the stronger the fortress.'

The first task for Wenger and his players was qualifying for the Champions League group stage. Although their opponents, Dinamo Zagreb, might have been relatively weak by European standards, the financial cost of failure was too great for the team to become complacent. The Champions League represented the main stage for any footballer in Europe and nobody in the Arsenal dressing room wanted to consider a season without it.

The players did not disappoint. Dinamo Zagreb were beaten in both legs as Arsenal racked up a 5-1 aggregate score and secured their place in the group stage draw. The draw placed the Gunners alongside Hamburg, CSKA Moscow and Porto in Group G. All three opponents would be challenging but Wenger knew Arsenal were favourites to finish in top spot. The squad that Arsène had assembled looked capable of enjoying a long run in Europe again but this had been true of many other seasons when the Gunners had fallen short. The team had to learn from their past mistakes and follow the example of the previous year.

The Premiership campaign began disappointingly for the Gunners at home to Martin O'Neill's Aston Villa. A 1-1 draw was not the desired result with which to start the Emirates era and it would have been a defeat but for a late equaliser. Things got worse over the next few weeks as Arsenal suffered a 1-0 defeat away to Manchester City.

Wenger was at least pleased to end the Ashley Cole saga at

the start of September when the Gunners sold their left-back to Chelsea in return for defender William Gallas and £5 million. The long-running row between Arsenal and the Blues, involving 'tapping up' allegations, had made it only a matter of time before Cole moved on. On a more positive note, Gallas was a very good acquisition and his partnership with Toure was a mouth-watering prospect. Unfortunately, the Frenchman's impact would be hindered by several injury problems. Another deadline day switch saw Reyes head for Real Madrid with Brazilian Julio Baptista moving to the Emirates in a loan swap until the end of the season.

On 9 September, Arsenal only picked up a point at home to Middlesbrough, again having to come from behind to avoid embarrassment in front of their own supporters. It was seemingly taking time for the Gunners to settle into their new stadium and opposition sides were taking advantage. The other title contenders were certainly looking stronger. Chelsea, boasting new signings Andriy Shevchenko and Michael Ballack, and Manchester United, who had added Michael Carrick to their squad, were setting the pace.

The Gunners' draw with Middlesbrough was not the ideal preparation for their next league fixture – against Manchester United at Old Trafford. United had taken maximum points from their first four Premiership games and looked ready to challenge Chelsea all the way this year. Wenger prepared his team thoroughly as always and hoped that his young side would have enough poise to rise to the occasion. It was the best Arsenal display of the campaign so far as the team silenced the United fans and grabbed a 1-0 win through Adebayor's goal from a perfect Fabregas pass. Arsène was delighted and struggled to hide his joy on the touchline. It really lifted the squad and Wenger felt that this would be the result that kick-started a good run of form.

Arsenal followed this three points with their first league win at the Emirates Stadium as Premiership newcomers Sheffield United were crushed 3-0. The team was starting to produce the type of football that Wenger craved. Porto were beaten 2-0 in the Champions League on 26 October, giving Arsène an early gift ahead of his tenth anniversary at the club later that week. It had been a truly memorable decade, packed with entertaining football.

There was no shortage of tributes from other managers, including Rafa Benitez. The Liverpool boss told the press: 'He is a good manager who has created good teams playing good football and he has won trophies for ten years here in England, which is not easy. As one of the first foreign managers in the Premiership maybe it was difficult for him at first, but he has given the rest of us more possibilities.'

Three consecutive wins followed against Charlton, Watford and Reading as the Gunners' pace and movement proved too much for opposition defences. It was this style of football that earned Arsenal the respect of so many neutrals. As Henry once revealed, people would approach him in public and, though they were not Gunners fans, applaud the way that Wenger's team played.

November, however, was a bleak month for Arsenal as frailties were exposed. For some reason, this month often let the Gunners down. The team failed to break through the CSKA

Moscow defence at the Emirates on 1 November and then lost 1-o to a late goal against West Ham at Upton Park. This was a significant moment in Wenger's season but sadly not for the right reasons as he argued and almost came to blows with then Hammers boss Alan Pardew. Pardew's celebrations after Marlon Harewood's winner upset Arsène, who could not contain his frustration and seemed to push the West Ham manager. It had not been a good afternoon and Wenger made things worse by refusing to shake hands with Pardew at the final whistle.

It was a rare sighting of Arsène losing his temper under pressure and one that he instantly regretted. Some criticised Pardew for celebrating so vigorously in front of the Arsenal bench but it was frustration at his team's inept display that really triggered Wenger's reaction. He could not believe what he was seeing as Harewood buried the winner.

Arsène was not winning any friends amongst his fellow bosses. That same weekend, Ferguson celebrated his twentieth anniversary as Manchester United boss and Wenger had caused an angry reaction by refusing to contribute to MUTV's tribute to Ferguson. Asked during the summer to give a message for the programme, the Frenchman turned down the request. To neutrals, this made Arsène seem bitter and mean-spirited. After all, surely he could have spared a moment or two to say a few words. But he has always been his own man.

Wins over Everton in the League Cup and Liverpool in the Premiership lifted the spirits at the club but a home draw with Newcastle on 18 November left Wenger once more impatient at his team's inability to finish off opponents. Perhaps the Emirates was a less intimidating venue than Highbury. The

Frenchman had worse to come as the Gunners fell to back-to-back league defeats at bogey team Bolton and London neighbours Fulham. Defensive problems were exposed and elements of the performance were distinctly below-par. Against Fulham, Arsène's side went 2-0 down after just thirteen minutes as they failed to switch on in the early stages.

Wenger called for improvement and challenged his players to respond to the criticism that was being directed at the team. A 3-0 victory over Tottenham on 2 December was the perfect reply but post-match Arsène had to deal with the delicate situation surrounding Henry, who had allegedly stormed out of the training ground after he was told he was not fit enough to feature in the derby. Wenger refused to speak about his striker's behaviour or Henry's criticism of the Gunners squad in an interview: 'I can't comment about things he is supposed to have said that I have not read. Ask him.'

A gritty 0-0 draw away to Porto followed on 6 December as the Gunners displayed plenty of determination and gave morale a much-needed lift ahead of a crunch match with Chelsea in the Premiership. It was a chance for Arsenal to claw back some ground in the title race – though in truth they were already too far off the pace. Arsène's relationship with Blues boss Mourinho was far from perfect and this added a subplot to the afternoon's game.

The manner in which the Gunners fought at Stamford Bridge was further evidence that they were back on track. Mixing sweeping football with tireless energy, Wenger's players made Chelsea work hard for every pass and soon silenced the home crowd. Arsenal's graft was rewarded when they took the lead through a goal from Flamini and suddenly a huge victory was within sight. But the Chelsea players were very proud of their unbeaten league record at home and threw bodies forward in search of an equaliser. That goal came with six minutes to go as Ghanaian midfielder Michael Essien curled a stunning long range strike into the top corner with the outside of his right boot. In fairness, it was the only way that a stubborn Arsenal defence was going to be breached that afternoon. Wenger felt a mixture of disappointment and pride at the final whistle – the win would have been most welcome but his side had performed admirably. They had arrived with a game plan and had executed it excellently.

With three wins in their next four games, new optimism swept around the Emirates Stadium. An away win at Wigan on 13 December brought a much-needed clean sheet and, although the Gunners drew 2-2 with Portsmouth at home, the players responded perfectly by hammering Blackburn 6-2 a week later. It was an emphatic display and it showed just how irresistible Arsenal could be on their day. Nobody could wipe the smile from Wenger's face, although at 3-2 things had looked a little worrying. Another win – 2-1 at Watford on Boxing Day – made it a happy festive period for Arsène and his team. They would have to step up their performances in the New Year, though, if they hoped to end the season with silverware.

Wenger came crashing back to earth on 30 December when his team was outfought in a scrappy 1-0 defeat at Bramall Lane against Sheffield United. It was the type of performance that the Frenchman felt he had eradicated. Arsène could only watch as his players were physically overpowered by Neil Warnock's side in a horrifying reminder that the Gunners still had much work to do. Instead of fighting back against the Blades, they had gone into their shells and succumbed to the intensity of the pressure.

The Arsenal boss would tolerate no more of this complacency. Things had to change and Wenger let his players know in no uncertain terms. His words paid immediate dividends as the Gunners returned to top form. Charlton were the first team to face the backlash on 2 January as Arsenal turned on the style to earn a 4-0 victory. It was the type of display that Arsène's team were famous for as the one-touch passing and lightning movement left Charlton defenders bewildered.

The goals kept coming as the team coasted to two important cup wins over Liverpool as Wenger demonstrated that he had the tactics to put Rafa Benitez's side to the sword. First, in the FA Cup third round, Arsenal outclassed their opponents in a 3-1 victory. Rosicky was the hero with two well-taken goals. In midweek, in the League Cup quarter-final, again at Anfield, the Gunners proved even more prolific as they dominated a 6-3 thriller. On loan forward Julio Baptista smashed a hat-trick and Arsène's side had silenced the Liverpool fans by dumping their team out of two competitions in three days.

It may have dented Benitez's hopes but it was a very positive week for Wenger. His team was playing beautifully and the goals were flowing. A league fixture with Blackburn at Ewood Park was the next challenge for the Gunners and, when Gilberto was controversially sent off in the first half, it became an even sterner test. But the spirit and fight in the team – that had been missing at times earlier in the campaign – came to the fore as Arsenal's class brought a 2-0 win. Toure's first half header gave the ten men a lead to protect and then Henry's stunning second sealed the points. It was hard to believe that this was the same club that had been rolled over at Bramall Lane in late December. Blackburn have often caused problems for Arsenal in the past but the Gunners were simply too good on this occasion.

It was around this time that the *Daily Express* reported one of Wenger's coaching secrets. According to the newspaper: 'The astute manager has worked out that seven minutes is the maximum time footballers can take on board advice and information from their coach.' It was approaches such as this that made Arsène unique as a manager.

Manchester United visited the Emirates Stadium on 21 January looking to extend their lead at the Premiership summit. Earlier in the day Liverpool had beaten Chelsea at Anfield and so Ferguson's side were hoping to take advantage. Wenger, meanwhile, got his players focused on defending their unbeaten home record and putting a dent in their opponents' title challenge.

After a goalless first period, United took the lead in the second half with a Rooney header but Arsenal heads did not drop. In the final twenty minutes they dominated possession and battered United into submission. Van Persie arrived on cue at the far post to equalise and bring the home fans to their feet. A point would have been a satisfactory result but the Gunners were not finished. Loose play from United gave Arsenal possession on the right flank and the cross from Eboue was perfect for Henry, who headed powerfully past Edwin van der Sar. The stadium erupted; Henry and Adebayor danced; Wenger smiled broadly. It was an incredible day for the Arsenal boss.

Arsène was gracious in victory, telling the media: 'This will be a big disappointment for Manchester United – but do not expect them to crumble because of it. But it is good for the Premiership because everybody still has a chance. We began nervously and United started with maturity but I knew after the break we would have a go.' Wenger was thrilled with the spirit of his 'lions' and this victory over the league leaders really lifted the morale of the squad.

Ferguson, unhappy to have thrown away the points, hit back angrily when days later it was suggested that Wenger had detected United's weakness in the final twenty minutes of matches. Arsène was rumoured to have told his players to exploit the visitors' weary legs late on. Sir Alex, though, was livid: 'I'm not sure what his point was. Maybe he was trying to make himself look great again – "I am the great Arsène Wenger."' It restarted the pair's feud, which had simmered down whilst Chelsea had been dominating the Premiership. All the attempts to smooth things over had apparently been in vain.

Almost as if the victory over United had overwhelmed the players, Arsenal stuttered in their next few games but showed plenty of character. A very youthful line-up fought back from 2-0 down to draw at Tottenham in the League Cup semi-final first leg. It was a performance that reminded Wenger once more that the future at the club was extremely bright. A 3-1 win in extra time in the return leg sent Arsène's youngsters into the Carling Cup final to face Chelsea at the Millennium Stadium.

Two draws in the league frustrated Wenger but a home victory against Wigan and another extra-time triumph – this time in the FA Cup against Bolton – gave Arsenal a boost going into their Champions League second round first leg against Dutch side PSV Eindhoven. It was a decent draw for the Gunners compared to other British clubs as Liverpool were forced to take on Barcelona and Celtic were paired with AC Milan.

The first leg, however, was a nightmare. PSV played well but Arsenal were out of sorts. The players had an off night and in the end the Gunners had to settle for a 1-0 defeat. Wenger struggled to understand why the display had been so disjointed but he knew that his side had enough quality to progress in front of a packed crowd at the Emirates Stadium in the return leg. 'We could have been punished more,' Arsène admitted.

The two weeks between the Champions League ties were not much better for Arsène and his squad. The youngsters fought hard in the League Cup final but Chelsea's experience edged a close match. Wenger was very proud of how far his players had progressed but was unhappy with the way that the match ended as Adebayor and Toure were sent off in a bitter final few minutes which also saw the dismissal of Chelsea's John Obi Mikel.

The Arsenal boss told the media after the game: 'I'm very proud of the performance of my team.' The Frenchman also referred to the fracas: 'Suddenly we lost it and they lost it as well and it became a brawl. I'm not sure the referee picked the right ones out but he made a decision.' Arsène was more scathing in his verdict on linesman Darren Cann, who advised referee Howard Webb to send off Adebayor. The Gunners boss labelled Cann 'a liar' and found himself in hot water with the FA.

While it was impressive that the club's young players had reached the final, Wenger had still desperately wanted to win the trophy. To make a bad week worse, Arsenal were then knocked out of the FA Cup by Blackburn in a fifth round replay.

PSV arrived in London desperate to cling on to their slender first leg advantage. Ronald Koeman, the manager of the Dutch side, hoped to subdue the Gunners as effectively as in the 1-0 win in Eindhoven. PSV fought hard but Arsenal eventually got the breakthrough to pull level on aggregate. Extra time was looming when the visitors won a rare corner. The delivery found Brazilian centre-back Alex (ironically, 'owned' by Chelsea) who headed home. The stadium went silent as Gunners fans worldwide sat in disbelief. Needing two goals now to reach the quarter-finals, it was all over for Arsenal. There would be no repeat of the 2005/06 Champions League final. Wenger shook hands with Koeman at full-time, knowing that his team really should have beaten PSV. To further Arsène's embarrassment, Liverpool showed in the next round that the Dutch team were very beatable on the way to an easy aggregate win.

Having lost in the League Cup Final, missed out in the Champions League and FA Cup and fallen behind in the Premiership, everything had suddenly turned sour for Wenger and Arsenal. Their league form was all that was left to focus on and so the Frenchman concentrated on plotting a strong finish to the season. That began with a 1-0 win at Villa Park. In fairness, the Gunners should have scored more but settled for the narrow victory against a toothless Villa side.

More woes on their travels left Wenger despairing again. A trip to Goodison Park on 18 March saw Everton beat a lacklustre Arsenal side 1-0 and two weeks later the Gunners returned to Merseyside and were thrashed 4-1 by Liverpool at Anfield.

Arsène had Gallas and Toure available again as a partnership in central defence but neither could cope with Peter Crouch, who grabbed a clinical hat-trick. Arsène was far from impressed with his team's defending.

Admittedly, there were no trophies at stake by now for the Gunners but Wenger expected his players to show more pride for the club. The rot continued with a first league defeat at the Emirates Stadium against West Ham. The Hammers were desperately fighting for their Premiership lives at the bottom of the table and their hunger for points was enough to secure a famous victory. Robert Green in the West Ham goal had a fantastic game and thwarted every Arsenal attack. A o-o draw at Newcastle ended the run of three consecutive defeats.

With Liverpool, Manchester United and Chelsea competing in the Champions League semi-finals and the latter two engaged in a thrilling title race, England was awash with excitement about the closing weeks of the season. But things were very subdued at the Emirates as Arsenal stumbled towards the end of the campaign. Back-to-back home wins over Bolton and Manchester City improved Wenger's mood but he wondered why his side had been so inconsistent over the course of the season. Clearly, when the players were on form, they could collect victories with ease.

Mid-April saw the surprise departure of David Dein from his role as vice-chairman. A statement from chairman Peter Hill-Wood explained: 'We sincerely regret that irreconcilable differences between Mr Dein and the rest of the board have necessitated a parting of the ways.' The news came as a blow to Arsène who was saddened by his friend's exit.

On 21 April, Arsenal headed to White Hart Lane and should have taken three points from the fourth and final North London derby of the campaign. Leading 2-1, the Gunners seemed to be in control of the game but a late Jermaine Jenas strike gave Tottenham a dramatic equaliser. Yet more points had slipped from Arsenal's grasp and there would be no bragging rights on this occasion for the supporters. Wenger's side then beat Fulham 3-1 at home to give the team their last win of the season.

When Chelsea came to the Emirates on 6 May, the Blues knew that only a victory would be enough to keep the title race alive after United had won the Manchester derby 1-0 at lunch-time the day before. It would be a tough task considering that Arsenal always raised their game against the top teams. Just before half-time, the Gunners were presented with a gift after sloppy defending by Khalid Boulahrouz. The Chelsea defender was outmuscled by Julio Baptista and then fouled the Brazilian in the penalty area. The referee awarded the spot-kick and showed Boulahrouz a red card. Gilberto scored the penalty and suddenly the Blues were trailing with ten men. A huge second half performance, led by Essien, brought Chelsea level late on but a winner proved elusive and United were champions again after a three-year wait. Mourinho was no doubt irritated that it was Arsène's side that put the final dent in the Blues' title challenge.

Wenger was already casting his mind towards the next campaign whilst carefully examining the quality of his current squad. A 0-0 draw away to Portsmouth in their last league match was a feeble way to finish but somehow it summed up the way that things had gone for Arsenal during the season.

Without the often injured Henry, the Gunners had struggled for goals at times – especially on their travels – and the team's supporters expected much more consistency next season.

So, United had lifted the Premiership trophy, Chelsea had achieved an FA Cup and League Cup double and Liverpool were beaten finalists in the Champions League. All this success for their rivals made the disappointments of 2006/07 even harder to bear for all those associated with Arsenal. Wenger tried to put the events of the campaign behind him because there was plenty of organising ahead during the summer if the Gunners hoped to return to the glory days.

There were question marks over the future of Henry and Fabregas and many felt that the lure of La Liga would see the pair heading to Spain. Wenger himself was the subject of much speculation because he had not yet signed a new contract and his current deal ran out at the end of the 2007/08 season. These were worrying times at Arsenal. On the positive side, some very talented youngsters had impressed Arsène and the run to the League Cup final suggested a lot of promise in the years ahead. When Wenger had a fully fit squad to choose from, he still felt that the Gunners were as good as anyone in the Premiership. Consistency would be the key factor for Arsenal in turning promise into prizes.

LIFE AFTER THIERRY

When Wenger and Arsenal agreed to sell Henry to Barcelona for £16.2 million during the summer of 2007, there was disbelief among Gunners fans. Immediately concern emerged over who could possibly fill the void that Henry would leave in attack. Henry, who had cemented his place in the club's history through his inspired years in London, boasted no end of admirers amongst the Arsenal supporters. His departure left a dark cloud over the Emirates Stadium and everyone watched intently to see Wenger's next move. Seeking another Thierry Henry would certainly be no easy task but, as with the departure of Vieira, the Arsenal manager had shown that he was not afraid to make changes.

Henry's exit had become inevitable. His mind did not seem as focused and in some matches he was fairly anonymous. The Frenchman had almost signed for Barcelona the previous summer, only to change his mind and stay at Arsenal. But now he had really gone and Arsène began to prepare for life after Henry. Wenger knew that Henry had been the team's star but he was also well aware that the squad contained many other talented players who were desperate to step up and take on more responsibilities. Watching the group in training, Wenger saw that the future remained bright, even without the club's record goalscorer.

The Arsenal boss explained: 'We have the potential to cope without Thierry. We will focus more on team play and sharing the responsibility. Thierry Henry had eight great years at the club and, at thirty, maybe he didn't have the patience to let the young team develop. You can understand that.' Henry would never be forgotten at Arsenal but it was time for a new era to begin in North London.

The feeling that the squad was good enough was not shared by all though. Some of the players shared their concerns with the media. Gallas was among them and said: 'What is sure is that several players are questioning the club's future. Around us, all the teams are recruiting but what is planned to compensate for the departure of Henry? It is necessary to recruit players of reputation because young players have many qualities but the season is very long.'

It was a tricky period at the Emirates. Wenger moved to assure his players that his plans were in place and the captaincy was passed on to Gallas. The French international defender was entrusted with leading a young team and bettering the fourth place finishes of the past two seasons. Gallas was full of confidence about the challenges ahead, telling the press: 'I know I am being called on to be one of the leaders of the team after the exit of Henry and I am prepared for that. I am one of the more experienced players in the squad and I am here to help the younger players in all aspects – and that is what I have told Arsène Wenger face to face. I am a born winner and always ask a lot of myself. My only desire is to succeed and I want Arsenal to be fighting for titles.'

In Fabregas, Wenger had unearthed a gem of a midfielder and it was he who would benefit most from stepping out of Henry's vast shadow. The diminutive Spaniard had shown Arsène that he could handle the pressure of dictating play from midfield and many felt that 2007/08 would see Fabregas move up to the next level in his development.

Arsène resisted the temptation to spend large sums on big name stars and instead made some of his typically shrewd investments. Eduardo Da Silva, the Croatian striker, and Bacary Sagna, the French full-back, were two of his signings. Neither were household names in England but few doubted that Wenger had unearthed yet more talented players. He now had strong options in defence with Toure and Gallas in the centre and Eboue, Clichy and Sagna fighting for the full-back positions. Da Silva gave Arsenal similarly good options in attack.

Elsewhere, the Gunners' title rivals had strengthened their squads. United had signed midfielders Owen Hargreaves, Anderson and Nani and had taken forward Carlos Tevez on a two-year loan. Liverpool had brought in several new faces, including prolific striker Fernando Torres, while Chelsea had improved their bench with the additions of Steve Sidwell and Claudio Pizarro amongst others. Would Arsenal be able to compete?

Wenger was in the strange position of being under pressure

as the 2007/08 campaign kicked off. He had not made a big name signing and some of his own squad had even questioned the lack of transfer activity. Arsène, though, continued with his job and stuck to his plans. He had not bought a player of Henry's stature but, in Adebayor and van Persie, Wenger had forwards who were improving all the time and now seemed ready to spearhead the attack.

There would be a change of philosophy now that Henry had left the club. As Wenger told *FourFourTwo* magazine: 'When you have a player of his importance with such a young team the play was always going to go through him. When he wanted the ball, he got the ball. Now he's not there anymore, everybody has to take the initiative and express themselves a little bit more.'

Some felt the Gunners were in the midst of a transitional period but Arsène had higher hopes. He told the *Daily Star* that his players 'can achieve what they want and desire. That means win the Premier League and win all kinds of trophies they want to win. The hunger in the team is strong, my hunger is stronger than ever and the talent and the potential of the team is very high.'

Arsenal made a winning start much to Wenger's delight. Fulham proved tricky opponents, taking a very early lead, and the Gunners left it late to claim a 2-1 win. Van Persie vindicated Arsène's youth policy by grabbing the equaliser before Hleb struck the winner. The youngsters had shown great spirit and had made the Arsenal manager very proud. Just like the previous season, the Gunners were leaving it late to salvage results at home but Wenger would settle for that so long as the victories kept coming. Arsène told the media: 'We had a horrible start and were playing against a good Fulham side and a good goalkeeper. Apart from that, we were resilient, didn't give up for ninety minutes, were physically and mentally strong.' Fulham boss Lawrie Sanchez, meanwhile, reacted angrily to what he felt were theatrics from the Arsenal side. A draw away to Blackburn – in which Lehmann gifted a goal to the home side – was followed by a string of impressive wins that forced the sceptics to re-think their negativity surrounding the Gunners' prospects.

Everyone associated with the club received further good news on 7 September when Arsène finally signed a new contract with the Gunners, ending months of speculation. Wenger explained: 'My heart is tied to this football club so signing a new deal was always my intention. Arsenal is the club of my life. I have been entrusted with complete freedom to implement and execute my plans on what will make the team successful. That means I have a responsibility to the fans to deliver silverware and also a responsibility to the players to help turn our potential into prizes.'

Chairman Hill-Wood echoed the feelings of all Gunners fans when he called the new contract 'excellent news'. Hill-Wood also told the media: 'With Arsène continuing to manage the team, I am sure we can look forward to more exciting football and success on the pitch. Arsène has a special ability to develop talented players and turn them into world class stars, a quality that is admired here at the club and indeed around the world.'

The new deal was worth £4 million-a-year, about £75,000 a week, putting his salary above all other Premier League managers except Chelsea's Mourinho. Most significantly, the contract would keep Wenger at Arsenal until 2011 and would give him plenty of time to continue his fine work with his young squad. The fear had been that if Arsène left, there might well be a mass exodus of the club's top players. Now, though, the future looked secure.

Former Arsenal left-back Winterburn, was adamant that this news signalled a bright future for his old club. Winterburn told *The Mirror*: 'It is a massive decision for the club and the fans. There was a lot of uncertainty and, with Arsène signing, it will take huge pressure off the club. They had to get Arsène to re-sign. I think he is a terrific manager.' He also pointed to the way that Wenger had spent transfer funds very wisely and had almost balanced the books during his time at the club.

The club was certainly in a strong position financially. But then Arsène had always taken great care over that side of his job. He had even predicted the rise in players' wages and planned out future contracts accordingly. At Arsenal, he was far more than just a manager.

Out on the pitch, Fabregas was proving a revelation in midfield and Wenger was thrilled to see the Spaniard getting on the scoresheet more often. An excellent 3-1 triumph in the North London derby against Tottenham on 15 September was the highlight of Arsenal's early season form. Adebayor bagged a brace as the Gunners took maximum points once again.

Martin Jol, the Tottenham manager, grudgingly praised Arsenal's composure in front of goal: 'The difference between them and us was their clinical finishing. We could have scored a second goal after we went 1-0 up, at 1-1 and when we were 2-1 down.' Wenger, meanwhile, admired his team's gritty display, telling the media: 'It shows our spirit and belief and I was very happy with our game and our mental strength and togetherness. We have showed them all again.' They certainly had.

Arsène was enjoying proving the doubters wrong as his young charges maintained their unbeaten record in all competitions whilst playing the type of free-flowing, attacking football that everyone had come to expect from the Gunners. It would be disrespectful to say that Henry had been forgotten, but certainly the Arsenal fans were enjoying life after Thierry a lot more than they had anticipated. The group stage draw for the Champions League also pleased the Gunners. Placed alongside Sevilla, Steaua Bucharest and Slavia Prague, Wenger felt very confident that his players would cruise through to the second round if they continued their fine form.

On 20 September, the news broke that Chelsea and manager Mourinho had parted company. Tensions had certainly been strained between Mourinho and owner Roman Abramovich but few had anticipated this outcome so early in the season. Despite his occasional arrogance in front of the cameras, the Portuguese would be missed by neutrals, the media and, most of all, those associated with Chelsea. Rick Wilkinson, a Chelsea season ticket holder, was quoted as saying, 'Yeah, I'm in mourning'.

The Chelsea players were equally dismayed, especially Frank Lampard, Didier Drogba and Ricardo Carvalho. Carvalho told the press: 'For me there is no doubt, Jose Mourinho is the best coach in the world and I cannot believe that we have lost him. He loved Chelsea.' Drogba was reluctant to commit himself to the club such was his disappointment over the way in which Mourinho had been treated. Abramovich had plenty to do if he was going to win over a number of concerned figures. His decision to appoint Avram Grant, an unknown Israeli coach, as Mourinho's successor was met with ridicule but Wenger certainly was not writing Chelsea out of the title race. He knew that they had too much quality not to bounce back.

His own relationship with Mourinho had been far from warm. The pair had clashed on several occasions as the Gunners attempted to keep pace with the rampant Blues. Wenger lashed out verbally a number of times as the Portguese succeeded in ruffling Arsène's feathers. However, the Arsenal boss claimed not to be glad to see the back of Mourinho. In a question and answer session with *FourFourTwo* magazine, the Frenchman admitted: 'It was a complete surprise as it came after the first difficult spell Chelsea have had. I still don't really know why he left but it wasn't a relief. I thought it would have been much more interesting this season if he had stayed.' It was certainly a shame for English football that the character and charisma of Mourinho had been lost.

The European campaign began at home to Sevilla, who were as fêted in Spain for attacking football as the Gunners were in England. Daniel Alves, the Brazilian right back, had attracted keen interest from Chelsea over the summer, and former Tottenham striker Freddie Kanoute had been a revelation since moving to Seville. But the Spanish side were no match for Wenger's team and the Emirates crowd were treated to a night to remember. A 3-0 scoreline told the story of an excellent, free-flowing performance. The elimination at the hands of PSV last season had been a painful shock and the players seemed to be responding with even greater desire.

With Chelsea struggling in the wake of the departure of Mourinho and Liverpool and Manchester United still to find consistent form, Arsenal took the chance to open a good lead at the top of the Premier League. Chelsea had already lost twice and Liverpool had recorded three draws. By the end of September, Wenger had the luxury of knowing that his side could open up a five point lead at the top if the Gunners could win their game in hand. Though Arsenal had not yet faced any of their closest title competitors, Wenger could not have envisioned a better start to the campaign.

Around this time, there was also much media speculation over Russian billionaire Alisher Usmanov's interest in buying the club. But the Frenchman shrugged it off in his usual nonchalant fashion. He had no real interest in a new owner or the transfer funds that this might bring. With his squad performing so well, Wenger made it known that a spending spree would not be on the agenda. It definitely gave the Arsenal players a lift to hear their manager speak so highly of their ability.

The road ahead was bound to be rocky but Arsenal looked ready to tackle any challenge in their path. Though many might have imagined that the Champions League would be Wenger's biggest aim – having never won the competition – the Arsenal boss made it very clear as to where his priorities lay. Dismissing the Champions League, Arsène claimed: 'It is overrated. It is a cup, it is not a championship. If it was a European championship over thirty-eight games then it would be different and you can say the team who wins that is really the best in Europe. I think it is harder to win the Premier League.'

But of course Wenger was looking to win both competitions with his young charges. Having gone so close in 2006, the coaching staff and the players all had their sights set on reaching the Champions League final again. Arsène looked at the AC Milan team that won the 2007 competition and felt that the Gunners would have been their equal. Sadly, the nature of knockout competitions means that some clubs have easier runs to the final than others.

After an excellent 1-0 victory away to West Ham and a gutsy win by the same scoreline in Romania against Steaua Bucharest, Arsenal extended their unbeaten run with a 3-2 win over a spirited Sunderland side. The Gunners raced into a 2-0 lead but when the Black Cats pulled level at 2-2, Wenger's players had to summon all their determination and skill to grab the winner. Arsène was impressed to see that heads did not drop when Sunderland equalised. Instead, the team responded with bags of attacking intent. The Frenchman was in such a good mood post match that he even grinned broadly when asked by a reporter whether Roy Keane, the Sunderland manager and ex-Manchester United captain, would be welcome for a post-match chat! Wenger replied that Keane would always be welcome!

With new Bolton manager Sammy Lee struggling to replicate the results of Sam Allardyce, the last thing he needed was to meet Arsenal on their current run of form. The Trotters defended in numbers but the Gunners eventually made the breakthrough as Toure fired a free-kick into the bottom corner from distance.

Rosicky added a second to seal the points yet the scoreline could have been worse for Bolton as Adebayor, amongst others, missed some guilt-edged chances.

Wenger was well aware that Manchester United were hitting top form again and that his side could not afford to get complacent. While the Gunners found life tough against Bolton, United clinically took Aston Villa apart at Villa Park as the Rooney-Tevez partnership in attack continued to blossom. With Ronaldo also back to his best, the Red Devils had recovered from their slow start and clearly meant business. Goalscoring had proved a problem earlier in the season but, with all their attackers now fit, United were finding the net at will.

Slavia Prague were treated to Arsenal at their best in the Champions League. The crowd of 59,621 at the Emirates Stadium saw the Gunners record a 7-0 victory and move to nine points out of nine. Fabregas struck twice, as did England starlet Theo Walcott who received a rare start. Wenger spoke proudly to the media after the game: 'We wanted three points and to play well but you can't predict that. Everything went for us. We scored the first goal with the first chance. I wanted Theo to start in a big game and he played well. He is calm and clinical in front of goal.'

It is one-sided matches like this that led Wenger to speak out against UEFA President Michel Platini's plans to include more European minnows in the competition. Weeks later, Arsène announced: 'You have to be careful not to change the Champions League too much by bringing in even more weaker teams, because you could find yourself with games five and six with no meaning. That would be very dangerous for the competition.' With Platini contemplating the idea of including domestic cup winners and more sides from less established European leagues, Arsène felt the need to voice his opinion. The Champions League has always been a very special competition for the Frenchman and he was desperate to ensure that it was not devalued.

Back in domestic action, Wenger took his players to Anfield for their biggest examination of the campaign. Liverpool had finished above the Gunners for the past two seasons and the neutrals wanted to see how Arsenal fared against the other top teams. In a tight Premier League title race, points dropped to such sides could prove very costly. But in 2006/07, Wenger's players had excelled against the big three – beating United twice, earning two draws with Chelsea and winning at home to Liverpool. The Arsenal team certainly did not hide on the big occasions and they would have to continue this trend because this away fixture on Merseyside would be followed by a titanic clash with closest challengers Manchester United at home.

Wenger refused to get carried away with the team's start, despite the inevitable comparisons with the Invincibles of 2003/04. However, if the Gunners could win at Anfield, it would be a massive statement of intent to send out to the rest of the league. Liverpool had made an erratic start to the season – one week superb, the next below-par – but the likes of Steven Gerrard and Fernando Torres thrived on pressure situations and would be desperate to repeat the 4-1 defeat that Arsenal suffered on Merseyside last season. Wenger preferred to recall the 6-3 victory that his team enjoyed in the League Cup when his players emphatically silenced the Liverpool fans.

The Arsenal side entered a hostile atmosphere at Anfield as they sought to preserve their unbeaten league record. As expected, Rafa Benitez had once more shuffled his squad for the game, choosing Torres as a lone striker. With van Persie out injured, the Gunners also lined up with a 4-5-1 formation, hoping to control the midfield areas with their fine range of passing. An early Gerrard free-kick put Liverpool ahead yet Arsenal were not to be denied. In previous years, Wenger's side might have folded under such pressure yet this group of players never lost focus. In truth, the Gunners dominated the contest throughout but had to wait until ten minutes from time before Fabregas popped up with an equaliser from Hleb's pass. It was a point that gave the side plenty of confidence ahead of the visit of Manchester United on 3 November.

Wenger admitted as much in his post-match press conference. He also revealed for the first time that he felt his players could challenge for the title: 'We have come out of our first big test this season stronger. We played without the handbrake on. We have the talent to fight up there for the championship. Overall we handled the game very well. After this performance we will be facing United much stronger.'

The Gunners' resilience was called into action again against United at the Emirates. Arsenal trailed twice against the champions but bounced back to claim a point in a gripping 2-2 draw. When Cristiano Ronaldo put United 2-1 up with less than ten minutes remaining, Arsène's side were staring their first league defeat in the face. But captain Gallas was the unlikely goalscoring hero with the second equaliser in stoppage time. The Emirates crowd was on its feet and the Arsenal players made no attempt to conceal their delight at denying United the three points.

It had been an enthralling afternoon, full of intriguing battles. Toure and Gallas had defended expertly against Rooney and Tevez while Fabregas and United's Brazilian midfielder Anderson had matched each other stride for stride. Clearly, both teams were equipped for a title challenge, although Matt Lawton of *The Daily Mail* suggested that the psychological points had narrowly gone to United.

Interestingly, Ferguson's side had been the first to slow Arsenal's flowing style. The neat, incisive passing was almost non-existent in the first half as Hargreaves and Anderson harried in midfield. The usual injection of pace was missing from the Gunners' attacks and United worked hard to frustrate the likes of Fabregas, Hleb and Adebayor. For once, Arsène's side found it tough to get into their rhythm.

Wenger reflected positively on the game and the manner in which his players responded to testing situations: 'Our character was tested twice. Just before half-time and with eight minutes to go. Overall, though, I believe it was a fair result. I am pleased that in two big games we had to run after the score and we did that both times. We are still in charge of the title race because we are top with a game in hand.' Two points out of six against their fellow title rivals was not bad, especially with van Persie still sidelined.

Yet Ferguson was furious that his side had surrendered their advantage and criticised the performance of referee Howard Webb. Sir Alex told the media: 'I think Howard Webb has a great chance to be a top referee but today was a big game and he favoured Arsenal. Their second goal came from him not giving a free-kick for a foul on Louis Saha. It should've been a foul for us.' The United boss also had complaints to make about the Arsenal supporters: 'On our bench, we were getting terrible abuse from people two or three feet away from us. There is a lack of security. It is absolutely disgraceful the abuse you and your staff take.' It became an issue for the FA to investigate.

Another strong display against Reading put Arsenal back at the top of the Premier League table. United's win over Blackburn the previous day had moved the champions above the Gunners but Arsène's side returned to the summit by beating Reading 3-1. Arsenal's second goal, scored by Adebayor, was vintage Wenger in the way that the team passed the ball in the build up and then cut through their opponents. Arsène felt his side had proved a point, telling reporters after the game: 'The players have shown they can cope with the pressure. This was the big test – would we have the nerves to deal with being the last team to play (over the weekend) with people expecting us to drop points? It was good that we just played the game like we are used to. We could have scored more goals.'

Adebayor's goal in the win over Reading gave the Togo striker a much needed boost. He had not scored for several matches prior to his strike against the Royals and he was well aware that he would be judged on his goalscoring statistics by most pundits – even though Wenger examined much more than merely a goal tally when assessing a player's contribution.

With van Persie due back from injury soon, Arsène would have all the attacking options at his disposal again and he would be able to return to the Adebayor-van Persie partnership which had been so profitable earlier in the campaign. There was no doubt that Adebayor had suffered during his strike partner's absence and the Togo front man welcomed the Dutchman's return to fitness. Rather than play a striker like Eduardo in place of van Persie, Wenger had preferred to play an extra midfielder and this left Adebayor more isolated. Arsenal fans hoped the system would would soon revert to 4-4-2.

With England's Euro 2008 qualifying campaign on the brink of utter disaster, the lack of home grown English players at top clubs became a topic of conversation yet again. UEFA president Platini felt the need to add his opinion on Wenger's heavy reliance on foreign players: 'I do not like the system of Arsène Wenger. If the best clubs buy the best fifteen or sixteen [year old] players that is finished for all the clubs in Europe.' The debate rumbled on with suggestions of a quota system being employed in English football to protect the future of the national team. Platini also took the chance to criticise England's planned bid to host the 2018 World Cup, suggesting that the country did not deserve the right to hold such an event.

Arsène certainly is not on the same wavelength as Platini on the notion of quota systems. The Gunners boss told *FourFourTwo*: 'I'll always fight fanatically against all the quota systems. I find them utter rubbish. I think that sport is just because it rewards the best. If you're good enough, my friend, you play – no matter what your name, colour or passport.' In the *Guardian*, Wenger went into more detail in defence of having no limit on foreign players at club level: 'A club is not a national item. The club is open to the world and the national team is representing the country. I give you the example of Ryan Giggs. How many World Cups did Giggs play? Zero. Was Giggs one of the best players in the world? Yes. He has chosen to play for Wales. Therefore, there is justice for these kinds of people. They can play with the best players in the world inside the club.' This issue has constantly hounded Arsène and it was destined to rumble on during the rest of the campaign. Some wondered: should the Arsenal boss take some of the blame for the struggles of the England national team? Had he damaged the game in this country with his transfer policies? Clearly, Arsène was adamant that he had done nothing wrong.

Wenger received a boost in mid November when Fabregas openly assured Gunners fans that he was committed to the club and had no interest in a move back to Spain. With Real Madrid and his former side Barcelona regularly linked with the player, Arsène was happy to see Cesc putting the record straight. The youngster told the press: 'I am not even thinking about returning to Spain. I do not listen to the offers that come in for me because I do not need anything that I haven't already got at Arsenal. And it's nothing to do with money – if it was I would have gone to Real Madrid last summer. I am not moved by money, I am moved by football.' The Spaniard added: 'I am playing and I am happy. Being a Gunner is very special, something that I am proud of. This is a small club on the inside, like a family, but it's huge on the outside.'

Wigan were Arsenal's next Premier League opponents and arrived at the Emirates after a turbulent few weeks. Chris Hutchings had been sacked as manager after a series of poor results and there had been much speculation over who would be appointed as the new boss. Steve Bruce was given the job and Wigan, eighteenth in the table, set out their stall predictably with a five-man midfield designed to frustrate the home side. Fabregas missed the contest through suspension while Hleb sat out through injury. Wenger's side left it late but took the three points thanks to goals from captain Gallas again and wide man Rosicky. The Emirates Stadium heaved a big sigh of relief. When news filtered through that Manchester United had lost away to Bolton, the victory became even more significant. The Gunners had a three point advantage and a game in hand.

The trip to Seville in midweek was less enjoyable for Arsène. He opted to rest a number of first team players with qualification already assured but Sevilla were intent on snatching top spot in the group from the Gunners. A neat finish from Eduardo put Wenger's side ahead only for the Spaniards to roar back, winning 3-1 and moving ahead of Arsenal in the table.

Fabregas was withdrawn in the second half as a precaution after he felt a twinge in his hamstring and Arsène himself was sent off for comments he made to the officials. The Gunners boss was confused as to what he had been punished for: 'I had no exchanges with the referee. I don't know why I was sent off, I was really surprised. The fourth official was really difficult for the whole game, I said to the referee "will you explain to me why I have been sent off?"' It was a rare blemish on his managerial record and reminded him of his touchline ban at Nagoya Grampus Eight.

All in all, it was a nightmare night in Spain for Wenger and his players. With one match remaining in the group phase, the

Gunners had to accept the fact that they might now finish second and find themselves facing a tougher second round tie. Arsène, though, showed little concern over the matter nor any regret at resting a number of first team players.

The loss also brought an end to the Gunners' unbeaten run in all competitions. But they were yet to suffer a defeat in the Premier League and this had to be Wenger's first objective. By resting Gallas, Adebayor, Sagna and several others for the match in Seville, Arsène would have a stronger squad for their league fixture at the weekend against Aston Villa.

The trip to Villa presented a potential banana skin. Martin O'Neill's side were in good form and Wenger was still without several first team players. The pace of Gabby Agbonlahor and Ashley Young on the flanks was identified by Arsène as a major threat but he remained confident that his back four would continue their solid league displays. In the build-up, the Arsenal boss explained that Villa would not be underestimated. Yet, having won 1-0 in the corresponding fixture last season, Wenger and his squad travelled to the Midlands with high hopes. With Manchester United not playing until Monday night, it was a chance for the Gunners to extend their lead at the top.

Villa scored first but goals from Mathieu Flamini and Adebayor ensured that Arsenal left town with all three points. The run continued. Wenger was gleeful post-match, telling the media: 'I think the first half was amazing. We were quick and sharp on the move, while in the second half we were resilient and showed commitment and calm to deal with the pressure. This was a big test for us. We were really tested when we were losing and we deserve a lot of credit.'

When under-fire Newcastle boss Sam Allardyce sent out his team against the Gunners, many expected a rout, with the Magpies' defence in hopeless form. But Wenger knew that Newcastle would have a point to prove and so when Adebayor opened the scoring early in the match, the floodgates did not open. Allardyce's players defended stubbornly and equalised in the second half through defender Steven Taylor. The Gunners were poor in the second half as Newcastle harried and chased and gave Arsène's side little time on the ball.

In the end, Wenger acknowledged that the 1-1 draw was a fair result and was probably content in the end to leave the North East with a point. The Frenchman told the media after the game: 'I must concede that overall Newcastle deserved a point. They battled hard and fought for every ball. My team gave absolutely everything tonight but we are a little bit frustrated.' His slight unhappiness came from the way in which his side responded to Newcastle's work-rate. Rather than playing their way out of trouble – which is usually the Wenger way – the Gunners began to play long, directing passes forward to Adebayor and surrendered possession too often. Newcastle boss Allardyce saw things a little differently: 'I feel very unlucky not to have won the game. We had the better chances but did not find the quality finish.'

Fabregas missed the trip to St James' Park due to injury – the third consecutive game that he had sat out – and Arsenal felt his absence, particularly in the second half. Unquestionably, the team's build-up play had suffered against Wigan, Newcastle and Villa with the little Spaniard unavailable. The vision and energy of Fabregas had been such a vital part of Arsenal's strong start and the midfield lacked penetration without him.

Manchester United closed the gap at the top of the Premier League table to one point by beating Derby 4-1 at Old Trafford, putting pressure on Arsenal again as they travelled to Teesside to face Gareth Southgate's Middlesbrough – a team always capable of rising to the occasion. Wenger's mood was not helped by the string of players carrying injuries. With Fabregas, Hleb, van Persie and Flamini struggling to be fit, Arsène was putting faith in some fringe players as the Gunners looked to open up a four-point gap again above United.

Arsenal have always prospered against Boro and any side containing Gallas, Toure, Rosicky and Adebayor ought to be full of confidence. However, this would be Middlesbrough's big day as Wenger's side lost their unbeaten league record. The home side got off to a terrific start, taking the lead from the penalty spot after a foul by Toure. Boro doubled their lead with sixteen minutes to go and Arsenal could only manage a consolation goal in stoppage time. It was a sloppy display from the Gunners and Arsène was very unimpressed. He bemoaned the congested fixture list that his squad had faced and claimed: 'We paid the price for it today. We were not very sharp. In fairness, Middlesbrough were sharper, played well and we lacked confidence at the start. We can't complain about the result.' A gap that had been six points after the win over Wigan had been reduced to just a single point now.

Arsenal were struggling at the wrong time. The next weekend, the Gunners would be entertaining Chelsea at the Emirates just hours after Liverpool and Manchester United collided at Anfield. Yet, rather than fearing his fellow title challengers, Wenger told the press that he welcomed the competition: 'It is super healthy. I believe without a doubt that this season will be the most exciting year in the Premier League.' He acknowledged Chelsea's quality and experience, Liverpool's eagerness and squad depth and United's individual brilliance but remained convinced that his own side could hold off all their rivals.

During the same week, Arsène also took time out to praise the appointment of Fabio Capello as the new manager of the England national team. He announced: 'It does not need me to tell anybody that Fabio Capello is a Rolls-Royce who will drive England through, not necessarily smoothly, but he will get the maximum out of the players. He has great experience, he's a strong man who will deal with the problems he has and try to find solutions.' Wenger also commented that there were some big problems with the England team and that he would be willing to discuss these with Capello if the new boss wished to do so.

As the nation settled down to watch the four biggest clubs in the Premier League square off in a massive day of football, Wenger went through his final preparations for the visit of Chelsea. He had publicly praised the performance of Avram Grant since the departure of Mourinho and knew that the Blues would make themselves hard to beat. However, the absence of Didier Drogba up front severely weakened Chelsea as Drogba had been the difference between the sides several times in the past. Arsène had had injury worries of his own but he hoped to have Fabregas, Flamini, Hleb and van Persie back.

News filtered through pre-match of the scoreline from Anfield, where in-form United had snatched a narrow 1-0 victory over Liverpool. It was not the best tonic ahead of kick-off.

Wenger was relieved to be able to recall Fabregas, Flamini and Hleb to the starting line-up with van Persie only fit enough for the bench.

The contest was fiery from the first whistle with plenty of crunching challenges yet the quality football took a while to come. The Gunners took the lead on the brink of half-time when Gallas headed in a corner that was woefully misjudged by Petr Cech in the Chelsea goal. The second half was gripping and both sides could have scored several times in the closing twenty minutes. However, it finished 1-0. Arsène felt his team had deserved their victory: 'We lost our first game of the season last weekend and this was a mental test. In the first half it was a game that was locked tactically. In the second half we had four or five chances to score the second goal. Overall, I felt that the three points was just about right.'

So having led the Premier League by six points just two weeks earlier and by a single point before Grand Slam Sunday (as it had been dubbed by Sky Sports), the Gunners were content to have maintained their slender advantage above United. The victory was a good way to end a poor week and provided a welcome boost. Many speculated that it was now a two-horse race for the Premier League title with Chelsea and Liverpool slipping out of contention. Benitez's team found themselves a huge ten points behind Arsenal, albeit with a game in hand.

A League Cup quarter-final with Blackburn, days later, and more vital league matches needed to be approached with the usual meticulous preparation. Against Rovers, the Arsenal youngsters showed first skill, then spirit to win 3-2 in extra-time with ten men – Denilson was red carded at the end of normal time. Wenger has always tried to blood younger players in this competition and they did not let him down. Eduardo bagged two, including the winner, while Lassana Diarra was immense in midfield. Arsène was ecstatic after his team held on to earn a place in the semi-finals, where they would face rivals Tottenham.

The North London derby was also the Gunners' next Premier League fixture. New Tottenham boss Juande Ramos had helped his club climb the table but a trip to the Emirates was a daunting task. In the end, Arsenal escaped with the three points but they might well have been beaten. Robbie Keane missed a penalty with the score 1-1 and substitute Nicklas Bendtner made an instant impact by heading home the winner. United won the next day and so the Gunners' advantage remained just one point.

The day before the Tottenham clash, the Champions League second round draw had paired Arsenal with last year's winners, AC Milan. It was not the tie that the Gunners had hoped for but Wenger refused to be pessimistic. The Italians were certainly experienced yet Arsène remained confident: 'It's an interesting draw. I believe we can do it if we play at our best. It's a good target for us to get stronger for the match. It's a big challenge but if you ask me do we have a chance to knock them out then I say "yes".' These two fixtures would make for gripping viewing as Arsenal's quick, passing game collided with Milan's patient, probing approach.

In the meantime, there were vital league games to occupy Arsène's mind. Trips to face Portsmouth have often resulted in impressive wins for Wenger's side but a 0-0 draw on Boxing Day was a bitter blow and saw Arsenal slip from the top of the

Premier League table. With Manchester United looking in ominous form, the Gunners needed to bounce back quickly and a 4-1 win away to Everton on 29 December was the perfect reply. Combined with West Ham's 2-1 victory over United, it was the ideal end to 2007. Arsenal were back at the Premier League summit and the Frenchman promised to fight Ferguson all the way for the title.

The only frustration as 2008 began was that Toure and Eboue would soon be heading off to Ghana for the three-week African Cup of Nations. Toure in particular would be hard to replace. On a more positive note, though, David Beckham was training with the Gunners to build his fitness for the new MLS season and Arsène hoped his experience and class would rub off on the club's youngsters.

Arsenal fans worldwide were holding their breath and hoping that 2007/08 would see Arsène inspire the team to one of the greatest campaigns in the club's history. There was so much to play for. After the years of anxiety over Henry's possible exit, the Frenchman had gone but clearly the show would go on.

Arsenal began 2008 with a solid 2-0 victory at home to West Ham on New Year's Day and morale was certainly high. Still involved in all four major competitions, Wenger faced the tricky task of looking at the bigger picture and keeping his big names fresh for the most important fixtures. The next two games saw the Gunners in cup action and Arsène took the chance to rotate his squad. Yes, these competitions were important – but they could not be compared with the glamour of Premier League or Champions League glory.

Despite fielding a weakened side, Arsenal saw off Burnley in the third round of the FA Cup then drew 1-1 with Tottenham in the first leg of the Carling Cup semi-final. In theory, this meant advantage Spurs with a second leg to come at White Hart Lane but it was impossible to discount the Gunners in current form and it would depend on which players Arsène picked on the night.

And on the whole, Wenger managed to keep his players focused over the next few weeks. A 1-1 draw at home to Birmingham was a disappointment, especially as United crushed Newcastle 6-0 the same day, but a classy 3-0 victory at Fulham steadied the ship again. Wenger knew there would be plenty more ups and downs as the title race wore on, especially as United looked to be on their tail for the long run.

The dream of winning four trophies ended on 22 January at White Hart Lane as Tottenham sent the Gunners tumbling out of the Carling Cup. Arsène opted to keep faith with his youngsters but watched in dismay as the hosts ran riot, winning 5-1 on the night to book a place in the final. To make matters worse, Adebayor was involved in a bust-up with team-mate Bendtner as Arsenal lost control.

The defeat might have only been in the Carling Cup, a competition that was low on Wenger's list of priorities, but the nature of it sent shock waves around the league and the incident involving Adebayor and Bendtner was particularly concerning. Critics suggested that the Gunners needed to become more gracious losers.

However, with some generous fixtures ahead, Arsène refused to become flustered. The side that lost at White Hart Lane had been largely second string, with the odd exception, and, sure enough, the return of all the big guns brought four straight wins. Newcastle suffered back-to-back 3-0 defeats at The Emirates as the second coming of the Kevin Keegan era on Tyneside continued to disappoint. Adebayor's double secured the FA Cup victory while Flamini's wonder strike sent Arsenal on the way to three points in the league meeting. Another win, this time 3-1 at Manchester City on 2 February, kept the pressure on United to match them stride for stride.

Wenger knew things were looking promising. If his youthful side could maintain their current form, the title would be within reach. However, United were usually flawless in the final few months and a sloppy patch from the Gunners could be enough to see the champions pull away. Arsène was pleased to see no complacency at home to Blackburn in a rare Monday night fixture as Arsenal moved five points clear at the top.

United had lost to rivals City on Sunday in the Manchester derby – an emotional afternoon owing to the 50th anniversary of the Munich air disaster – and the Gunners had cashed in. However, Wenger refused to get too carried away. Speaking after the Blackburn game, the Frenchman told the press: 'There is still a long way to go. We didn't expect to be where we are after this weekend. But it is important to keep some humility. This league is very tight.'

A huge FA Cup fifth round tie against United at Old Trafford was the next challenge in Wenger's sights and the Gunners boss was well aware that there were psychological points on offer, even if the Premier League and Champions League offered more glamour in many people's eyes. Both managers sought to rotate weary squads but it was United who looked more up for a battle. With Rooney on song, Arsène watched his side fall three goals behind in the first half before Eboué was sent off for a high challenge on Evra. Fletcher completed the 4-0 victory and Wenger was left to pick up the pieces as his troops trudged back into the dressing room.

The young Gunners had been humiliated and the Frenchman wanted to see more fight in their eyes. The media relentlessly attacked the feeble display and Wenger had to deal with claims that he and his players did not value the FA Cup. Several newspaper columns condemned the attitude of Arsène and the team he had picked on the Saturday.

The return of Champions League football could not have come at a better time in some respects. The Arsenal players wanted to bounce back and make a big statement – perhaps the atmosphere of European football would be the spark. Their opponents in the second round were AC Milan, the holders. Carlo Ancelotti's men had all the experience; the Gunners had the pace and movement. It was all set up to be an intriguing battle.

Back in December, when the draw was made, Wenger had refused to take a backward step. And he had not changed his stance since. The Italians had many qualities, including the skill of Kaka and the vision of Andrea Pirlo, but Arsène knew that they were vulnerable against teams that attacked with pace and he urged the likes of Hleb, Fabregas and Adebayor to be the difference-makers.

But the first leg, at the Emirates, ended goalless. After all the build-up and planning, Wenger was disappointed that his side had failed to score, especially as Adebayor headed against the bar when well-placed late-on. Maldini and company had produced the type of gutsy defensive effort that they were famous for and Arsène was left to fret over his side's chances of scoring in the San Siro.

He admitted to the press, 'We didn't take advantages of the chances that we created. We were a bit forceful and a bit nervous in the final third or our finishing situations. Milan defended with a lot of experience. They adapted to the situation in thinking they would be under pressure and that they would have to defend well, which is what they did. But, overall, we played a fantastic game and it's a shame that didn't get us a goal. On a night when everything goes for you, you would get two or three. The positives are that we put them under pressure for a big part of the game and that we didn't concede a goal.'

This last point was key. For all Wenger's frustration over the o-o draw, he backed his young charges to produce a moment of magic in Milan and if the Gunners scored, the hosts would need two goals to go through. The Italians were now favourites to progress but Arsène remained positive.

If the draw in midweek was a slight setback, events at the weekend delivered a far more damaging blow to Wenger and his players. Just three minutes into the clash with Birmingham at St. Andrews, Arsène was rocked by a horrific injury to Eduardo. After a tackle by Martin Taylor, the Croatian required oxygen and seven minutes of treatment before being rushed to hospital with a badly-broken leg. Wenger looked pale and his players initially froze.

Birmingham went ahead through James McFadden but Walcott came to the rescue, netting twice in five minutes. However, there was another sting in the tail as Clichy fluffed his lines and brought down Stuart Parnaby in the box. Ten-man Birmingham grabbed a point as McFadden fired home the spot-kick but the most worrying sign was the reaction of Gallas, who berated Clichy and promptly marched up to the other end of the pitch as the penalty was taken.

The Gunners defender – the team's captain no less – then sat in the penalty area for several minutes after the game until Wenger coaxed him back into the dressing room. Arsène chose to shrug it off as understandable disappointment.

Villa came to the Emirates and took advantage of the rattled side, with Arsenal needing a late Bendtner goal to snatch a 1-1 draw. Meanwhile, United were ploughing on and had cut the gap to a single point.

It was far from ideal preparation for the trip to Milan for the second leg but, then again, Wenger had always relished the big stage and the chance to prove his critics wrong. And he had passed this onto his players. The Frenchman had billed this as the ultimate test of his young side's character – and they did not let him down.

The Gunners were the better side and again subdued the attacking threat of Kaka and Alexandre Pato. Fabregas was everywhere in midfield, Hleb roamed freely and Adebayor proved a handful for the Milan back four. But the killer goal just would not come and a tense period of extra-time seemed inevitable.

Then Fabregas struck. With just six minutes to go, he collected possession just inside the Milan half, drove forward and, with no red and black shirt coming close to him, he unleashed a crisp, low drive into the bottom corner from 30 yards. The San Siro fell silent while Wenger and his players rejoiced. And just for good measure Walcott burst through and teed up Adebayor to clinch a 2-0 victory. The party could begin.

After heaping praise on his players as they headed off the field, Arsène did likewise when speaking to Sky Sports News. He said: 'He [Fabregas] was outstanding, but tonight it is very difficult to single one out. I believe the whole team defended well and attacked well, it was a complete team performance. Of course I'm very, very happy tonight. I'm very proud of our performance; we were under pressure to score goals.'

After the woes of the past few weeks, Wenger had done brilliantly to pull his squad together again and it spoke volumes for his man-management and tactics. They still had their noses in front in the league and all Gunners fans hoped that the buzz from winning in Milan would carry over to the next few games. However, for whatever reason, there was no sign of the heroic performance in the San Siro when Arsenal took on Wigan and Middlesbrough.

A 0-0 draw at the JJB Stadium was a blow and handed the initiative to United. A week later, Aliadiere hit back at his former club as Boro almost took three points at the Emirates. Toure's equaliser earned Arsenal a point but they were running out of steam at the worst possible moment. They had not won in their last four league fixtures but Wenger refused to be downcast. Others, though, showed more concern and pointed to the team's recent average run of results. Were the team now lacking leadership on the field?

The Gunners boss ignored the criticism and prepared for another huge game – against Chelsea at Stamford Bridge.

United were facing Liverpool at Old Trafford earlier in the day and, when Ferguson's side romped to a 3-0 victory, the pressure was really on. Arsenal and Chelsea both knew that they would have an uphill battle on their hands if they failed to take three points.

After a nervy and goalless first half, Wenger was out of his seat to celebrate the opening goal just before the hour mark as Sagna chose the perfect time to score his first goal for the club. The full-back rose well to head home Fabregas's corner and the title race was seemingly back on for the Gunners. But there had always been question marks over the resiliency of Arsène's players and whether they had the know-how to close out big games. Unfortunately, the Frenchman's big names let him down again as Chelsea recovered to steal an unlikely victory with two Drogba goals.

It was a bitter pill to swallow for Wenger. He had been 17 minutes away from celebrating a huge win but the Drogba late show meant it was the Blues who now sat second, with Arsenal falling to third. United were five points above Chelsea and six above the Gunners. Could the Gunners muster one more big surge?

Wenger looked shell-shocked in front of the media but refused to count his team out of the title race. He claimed: 'We will fight until the end and we are not worried about the future but are disappointed now, obviously. Today we were unlucky and I thought we played well. We were 1-0 up and were unlucky with their first goal, which I thought was really offside.'

One thing was for sure – there could be no more slip-ups or else a slim chance would become no chance. Wenger needed to mastermind a flawless run-in and then cross his fingers that United suffered a bad patch. However, by half-time at Bolton on March 29, such an outcome looked ludicrously optimistic. The Trotters were 2-0 up and Diaby had been sent off. Yet Arsène rallied his troops, pointed to the kind of play that had kept them in the hunt all season and sat back to admire a brilliant second half.

His players responded and turned the deficit into an inspired 3-2 victory, reminding everyone of their attacking potency and in the process dismissing the suggestion that they were out of the title race. Gallas grabbed the first before a van Persie penalty and a Jlloyd Samuel own goal completed a gutsy comeback. Wenger was delighted, telling the media: 'I can't remember a better comeback, being 2-0 down and with ten men. We knew at half time that 2-2 would not be good enough but we showed our mental strength and kept on going.' The first half had been a horror show yet the players had shown great spirit to fight back and Arsène could not have been prouder of his youngsters.

All Wenger's attention was on Liverpool now. In addition to a league meeting, the draw for the Champions League quarter-finals had paired Arsenal with Benitez's side, with the winner facing the victor from the Chelsea-Fenerbahce tie. So Arsène prepared to face Liverpool three times in a single week.

After the draw, the Gunners boss had sent out a rallying cry, telling reporters: 'We were strong enough to knock the holders out, so let's do it against Liverpool. I said ideally you would like to play a foreign team because it's Europe but I prepared myself to play anyone. We are highly determined to go through.' Now, though, the time for talking was over.

In the first leg, played at the Emirates, Arsène sent out an attacking line-up, hoping to stun the visitors with a fast start. And after 23 minutes, his ambition was rewarded as Adebayor headed the Gunners in front. But his joy turned to despair three minutes later as Kuyt levelled after a brilliant run from Gerrard. The Arsenal boss knew that throwing away a lead so quickly was a major error.

And Liverpool defended well thereafter but the Gunners should still have won on the night. The match ended 1-1 yet Bendtner managed to block a goal-bound effort from Fabregas and Arsenal had a penalty appeal denied. Like against AC Milan, Wenger could not help wondering what might have been. They had had the chances to settle the tie.

Arsène claimed the Gunners were still a threat. He told reporters: 'It will be a test for us, but we have the desire to do it. I feel we were not rewarded for what we produced – and we had the chances to win it. We were a bit unlucky with a big decision of the referee on the penalty. It's difficult to take, but we have to swallow it.'

A 1-1 draw at home to a largely second-string Liverpool side at the weekend put another nail into the Gunners' title bid as Wenger became increasingly irate and desperate on the touchline. 'In my brain it is not over, because it is not over mathematically. It depends on the results of the other teams. With our situation in the table victory was needed but you never know, you hope for the best. I hope we're not too far behind on Monday.' United were held at Middlesbrough, giving Chelsea hope, but the trophy still looked beyond Wenger's players.

The third clash of the week with Liverpool ended up being the most enthralling. Arsène took his players to Anfield knowing that they needed to score but that had never been a problem for the Gunners. It was at the other end that there were obvious concerns, with Gerrard and Torres looking the main threats.

The Gunners started brilliantly, producing arguably their best half-hour of the season. They kept possession, worked tirelessly and stretched the Liverpool defence to the limit. And, through Diaby's rocket strike, they took a priceless lead. It was all going their way and Wenger prayed that he could put a nightmare six weeks behind him with a place in the semi-finals.

But Liverpool eventually settled and Hyypia's header levelled things on the night and on aggregate. Losing van Persie to injury had taken its toll on the Gunners but Hleb, Diaby and Adebayor all looked menacing. Yet defensive instability again haunted Arsène, with Torres exploiting a mismatch on the deck against Senderos to make it 2-1. But Wenger's fearless youngsters could not be accused of lacking spirit on this occasion as Walcott's bold run ended with Adebayor equalising in the 84th minute. It put Arsenal in the box seat, leading on away goals.

However, very little had gone right for the Gunners since Eduardo's injury in late February and that trend continued in the last five minutes at Anfield. Referee Peter Frojdfeldt awarded the hosts a contentious penalty as Ryan Babel and Toure fell in the area. Gerrard converted and then, with Arsenal charging forward, Babel added a fourth on the counter attack. Wenger had just watched another trophy slip through his fingers. In January, all four trophies were up for grabs still. Now, the likelihood was that Arsène and his players would end the campaign empty-handed again.

A dejected Wenger told the press: 'I felt the game was over at 2-2. Then there was a dodgy penalty and we started to lose concentration. Over the two games this is hard to swallow. The big decisions over penalties have gone against us. It is difficult to take. The players in the dressing room are very down because they believe week after week the decisions are going against them.'

More misery was around the corner for Arsène, though, as his mood darkened and the stress of the season started to catch up with him. On 13 April, he took his players to Old Trafford. Most pundits had discounted Arsenal from talk of the title now but there could be no doubt that the Gunners' hopes would be over if they failed to beat United. As at Anfield, Fabregas and company did their manager proud for large chunks, particularly in the first half. Just after the break, Adebayor put Arsenal ahead and the title race debate was re-ignited. The Togo striker appeared to deflect the ball home with an arm but the goal stood and, after the decisions that had gone against them recently, it was hard to begrudge Wenger's side this opener.

Typically, though, the Gunners' soft centre was exposed again. They would always give opponents a sniff unless they became more ruthless. Gallas conceded a penalty, Ronaldo scored it and the lead was gone. It had lasted a mere six minutes. And the final nail was hammered into the Arsenal coffin in the 72nd minute as Hargreaves' free-kick settled the contest and slammed the door shut on Wenger's title dreams. United were now six points clear at the top.

Yet Arsène stood by his players. He has been criticised at times for his endless defence of his squad but on this occasion their tireless effort was worthy of praise. He told reporters: 'This team is amazing. They keep going and I am so proud of all of them. We are out of the title race, of course; we know that. We played with quality and spirit, but what can you do about the result now? We had plenty of chances and I feel we were very unlucky not to win the game, but we have to accept what happened. In the last two months we have had a blip, but we have not had much luck either and you could see that again today. I believe this team is good enough to win things and our biggest target now is to keep the group together.'

Maximum points from what Wenger had always identified as a gentle four-game run-in did little to subdue the feeling that Arsenal had missed a big opportunity for silverware. A 2-0 win over Reading, followed by a 6-2 demolition of woeful Derby and 1-0 victories at home to Everton and away to Sunderland brought the campaign to an end but it was United who were enjoying their big day, beating Wigan to hold off Chelsea and lift the trophy for the second year running.

Despite the disappointing final few months, the Frenchman was full of praise for his squad when talking to the media at the Stadium of Light. He said: 'Quality-wise, we've been remarkable the whole season. We lost a 100m race by a fraction of a second. It doesn't mean we have not made a good 100m. To have a great 100m, you need three or four who compete for the final place. This year, the Premier League, for maybe the first time in the last four or five years, was exciting until the last day of the season, and we have contributed to that. My message to Sir Alex Ferguson is congratulations for the achievement – and get ready for the fight next year.'

But for Arsène there would always be 'what-ifs' surrounding 2007/08. What if Eduardo had not got injured? What if van Persie had been fit for more games? What if several dubious penalty decisions had gone Arsenal's way? But ultimately such questions were pointless. The Gunners had fallen short and would need to reassess their options over the summer.

It was easy to forget that Wenger's side had not been fancied by many to make an impact that season when predictions were being thrown around in August. They had come a long way and, if he could keep the group together and fight off interest in Adebayor and Fabregas in particular, next season had the potential to be a huge one in the club's history. This was the target Arsène had in mind as he headed off for a short summer break before returning to the hot seat.

ADRIFT FROM THE PACK

Bouncing back from the disappointments of the previous season was never going to be easy for Wenger. Despite all his experience at the highest level, missing out on silverware always scarred him deeply – especially when he felt his team were so close to pocketing a string of trophies.

However, Arsène found a way to shift his focus to the challenges ahead. A new season meant a full set of trophies were once again up for grabs but the summer had been far from ideal for the Gunners. Flamini, such a lynchpin in midfield during Arsenal's promising run, had opted for a switch to AC Milan on a free transfer. The Frenchman had been a tireless worker and suddenly there was a gaping hole in the central areas. Normally, Gilberto would have been the obvious choice to fill in but he too headed for the Emirates exit, moving to Greek side Panathinaikos.

While Wenger was able to hang onto Fabregas and Adebayor

– arguably his two most precious talents – the midfield looked very lightweight as the new season approached. And there were concerns over Adebayor's attitude after the player was denied a summer move to Barcelona. And things went from bad to worse when Hleb became the third midfielder to leave north London, sealing a dream move to Barcelona. Arsène temporarily appeased the club's fans with the signing of skilful young Frenchman Samir Nasri from Marseille for a reported £12 million fee. Meanwhile, United strengthened their hand by buying Berbatov from Tottenham and Chelsea brought in Portuguese duo Deco and Jose Bosingwa.

Of course, future results would ultimately decide the wisdom of Wenger's dealings in the transfer market. If Arsenal made a bright start, with several young players to the fore, he would be hailed a genius and he was well aware of this fine line as he oversaw the final weeks of pre-season training. However, many pundits felt the Frenchman had missed a trick by not adding more steel to the defence and midfield. They questioned whether a squad that was small in comparison to Manchester United, Liverpool and Chelsea could really last the pace. Even more pressure would be placed on the shoulder of Fabregas.

Pre-season wins over Stuttgart and Real Madrid suggested Arsenal would still be a force to be reckoned with and Arsène remained bullish about his side's chances. The Champions League remained a big target and he was delighted to see his players comfortably handle the qualifying round tie with Steve McClaren's FC Twente. Gallas scored a goal in each leg as the Gunners racked up a 6-0 aggregate win.

Wenger told the media: 'We needed to be organised because

they play a little with your patience. We were disciplined and focused and we were never really under threat. I felt the whole team was sharp.'

Meanwhile, though, Arsenal's Premier League campaign had got off to a wobbly start. A far from convincing 1-0 win over newly-promoted West Brom, courtesy of a Nasri strike, was followed by a woeful defeat at Fulham as Brede Hangeland grabbed the only goal of the game. Wenger fumed post-match, telling reporters: 'When you want to play at the top you must start the game with the right attitude and personality. That's what we didn't do and that's a good learning lesson. It was the kind of game where you couldn't afford a mistake at the back or at a set piece. I believe they wanted it a bit more than us in the first half and the corner [when they scored] shows that.'

And the Frenchman got his response in the next league game as a van Persie-double sunk beleaguered Newcastle. This was the Arsenal of old, playing the type of football that had made Arsène a world famous manager. Wenger praised his players for 'playing the game we love' with their perfect passing and movement. Newcastle had had no answer to it.

Blackburn fared even worse a fortnight later, going down 4-0 as Adebayor put a sluggish start to the campaign behind him with a clinical hat-trick after van Persie's opener. Walcott continued his fine run of form with some dazzling work out wide and Arsène's footballing principles again bore fruit. He was quick to point out that the title race appeared wide open and he knew that the defeat at Fulham had not done any lasting damage. New Rovers boss Paul Ince, the Premier League's first black manager, summed the day up when he told the media:

'The good thing is that we won't be playing Arsenal every week.'

Wenger then looked ahead to Europe, where Arsenal had been drawn in Group G alongside Dynamo Kiev, Porto and Fenerbahce. On paper, it appeared plain sailing. The Gunners kicked off this stage of the competition in Kiev and came away with a creditable point thanks to Gallas' late equaliser. Arsène was left to reflect on a decent performance but one that lacked the clinical finishing to punish inferior opponents and this was a familiar story for the Gunners in Europe. His team were just not set up to score scrappy goals and it often cost them on their travels. Better teams would punish them.

The unbeaten run stretched to five games as Arsenal overcame Wenger's bogey team Bolton on the road. Kevin Davies' opener provided a real test of the Gunners' spirit and character but they responded with two scintillating goals in as many minutes. First, a sweeping move allowed Bendtner to tee up Eboue for an equaliser – the Ivorian's first Arsenal goal. Then a minute later Bendtner was on the score sheet himself as he netted from Denilson's cross. The Brazilian later secured the points with a third, four minutes from time.

Having been out-muscled so often in Lancashire over the years, Arsène was pleased to see his players pass their way out of trouble. Denilson was impressive in midfield and Fabregas was proving to be his typical, steady self since returning from injury. Most significantly, the victory put the Gunners top of the table and Wenger told the media: 'I thought it was a convincing, united, classy performance with strengths everywhere.' There was a long way to go but the doubters were having to re-think their assessment of Arsenal's chances as Arsène seemed to have managed yet another masterstroke. The personnel might have changed but the quality of the football was just as mesmerising when his team were on-song.

And the youngsters showed how bright the club's future was in midweek with a sumptuous display against Sheffield United of the Championship in the Carling Cup. The Blades were put to the sword as young Mexican Carlos Vela bagged a hat-trick and Bendtner added another two in a 6-0 rout. Arsène's youth system was clearly still bringing through some frighteningly-gifted players and he took great pride in the glowing reviews. He had certainly lost none of his knack for spotting young talent.

However, the Gunners were brought crashing down to earth at the weekend as Premier League new-boys Hull arrived at the Emirates and left with all three points in the biggest surprise of the season to date. A scrappy Paul McShane own goal gave Arsenal the lead early in the second half and, despite the plucky nature of the Tigers' display, many expected this to open the floodgates. But the reaction was quite the opposite. Hull levelled 11 minutes later as Geovanni thundered in an unstoppable 25-yard rocket to silence the Emirates. Wenger urged his players to regroup and regain control, but the visitors completed their fight-back as Daniel Cousin headed home Andy Dawson's corner.

Two goals in four minutes had turned the match on its head and, though Arsène tried to break through with the introduction of Bendtner and Vela, Arsenal found no response. The feeling of invincibility had been shattered. Wenger was visibly angry after the game, knowing his side had thrown away vital points, and the Frenchman called it a shocking defeat.

Porto felt the effects of Wenger's frustration in mid-week as the Frenchman sent his players out on a mission to make amends. Van Persie and Adebayor scored two apiece and Arsenal made it four points out of a possible six with a 4-0 win. However, the attackers found life much tougher at the Stadium of Light against Sunderland at the weekend. Much of the match was a stalemate, though the home side marginally held the upper hand and a goalless draw appeared the likely outcome.

But Wenger was left in dismay in the 86th minute as Grant Leadbitter fired Sunderland ahead with a superb shot off the underside of the bar. Fortunately for Arsène, Fabregas bailed the Gunners out, heading in an equaliser in the third minute of stoppage time. Wenger attempted to find the positives after the match but, while he had other ideas, many felt that his team had been fortunate to escape with a point after a below-par display.

Back-to-back wins over Everton and Fenerbahce boosted morale at the Emirates. Three second-half goals sunk the Toffees while five different scorers helped Wenger's side demolish the Turks. The Gunners, fearless and flashy in everything they did, were starting to find their stride again going forward but there were defensive concerns to address. Excluding the Carling Cup, Arsenal had managed one clean sheet in their past seven games. While this sequence included just a single defeat, Arsène saw that improvements were needed in order to keep up with pace-setters Chelsea and Liverpool.

As the campaign neared the end of October, the Gunners' form became increasingly erratic. Wenger watched in agony as his side veered from sublime to error-strewn and back again. A

2-0 victory over West Ham at Upton Park ensured that Arsenal lost no ground on leaders Liverpool. The win owed much to the relentless desire of Arsène's players, who put a string of misses behind them to seal the points courtesy of a Julien Faubert own goal and a late Adebayor strike. Wenger had kept the Togo front man on the bench until the 67th minute and it looked an inspired move when Adebayor exploited weary legs for his goal.

But while Arsène hailed this 'big win', he was less than happy in midweek as a comfortable north London derby soured, further highlighting his team's soft centre. After falling behind to a David Bentley wonder-strike, the Gunners rallied well and moved into a comfortable lead through goals from Silvestre – signed from United in the summer – Gallas and Adebayor. Tottenham made it 3-2 through Bale, only for van Persie to restore the two-goal cushion with more than 20 minutes remaining. Seemingly, the three points were safe.

Tottenham, though, were not done. Looking a revitalised side under new boss Harry Redknapp, they pressured Arsenal and Wenger shuddered as his players wilted under the strain. A mistake from Clichy allowed Jenas to cut the deficit and the Gunners boss' night was truly ruined as Lennon pounced in the final seconds of added time to snatch a point. For everyone associated with Arsenal, it felt like a defeat.

Wenger cut a distraught figure as he spoke to the media after the match. He admitted: 'Unfortunately we were not rewarded because we lack maturity and instead of being efficient we became a little too negative in the last ten minutes. The potential is outstanding in the side but the result is down to inexperience.' He was pleased with the attacking intent on show but again the defence had wobbled under pressure. The best teams domestically and in Europe would punish such lapses severely. It was not a new issue but it needed to be addressed as soon as possible.

Perhaps still suffering a hangover from dropping these two points, Arsenal stuttered again at Stoke on 1 November. Gone was the breathtaking movement that had left West Ham and Tottenham chasing shadows. In its place were hesitation and a lack of confidence. The swagger was nowhere to be seen. The Potters put in a typically gutsy, in-your-face display, combined with Rory Delap's dangerous long throws. It proved a potent mix for the Gunners, who succumbed 2-1. To rub salt into the wounds, Wenger lost more than the three points as van Persie saw red for a needless challenge on Sorensen while Adebayor, Walcott and Sagna all left the field with injuries. Wenger was livid and while he was willing to acknowledge that Stoke had exploited an Arsenal weakness in dealing with the long ball and long throws, he told the press he felt some of the challenges had been unnecessarily aggressive.

A 0-0 draw with Fenerbahce in midweek completed a miserable seven days. It would be an overstatement to suggest that the Gunners' season had headed off the rails but the cracks were starting to show. All this meant that the visit of champions Manchester United took on a greater significance. It was almost a must-win game, even if the season was only in November.

Thankfully for Wenger, his players rose to the challenge in style and produced a performance worthy of the great Arsenal teams at the start of the decade. There was passion, pace, flair and some stunning passing moves. Clearly, Arsène had given his team the perfect motivation and all the tactical planning paid dividends.

Nasri was the star man as he scored both goals to secure a fine 2-1 victory. It was a gripping contest and United played their part. Had Rooney and Ronaldo been more clinical in front of goal, it could have been another bleak afternoon at the Emirates for Arsenal. Wenger was on his feet to celebrate the opener in the 22nd minute as Nasri's strike deflected home off United skipper Gary Neville, who endured a torrid afternoon against the young Frenchman.

Nasri doubled the lead with a second well-placed strike just after the break and, though Brazilian starlet Rafael Da Silva's volley gave United a lifeline, Arsenal held on for a priceless win. The celebrations at the final whistle told their own story and Wenger wore a look of joy and relief.

The Gunners boss told the media post-match: 'I am very proud of the performance. It was a fantastic game and we won against a great side, who were very dangerous going forward. The team was not faultless, but we were spot-on spirit-wise. Now we want consistency and to keep winning.'

The youngsters took these words on board and kept up the good form in midweek, beating Wigan 3-0. But the senior players returned at home to Aston Villa at the weekend and produced a sluggish performance that destroyed the fine work against United seven days earlier. Martin O'Neill's flamboyant young side strolled in and took the points playing the Arsenal way, with pace and movement in attack and with plenty of grit defensively. A Clichy own goal and a late Agbonlahor strike handed Villa the points.

Wenger despaired as he watched his side's title pursuit veer off track. And things were about to get much, much worse as the dressing room dynamic unravelled to devastating effect. The drama centred around Gallas, who criticised one of his team-mates. Wenger, renowned for his desire to preserve the club's privacy, was furious. Airing such grievances in public brought the inevitable media attention. Pundits were having their say and putting Arsenal's trophy hunt under even greater scrutiny. Arsène acted decisively, stripping the captaincy from Gallas and banishing the defender from the squad prior to the match at Manchester City.

It was chaos. The media swarmed around the Emirates and Wenger could do nothing to prevent his team's demise being discussed on all the back pages. The trip to Manchester just added to Arsène's woes as the damage became clear. The Gunners were flat and Robinho ran rings around a side lacking leadership and belief. Almunia took over the armband for the match but was beaten three times as Wenger watched his side slump to another defeat.

With Villa on the rise, Champions League qualification was very much in jeopardy for the Gunners. Arsène sought to remedy the situation by naming Fabregas, who had been suspended for the City game, as the new club captain. It was a sensible move – the Fabregas era began with three points against Dynamo Kiev at the Emirates as Wenger allowed himself a smile for the first time in several weeks. The 1-0 win was gratefully accepted. Arsène was facing one of toughest challenges since arriving in north London. His team were losing belief fast and, in the process, their grip on a top four spot.

Back in domestic action, they faced the prospect of heading to Stamford Bridge to take on Chelsea on November 30. The Blues had seen their stunning 86-game unbeaten home run in the Premier League ended by Liverpool in late October and were keen to start another streak. It was the last fixture that Arsène would have chosen with his team's spirits flagging.

But the Gunners rose to the occasion and put all the negative press behind them. Fabregas' influence was a factor and all over the pitch Arsenal looked a united team, particularly in the second half. Then a Djourou own goal gave Chelsea the lead and many Gunners fans feared the worst as the hosts took control.

Arsène rallied his players at half-time, pointing out that they were just a goal down and urging them to make a fast start after the break. Sparked by Wenger's team talk, Arsenal stunned Terry, Lampard and company with two goals in three minutes to turn the match on its head. In truth, the Gunners had offered little goal threat prior to the 59th minute but grabbed an equaliser when van Persie, who appeared to be offside, fired past Cech.

Chelsea appealed in vain and, perhaps still rattled by the nature of the equaliser, conceded again three minutes later. Van Persie popped up in the box, turned neatly and drilled a low shot into the far corner. The Bridge went silent; Wenger was on his feet. The Gunners continued to work brilliantly as a team to hold onto their lead as Arsène watched on proudly. The final whistle went and the celebrations could begin. It was a massive moment in an up-and-down season.

The Frenchman said: 'It was a fantastic win. There's no better test of character. I told the team to keep the pace and last longer than they did and keep strong.'

A disappointing 2-0 defeat to Burnley in the Carling Cup was a setback for the Gunners but, more importantly, a 1-0 victory over Wigan, courtesy of Adebayor, maintained their title push. There was a lot of ground to make up but there were plenty of fixtures left. While Wenger was encouraged by the improved league form, a 2-0 defeat to Porto in the Champions League saw the Gunners finish second in the group and face a tougher second round tie. It was not ideal but it had been a similar story last season and Arsène had overseen a victory in the San Siro against AC Milan so it was hardly make or break.

Manchester United, Liverpool and Chelsea were leading the way domestically and Wenger was well aware that a winning streak was required if Arsenal were going to force their way into the hunt. However, the Gunners managed just three points from their next three games, falling further behind in the process. First, Wenger's side squandered the lead to draw 1-1 at Middlesbrough then a week later van Persie's strike was cancelled out by Robbie Keane as Arsenal were held at home by Liverpool.

In truth, the point against Rafa Benitez's side was a solid result for the Gunners after losing Fabregas to injury at half-time then seeing Adebayor sent off for a second yellow card. Wenger was furious but the tenacity of his side's rearguard action slightly improved his mood.

Sandwiched between the clashes with Middlesbrough and Liverpool, the draw was made for the second round of the Champions League. Having finished second in their Champions League group, the Gunners were paired with Italian side Roma in the last 16 and after showing that youth and pace could conquer experience last season against AC Milan, Arsène appeared excited by a similar kind of tie.

'Of course we have a great chance of winning the competition, like any team at that level,' he said, refusing to be drawn on his team's chances. 'But now the Champions League becomes a different competition, like a cup competition. If you miss five minutes of the 180, you are out.'

Roma boss Luciano Spalletti insisted he was happy with the draw, adding: 'That does me just fine. There's no point in talking about it now we must simply show what we're made of and how we're prepared to make sacrifices. To Arsenal I want to congratulate them for their system. They have many young players on their way to becoming great players who are being chased by all the big clubs in Europe.'

Continuing with league action, Wenger was raging again on Boxing Day as he watched his team surrender a promising lead yet again – this time against Aston Villa, who were threatening to snatch fourth place away from Arsenal. Arsène knew this fixture was a perfect opportunity to regain the initiative in the race for Champions League spots and his team responded, taking a two-goal lead through Denilson and Diaby. But the team's soft centre was exposed once more as Barry pulled one back from the penalty spot after Gallas fouled Agbonlahor and then Zat Knight equalised in the last minute.

O'Neill claimed his team deserved more than a draw and the Frenchman said: 'In the first half Villa created good chances and we were lucky, but in the second half we were never in trouble. It is frustrating.'

On 28 December, Arsenal hosted Portsmouth and returned to

winning ways with a 1-0 victory but they made heavy weather of it. Without Fabregas, there was little creativity and it was only in the 81st minute that Gallas scored the decisive goal. Wenger urged his side to be more clinical.

Three consecutive wins followed as the Gunners stumbled into better form. A 3-1 victory over Plymouth in the FA Cup was followed by a 1-0 win over Bolton on 10 January. Again, though, it was only late on that Arsenal broke through as Bendtner struck an 84th minute winner. Still, it was the result that mattered and Wenger was encouraged to see his team fighting until the final whistle. And the next weekend, the Gunners avenged the humbling loss to Hull at the Emirates by travelling to the KC Stadium and bagging a 3-1 victory – again leaving it late as Nasri and Bendtner both scored in the final eight minutes.

The points haul had been pleasing in the past few weeks but the performances remained well short of Wenger's expectations. He knew that the Gunners could not keep scraping through with late goals but the players seemed unable to lift their performances, emphasising again how valuable the injured Fabregas was to the team. Four consecutive draws left Arsenal supporters, and Arsène himself, dismayed.

The Gunners were held to a 0-0 draw at Cardiff in the FA Cup Fourth Round then required a last gasp van Persie equaliser to snatch a point against Everton at Goodison Park. It was scary to think where Arsenal would have been in the table if they had not scored so many late goals during the campaign. Wenger admired the spirit but, as he often stressed, this was not enough to win titles.

Another goalless stalemate followed at the Emirates against

Gianfranco Zola's West Ham. Arsène tried everything to engineer a breakthrough but the Hammers defended in numbers, making it another frustrating afternoon for everyone associated with Arsenal. Goals were proving hard to come by at the moment and Adebayor's slump was putting more pressure on others to make contributions.

The January transfer window had been a quiet one up to this point for the Gunners but numerous rumours had been flying around about potential targets. Many felt Wenger would look for a centre-back or a defensive midfielder to toughen up the team's lightweight spine but the Frenchman had other ideas. When Arsenal finally made their move it was for an attacker, the Russian Andrey Arshavin, who signed from Zenit St Petersburg for around £15 million. Arshavin's inspirational displays had lit up Euro 2008 and Arsène hoped for more of the same at the Emirates.

A 0-0 draw in the north London derby with Tottenham on 8 February meant Wenger's usually free-scoring side had netted once in the last four games. The cause was not helped by Eboué's senseless red card, picking up bookings for dissent and then for kicking out at Luka Modric before half-time. The Ivorian had been a dismissal waiting to happen ever since seeing an effort disallowed early on. With the Gunners defending in numbers, there would be no debut for Arshavin who remained on the bench. Ultimately, it was probably a point gained considering the circumstances but Wenger was far from pleased, especially as Adebayor limped off with a hamstring injury.

The Frenchman refused to be sucked into debating the Eboué red card, though he claimed the first yellow was harsh. Instead, he hit out at referee Mike Dean for disallowing Eboue's goal. He told the media: 'I'm very angry, I am pleased with my team, but very angry with the decision of the referee to cancel a goal like that. The goal we scored is completely normal, how can you cancel a goal like that? It's just not acceptable, this kind of decision. He must have seen a clear-cut foul to cancel a goal like that. I would like our opponents to have goals cancelled like that when they play at the Emirates.'

A fairytale return for Croatian striker Eduardo brightened the world of football on 16 February. He was back with a bang, scoring twice as Arsenal dumped Cardiff out of the FA Cup, winning the replay 4-0. However, the Premier League woes continued with a 0-0 draw against Sunderland. It was a fourth goalless draw in the past month and the supporters were becoming restless. Wenger could not understand why the goals had dried up. Even Arshavin, making his league debut, could not break through, though he had several good efforts on goal.

Arsène put on a brave face in front of the cameras, telling the press: 'We had the chances but we could not get the goal that would have made us happy. We don't concede goals but we want take advantage of the chances that we create – we need to play with a little bit more freedom.' But the frustration was clear in his voice. Villa had lost 1-0 against Chelsea and the Gunners had missed a golden opportunity to crank up the pressure on O'Neill's side. The Midlands club still held a six-point cushion in fourth place and Wenger knew that his players faced an uphill battle to claw their way back into contention.

The news that Fabregas was nearing full fitness boasted the morale at the Emirates but if the talismanic Spaniard's absence proved one thing in particular, it was that the Gunners relied too heavily on him. Wenger wanted more from his other star players, especially with some massive games on the horizon.

The first leg against Roma was up next and the Arsenal players set about gaining a solid lead at the Emirates to take to Rome. As expected, Wenger sent his team out to attack from the first whistle and the visitors were overwhelmed by this positive approach. Had the Gunners been more clinical, the tie might well have been over inside the first half. As it was, a penalty from van Persie after a foul by Philippe Mexes was all that separated the sides over the 90 minutes.

Though a 1-0 advantage was far from a bad night's work, Arsène fretted over the missed opportunities. He told the press: 'That is the regret we have tonight. I'm happy with our performance but there was room to score more goals – we know we can create chances. One of the positives is we didn't concede a goal and our pace gave them problems in the first half. In the first 20 minutes of the second half, we had one chance after another.'

But they would fancy their chances of bagging a goal at the Olimpico which would leave Roma needing three to go through. In the meantime, there was a lot of work to do domestically to resurrect their hopes of a top four finish. But there was more frustration ahead as Fulham, enjoying a fine season under Roy Hodgson, secured a 0-0 draw at the Emirates. In an open game, the Gunners' inability to kill off opponents was highlighted again. Despite ending the match with van Persie, Arshavin and Bendtner on the field, Arsenal could not find a breakthrough. Wenger prayed that he would have Adebayor and Fabregas available again soon. His side were looking clueless without them at times.

Typically, Arsène refused to become flustered after the stalemate. He told the media: 'We are not scoring goals and the offensive confidence of the team is not high and as a result the players are becoming a little anxious. The fans are frustrated and so are we. We have to take the result on the chin and continue to fight.'

And in midweek West Brom were floored by a pumped-up Arsenal side. Wenger had left his players in no doubt that their finishing needed to improve and two-goal Bendtner had an evening to remember. There were a few nervy signs defensively but Arsène enjoyed a relaxed night, thrilled to see his side move within three points of Villa. The Gunners had played a game more yet there would be extra pressure on O'Neill's side now.

Wenger shuffled his pack against Burnley in the FA Cup but his younger charges answered the call and Eduardo, one of the more senior men and captain for the day, netted the second in style to set up a 3-0 win. Now, the Gunners' boss turned his attention to Roma – but not before hailing the character of the Croatian striker.

Arsène had been hugely supportive throughout Eduardo's recovery and was delighted with the way the striker had settled back into the team. Wenger admitted to reporters: 'I didn't expect him to come back like that. It's a tribute to his personality. He's never complained and that is a big example in our world.'

Despite his own concerns about the delicate nature of the tie, Wenger was publicly upbeat ahead of the trip to Rome. His young charges, including Bendtner, Denilson and Eboue, were sent out full of belief while Roma strapped up talisman Francesco Totti, who was nursing an injury.

Things began disastrously as Brazilian defender Juan fired Roma ahead after ten minutes following a breakdown in communication between Gallas and Toure. Conceding early on was a hammer blow and, with the stadium rocking, Wenger was powerless to help his players. He just hoped they would stick to the game plan and play with their usual poise. However, Arsenal were below-par, failing to string passes together and looking disjointed in attack. The Gunners were terrified of making the decisive mistake and it took all their resolve to force penalties. Now their mettle would really be tested.

Almunia and Doni had the chance to be the hero and it was the Roma stopper who made the first move, diving to claw out Eduardo's spot-kick. It was a bad start, made worse as David Pizarro netted Roma's first penalty. But, after van Persie scored, Almunia threw Arsenal back into the mix with a save from Mirko Vucinic's overly-casual effort. Successful spot kicks from Walcott, Nasri and Denilson were matched by the Roma takers and the shootout headed into sudden death locked at 4-4.

Wenger looked pale but his players retained their composure. Toure scored, only for Alberto Aquilani to level; Sagna scored, only for Riise to square things again. But the end eventually arrived. Diaby slotted home his spot-kick and the Gunners' boss could celebrate as Max Tonetto blazed over the bar. Arsenal were into the quarter-finals.

It was a hugely significant night in the development of Wenger's youthful squad and one that he would not forget. They headed over to applaud the travelling Gunners supporters and the Frenchman told the media: 'After conceding an early goal and missing the first penalty, you need something special, mental strength to come back and win it. I am proud of the mental strength because it has been questioned a lot.

Maybe this boost would kick-start a return to top form in the Premier League. It certainly seemed so as Wenger's side hammered relegation-threatened Blackburn 4-0 at the Emirates to leave Villa trailing in the race for fourth place. The buzz from midweek was still running through the players – and Arsène himself – and at the moment they felt they could do no wrong. And the fixtures kept coming as Arsenal continued to pursue FA Cup glory.

Hull, who had achieved that famous victory at the Emirates earlier in the season, were the opponents in the FA Cup quarter-final but could not repeat their previous success despite going in front through Nick Barmby. Van Persie equalised before Gallas headed in a controversial winner with six minutes to go to set up a semi-final with Chelsea. Hull boss Phil Brown fumed as replays showed the French defender appeared to be in an offside position.

The protests continued after the game but Wenger preferred to switch his focus to the trip to beleaguered Newcastle on March 21. Arsenal had not lost in the Premier League since the disastrous 3-0 result at Manchester City on 22 November and Wenger knew that if they had turned some of the draws during that spell into wins, the Gunners might be in the title picture. The Magpies, however, were in dire straits and succumbed to a 3-1 defeat despite some decent chances. Martins' penalty was well saved by Almunia and, though the Nigerian quickly equalised Bendtner's opener, Newcastle paid the price as Diaby and Nasri helped Arsenal pull clear.

Villa were busy self-destructing and the Gunners had ghosted into the top four. They also still had their eyes on the Champions League trophy after seeing the draw for the next two rounds prior to the Newcastle fixture. Arsenal were paired with Villarreal in the last eight, with the winner facing either Manchester United or Porto. No outcome could be seen as favourable at this stage of the competition but Wenger knew things could have turned out far worse.

He told the media: 'It is maybe a good opportunity to play the first game away from home, but at that level it is very difficult to be creative in your statement. It will depend on the quality of your performance and the players available as well. We have learned that to knock any Spanish team out is very difficult. There are many big clubs in Europe who are not in the quarter-finals. We are one of the five clubs who have for ten consecutive years qualified for the Champions League, so to go to the end of it is our immense desire.'

It threw up some intriguing scenarios. Firstly, Wenger would be re-united with former Gunner Pires who was enjoying a second wind at Villarreal. And then there was the possibility of an all-English semi-final against rivals United. There were some mouth-watering weeks ahead for Arsène.

On 4 April, after an international break, Arsenal's unbeaten run in the Premier League continued with a 2-0 win over Manchester City, banishing memories of their meek surrender at the City of Manchester Stadium. Wenger was delighted to have Fabregas and Adebayor back in the starting line-up and the Gunners were purring as a result. The Togo front man bagged both goals and, with key players appearing fit and fresh, pundits began to see Arsène's team as serious contenders for both the FA Cup and the Champions League.

Wenger was able to withdraw his captain and star striker before the end and keep them fresh for midweek when Villarreal arrived in the capital. Playing at home in the first leg had worked against Roma but Arsène was happier knowing that this time the Gunners would benefit from the support of their own fans in the decisive second leg. He simply focused on the preparations and ensuring his players were tactically set up to deal with the Spaniards, who were formidable at home.

However, rather like in Rome, Arsenal began slowly. Wenger had spent much of the build-up urging his players to expect a fast start from Villarreal and warning against letting the home crowd become a factor. But after ten minutes, Spanish midfielder Senna drilled the hosts ahead with an unstoppable 30-yard rocket. It left the Gunners facing the kind of atmosphere Arsène had feared and things got worse when first Almunia, then Gallas limped off.

But the experience in the last round seemed to have given Arsenal more steel and steadily Wenger watched his charges gain a foothold in the match, with Fabregas starting to pull the strings. And in the 66th minute, Arsène was rewarded for the positive mindset that he had instilled in his squad as Fabregas' pass picked out Adebayor and the striker equalised with a breath-taking overhead kick. The Gunners held on and were most people's clear favourites to progress.

Of course, Wenger stopped short of such a verdict but he admitted his players had done him proud. He revealed to reporters: 'It puts us in a great position, but we want to qualify at home and to repeat the type of performance we did in the second half. I am confident, after the quality we have shown added to the mental strength and desire we have shown. We know Villarreal are a good team as well, so we will be on our toes and focused at the Emirates. We have a little chance to recover some players who are out as well.'

Whether Arsène was prepared to say so or not, things were bubbling up nicely. A 4-1 win at Wigan emphasised the attacking prowess as four different players got on the score sheet. Most importantly, the team were not overworked ahead of the return game with Villarreal, meaning there were no new injuries to add to Wenger's list. He was uneasy about approaching the second leg without Almunia, Gallas and Clichy – out with a back problem – but he believed there was enough quality in the side to get over the line.

And he was proved right as the Gunners shrugged off Villarreal with relative ease. Walcott settled Arsène's nerves with the opener after ten minutes and second-half goals from Adebayor and van Persie, from the penalty spot, wrapped up the tie. Wenger could now look forward to a titanic clash with Manchester United, who squeezed past Porto 3-2 on aggregate courtesy of a stunning Ronaldo strike.

Post-match, Arsène was jubilant, telling the press: 'We used our passing well and gave them a lot of problems. We were explosive on the counter-attack. We sent out a very offensive team and we played in a convincing way. I was impressed with our quality and speed. Villarreal have a good technical level but we gave them problems they didn't like.'

The big games kept coming but, with several players still sidelined, Arsenal ran out of steam in the FA Cup semi-final with Chelsea, played on a less than ideal Wembley surface. Walcott put the Gunners in front but the power of Drogba haunted Wenger once again. He had worked hard on plans to keep the striker in check but, having seen Malouda level, Arsène was left exasperated as Chelsea gained control. Then Fabianski made the fatal error. He raced from his line only to see Drogba reach the ball first, round him and shoot the Blues into the final.

The Gunners boss told reporters: 'It is disappointing because we had a good start and after we dropped off. When you go a goal up you never feel the game is finished, but it looked as though it would finish as a draw. I felt we gave two cheap goals away and in a game like that it matters hugely. Any mistake can be costly. The pitch doesn't decide who wins and who loses, but when people pay money to watch people play football you have to give a good pitch.'

With fourth place all but assured, Arsenal travelled to Anfield to face title-chasing Liverpool and Wenger made it clear that all the pressure was on the home side. And, in Arshavin, Arsène had a man who loved this kind of stage. In a pulsating game, the Russian struck four times but it was still not enough to secure the win as the teams played out a 4-4 draw, which put a big dent in the Reds' title hopes.

The Gunners boss told the media: 'It was a game at a frenetic pace of top quality technically and you could see both teams created many chances. We are half happy because we scored four goals and half unhappy because we conceded four. [Arshavin] scored four goals but he was at the end of some good combination play. He has a lot of tricks and a short back-lift and that makes him very dangerous.'

A 2-0 victory over Middlesbrough kept Arsenal's spirits up ahead of their huge Champions League semi-final with United and Wenger knew that this was all the Gunners really had to play for. Fabregas struck twice against Boro as Arsenal extended their run to 20 games without defeat in the league and cranked up the pressure on Chelsea in the race for third place. However, the name of the game was avoiding injuries and getting ready for Europe.

Looking ahead to the first leg at Old Trafford, Wenger promised that his side would be positive. He revealed to the media: 'What I want is for my team to play with belief and certainty and with a desire to score goals. This is the moment we've waited for. This is the moment we want to show we have what's needed to take advantage of this first game.'

And so, all eyes turned to Manchester on 29 April as Wenger took his Arsenal side to Old Trafford for the huge first leg of their semi-final. There had been little sign of the old Ferguson-Wenger rivalry in the build-up, but most pundits anticipated a tense battle. Arsène was without several key men, including Gallas, Clichy and van Persie, who was again missing key games through injury. Yet Wenger remained positive, hoping that Fabregas, Nasri, Walcott and Adebayor could help conjure a priceless away goal.

But United started in rampant form, pegging Arsenal inside their own half. Tevez was brilliantly denied by Almunia before

O'Shea fired the hosts ahead in the 18th minute. In fact, Wenger knew that but for his goalkeeper's fine display, the Gunners could have been trailing by three or four at the break. Almunia bailed out his team-mates on numerous occasions, denying Ronaldo and Rooney with vital stops.

At the other end, van der Sar was untroubled and Wenger was disappointed to see the lack of fight within the side. Adebayor was anonymous, Fabregas was subdued and United never looked in danger. However, they could only manage a 1-0 victory, letting the Gunners off the hook. Considering the one-sided nature of the match, Arsène was a relieved man.

He told reporters: 'I believe that we have a good chance to reverse the result. I am convinced you will see a different Arsenal team at the Emirates. United can have regrets because they didn't score a second goal. It's down to us to make sure they regret they didn't score a second goal.' He also acknowledged that Almunia had really come up trumps.

Meanwhile, Ferguson added: 'We played at a good high tempo and maybe we should have scored four goals but before the game I wanted to win without losing a goal. We know we can go there and score and that is the big problem Arsenal have.' It was certainly set up for a cracking second leg and deep down Ferguson must have been fretting that he would rue the missed chances at Old Trafford.

Back in league action, Arsenal were far more comfortable on the way to a 3-0 victory away to Portsmouth as Arshavin kept up his hot streak, running riot and helping Bendtner grab a brace. The Dane's second came from the penalty spot after Arshavin fell under Sean Davis' challenge. The Russian tried to tell referee Lee Mason that it was a fair challenge but the penalty was awarded regardless. The Gunners headed into cruise control and this three points clinched Champions League qualification for next season.

Wenger looked relaxed post-match and allowed himself a wry smile when discussing the Arshavin penalty incident. The only disappointment was that the Russian was ruled out of the Champions League due to his involvement with Zenit earlier in the competition. Gunners fans would have felt more confident if Arshavin had been able to support Fabregas, Adebayor and van Persie in the all-important second leg.

Facing United, a dominant start would be crucial. If the Emirates was rocking after an early Arsenal goal, Ferguson's players would face an uphill battle. Wenger was well aware that it was 27 games since the Gunners had lost at home in the Champions League and, in a pre-match press conference, he admitted: 'There is no mission impossible for us. I believe that when we've beaten Manchester United at home in the Premier League there have been plenty of opportunities for us. We have a good opportunity to enjoy it. We have a good opportunity to play the football we love. What I want to do is go to the final – and I believe we will do it.'

It took United just 11 minutes to blow those dreams out of the water. Park and Ronaldo silenced the Emirates as a despondent and devastated Wenger watched the champions fly out of the blocks into a two-goal lead, leaving Arsenal in need of four goals to qualify. Young Kieran Gibbs, deputising for Clichy, had slipped to hand Park the opener and Almunia was beaten from more than 40 yards for United's second. Game over.

Wenger tried to lift his players at the break, urging them to restore some pride. But Ronaldo grabbed another after a sweeping counter attack and Arsenal only got on the scoreboard when referee Roberto Rosetti awarded a penalty for a Fletcher challenge on Fabregas. The Scot appeared to have won the ball but was shown a red card, meaning he would be suspended for the final. Van Persie netted the spot-kick but most Gunners fans had long since headed for the exits while Wenger contemplated how things had gone so badly wrong.

There were some huge decisions to be made over the summer. Most critics agreed that Wenger needed to open his chequebook and bring in an aerially-dominant centre-back, a ball-winning midfielder and possibly another striker, depending on what he decided over Adebayor's Arsenal future. It would all hinge on the size of his transfer kitty.

Though the Gunners were deflated – no one more so than Wenger – there were a few league fixtures to think about first. The visit of Chelsea was probably the ideal game after the midweek despair. The Blues had suffered an even more agonising exit, with Barcelona netting an equaliser in stoppage time to progress on away goals, and a big match of this nature would force both sides to switch on again. However, it was Guus Hiddink's Chelsea who bounced back strongest.

The whole ebb and flow of the game summed up the Gunners' season. The players produced the kind of football that Wenger loved to see but there was no end product. Walcott was guilty of wasting several good chances but he was not alone. Then, having ridden the storm, Chelsea struck twice before half-time on the way to a 4-1 win. An own goal from Toure left a sense of déjà vu in the air after Arsenal's capitulation against United in Europe and every time the camera focused on Arsène he had a look of dismay on his face.

After the game, Wenger told reporters: 'We have experienced a little bit of everything in football this week and only on the bad side. We created plenty of chances and should have been 2-0 up but we find ourselves 1-0 down. But the positive is going forward we did well, although defensively we certainly did not do as well.'

At the same time, he did not hide from the fact that this was a fourth season in a row without a major trophy. He added: 'Certainly we will try to strengthen the squad in the summer. We'll look to sign one or two players. We are prepared to spend the necessary money to get the players we want. I remain confident that we can win silverware next season and that's why we will continue to work hard.'

This was a bold statement considering their recent failings but it proved that Wenger had lost none of his passion for the job. In previous years, by his own admission, Arsenal had not managed to fill some of the holes in their squad. There could be no excuses for making those same mistakes again. The summer ahead promised to be one of the most important in Wenger's managerial career.

A trip to Old Trafford to face the team who had knocked the Gunners out of Europe was not exactly the ideal next fixture. On top of that, United needed just a point to clinch the title and Wenger had to face up to the possibility of watching on as Ferguson and his players lifted the trophy. And so it turned out. The Gunners contributed plenty to an eventful 0-0 draw but could not find the cutting edge to spoil the champions' party. Gary Neville lifted the trophy and pundits were left to reflect on how United had continued to improve on last season's efforts.

Arsène had taken all the criticism on the chin during the campaign but his comments prior to the United game showed that cracks were appearing. The lack of silverware was hurting him and he needed the fans to buy into the youth policy. The big question now was: how would the Gunners boss use the summer to close the gap between Arsenal and the top three?

There was no doubt that the unrest among the Arsenal supporters continued to hurt Wenger. Having achieved so much at the club, he had hoped the fans would show more faith in the building project. Finishing in the top four and reaching the FA Cup and Champions League semi-finals was hardly a poor season, he reasoned. Addressing reporters about comparisons between the Gunners and United, the Frenchman went further, saying: 'When you look at people assessing the situations of the clubs, it has become ridiculous. You sit here, you are in the last four in Europe, and every day, you feel you have killed someone. If you do not take a distance with it, you think what kind of world do you live in? We lost against United who have ten times more resources, they are the best in the world. In sport, you have to accept that. It is like they [the fans] are ashamed to be fair. There is no shame to say, "Yes, you are the best." We were in the last four with a very young team – that is the reality. We have to keep a little bit of common-sense. Our average age in midfield is 22 – normally you play not to go down in the Premier League with a team like that.'

Shortly after, reports emerged linking Wenger yet again with the Real Madrid job. For Arsenal fans, this speculation was nothing new, with the Spanish giants long-term admirers of the Frenchman's work. Yet this time there was something different about the scenario. Arsène had admitted that the proposition was 'interesting' while an aide added: 'It is more of a possibility now than it's ever been before.' No one doubted the talent within the Arsenal squad but too many weaknesses had been highlighted and suddenly his tenure in north London appeared to be on the rocks.

BACK IN CONTENTION

Wenger would stay put at the Emirates but there were other issues to deal with. The feeling among Arsenal fans and pundits was that the Gunners needed to be active players in the transfer market. Though Wenger would never admit it, finishing fourth indicated that Arsenal had a lot of ground to make up and that the squad was simply too young and too threadbare. Manchester United and Chelsea could turn to world class substitutes when injuries struck, the Gunners could not and this was a key area to address.

However, Arsène left supporters open-mouthed by instead seemingly weakening his squad during a summer that brought a frenzy of transfer activity. Elsewhere, Real Madrid finally got their man as Cristiano Ronaldo completed an £80 million move to La Liga, levelling the Premier League playing field in the process. Manchester City's push to break into the top four gathered momentum as Tevez and Gareth Barry joined the revolution at Eastlands.

And Wenger would make headlines by selling Toure and Adebayor to City for a combined fee of around £40 million. The Gunners had finished well adrift from the top three the previous season and now Arsène had sent two of his more talented and experienced players to one of Arsenal's rivals. It prompted a lot of head scratching.

Frustratingly for Gunners fans, this was not the cue for a spending spree. Wenger agreed a £10 million swoop for Ajax defender Thomas Vermaelen – an upgrade on Toure – but no other big names followed, despite interest in classy Brazilian defensive midfielder Felipe Melo. Though it was never wise to question the Frenchman, it appeared to have been another damaging summer. If van Persie, Fabregas or Gallas picked up an injury, who would step into the void? And what would this trio make of the summer moves?

But nothing could change Wenger's positive outlook. He told the media: 'I'm very optimistic about the season and I'm very positive about this team. We always have to listen to people's opinions but you also have to trust what you see in the games and in training.'

Arsène loved proving the doubters wrong and his team started the season as though they shared this sentiment. After a free-scoring pre-season, the Gunners carried that form into the early weeks of the new campaign. Arsenal began by dismantling Everton at Goodison Park, making a mockery of some of the gloomy predictions. Fabregas scored twice as the Gunners produced the kind of flowing football that Wenger lived for.

Victories in both legs against Celtic in their Champions League qualifier and a 4-1 demolition of Portsmouth continued the hot streak and set Arsenal up perfectly for an early test against United at Old Trafford. Wenger relished his battles with Ferguson and knew that taking three points in the champions' backyard would emphatically prove that his team should be taken seriously as title contenders.

At half-time, the Frenchman could not have been happier. Arshavin's rocket strike had put the Gunners in front and United were struggling to threaten Gallas and Vermaelen. But the fragility factor came back to bite Arsenal yet again. As United cranked up the pressure, Arsène watched his players wilt. There was no obvious leadership and the lack of a world class ball winner in midfield harked back to Wenger's transfer dealings in the summer. Rooney levelled from the penalty spot before Diaby inexplicably headed into his own net to hand the points to Ferguson's men.

For Arsène, it was too much to stomach. After Gallas had a late goal disallowed, Wenger saw red. The Frenchman kicked a water bottle and was sent to the stands to complete a disastrous second half. His post-match interviews were characteristically cutting as he hit out at the penalty decision and, bizarrely, highlighted Darren Fletcher's physicality in midfield. Referring to his dismissal, Arsène admitted: 'I didn't kick the bottle because I thought Gallas had been onside, I kicked it because I was disappointed. I did not know that was not allowed.'

Critics were quick to point out that the same old problems – namely a brittle response under pressure and a lack of experience – had hurt the Gunners. It was also noticeable that while Ferguson had the luxury of sending on Berbatov and Ji-Sung Park off the bench, Wenger had to rely on youngsters Ramsey and Bendtner.

329

One defeat was hardly a major setback – after all, United had already lost at Burnley – but when it became two in a row after the international break, question marks predictably emerged. Arsenal were back in Manchester on September 12 to face a rejuvenated City side and it was always destined to be a tense, feisty occasion as Wenger's players took on familiar faces Adebayor and Toure.

Adebayor's departure in the summer had been somewhat acrimonious, with the striker and Wenger offering up contrasting stories of the transfer discussions. Of all the players on show, no one was more pumped up than Adebayor. When van Persie cancelled out Micah Richards' opener, Arsène hoped the momentum had swung the Gunners' way but just over 20 minutes later City were 4-1 ahead and Eastlands was rocking, largely due to Adebayor.

The former Arsenal striker struggled to keep his emotions in check all afternoon and, after heading home City's third goal, Adebayor raced over to the Gunners fans and celebrated by sliding to his knees. He had endured taunts from the away end all game but this was a moment of madness that would earn Adebayor criticism and FA punishment. Rosicky pulled a goal back late on but for the second straight game Wenger was furious as he left Manchester, in part because Adebayor had appeared to stamp on van Persie earlier in the game.

The Frenchman could not bite his tongue about the controversial moments in the defeat. In midweek, discussing the challenge on van Persie, he told reporters: 'Emmanuel Adebayor deserves to be charged for what he did. I was surprised there was such animosity in his attitude towards

Arsenal because, in a few years, he will realise Arsenal have been a very positive influence in his life. That is why I was deeply surprised and shocked.

'We are disappointed because when you go to the head, you are always scared for people. You never know how it will affect their health. You want to be protected.' He added that the provocative goal celebration 'doesn't look good either'.

One of the problems for Wenger to deal with was the Gunners' tendency to let one loss affect their mindset in the next. This was apparent as the Champions League group stage kicked off, just four days after the City defeat. Arsenal found themselves in Group H with Olympiakos, AZ Alkmaar and Standard Liege, which on paper looked the easiest group of the draw. But they got off to a nightmare start.

In Liege, Wenger's men were shell-shocked by the Belgians' strong start and after five minutes the hosts had a 2-0 lead. For 45 minutes, the hangover from the City game lingered on but Bendtner's strike just before half-time gave the Gunners hope. Two goals in three second half minutes put a smile back on Arsène's face as they escaped with a 3-2 win.

Wenger knew that the nature of the victory might just be a pivotal moment in their season. He claimed: 'When you're at a big club, you cannot afford to have too many defeats on the trot. After being 2-0 down, this will strengthen belief within the group.'

And the comeback did seem to flick a switch for the Gunners, just as Arsène had predicted. In fact, it sparked a 13-game unbeaten run in all competitions. A run of four straight clean sheets settled a nervy defence, with a 4-0 victory over Wigan the highlight of that stretch. Despite all the talk of Wenger's limited summer spending, the Gunners were still shredding opponents with their slick passing and clever movement. The cast might have changed but the script remained the same.

A 6-2 thumping of Blackburn was the perfect way to kick off October, with six different players on the scoresheet. Contributions from defence and midfield were certainly taking the pressure off the strikers. By the time Tottenham visited the Emirates on October 31, Wenger had masterminded a win over Liverpool in the Carling Cup and the Gunners were well-placed in their Champions League group. Arsène was quick to remind his players of the tests that lay ahead but with each passing day he became more convinced that the current squad was equipped to land a major trophy. A van Persie double clinched the North London derby as Arsenal pulled to within five points of leaders Chelsea with a game in hand.

Cruelly, van Persie would make few further contributions for the Gunners during the 2009/10 campaign. An ankle ligament injury while on international duty with Holland put the striker on the treatment table and left Wenger fuming. Van Persie had become such a key cog and it left Arsène with some serious headaches for the months ahead.

When the unbeaten run was finally ended at Sunderland, Wenger saw his team fail to score for the first time that season. Despite enjoying 57% of the possession, there was no end product and it was clear that the absence of van Persie was hurting the Gunners. Arsène's failure to strengthen his attack in the summer months was looking costly as Arsenal fell eight points adrift of Chelsea.

Though Wenger's game plan was working perfectly in Europe,

it was a different story domestically. On November 29, Chelsea visited the Emirates, presenting the Gunners with a chance to claw themselves closer to the league leaders. Instead, Drogba terrorised Arsenal yet again and put a major dent in Wenger's title ambitions. The same flaws continued to prevent the Gunners taking the next step and the Frenchman had repeatedly ignored them. Chelsea were stronger in midfield, had more options going forward and were clinical in front of goal. Carlo Ancelotti's men thoroughly deserved their 3-0 win.

Suddenly, before the campaign had even reached December, Arsène found himself denying that his team was out of the title race. He said: 'We are fighters and we have to show that in the next game. We are still in a very strong position. Chelsea can drop points, I am convinced of that.' Wenger also pointed to a disallowed goal that might have changed the course of the game.

The bottom line was that Chelsea held an 11-point advantage over Arsenal, who were leapfrogged in third by Tottenham after this loss. A 3-0 loss to Manchester City in the Carling Cup capped a hugely disappointing few days. But as Wenger had hoped, his players responded with real character. The Frenchman tried to boost morale on the training ground, and it paid dividends. Arsenal would not lose again in the league until the end of January.

A 2-0 win over Stoke kick-started the run, with goals from Arshavin and Ramsey. And that man Arshavin was at it again a week later against Liverpool. The Russian had shown a liking for Anfield the previous season with a four-goal masterclass, and he grabbed the headlines again – but not before Wenger had torn into his players.

Arsène seethed as Liverpool took the lead just before half-time with the Gunners far from their best. Back in the dressing room at the break, the Frenchman exploded, questioning his players and demanding an instant improvement. Perhaps shaken by a rare sighting of Wenger's angry side, the Gunners levelled within five minutes then Arshavin netted what would be the winner just before the hour mark.

The turnaround was impressive and the players attributed it to Wenger's fiery team talk at half-time. Fabregas told the media: 'I have never seen him like that. It worked, maybe he should do it more often.' It was a crucial moment as Arsenal capitalised on a Chelsea draw and a United loss that weekend.

Arsène was keen to gloss over his outburst, admitting: 'I believe that sometimes you have to respond to what the team needs. I try to be composed. It was good to be able to surprise the players after 13 years.' On this evidence, his players needed to receive a dressing down more regularly.

Sadly, the joy did not last as the Gunners dropped two sloppy points at Burnley. And more worryingly, Fabregas limped off with a hamstring injury after putting Arsenal in front. Without their skipper, Arsène's side floundered. Until his players provided greater consistency, Wenger knew he would convince nobody that the Gunners could win the title.

Ten goals in the next three goals was a reminder of what most people already knew – Arsenal could steamroller teams when they were in the mood. With Fabregas on the treatment table, the Gunners beat Hull 3-0 and, until the Spaniard returned, his team-mates would need to continue to step up.

There was little margin for error, even as early as December, and Wenger knew it. With the Gunners drawing o-o at home to a stubborn Villa side, Arsène made the drastic move to send on a seemingly half-fit Fabregas. The sight of a Fabregas-less line-up looking out of sync clearly highlighted the lack of depth at Arsène's disposal and, sensing this, he gambled by throwing his captain into the fray. The Frenchman is as studious as any manager when it comes to statistics and he was fully aware of the consequences of dropping points at home. Nonetheless, the decision was bold and desperate in equal measure.

And Fabregas turned the game around. Scoring twice, the Spaniard vindicated his manager's decision. But it came at a price. Wenger cringed as the midfielder aggravated the hamstring injury and limped off late on. It was a constant topic of conversation but it was hard not to feel that Arsène's unwillingness to strengthen his squad had forced his hand by taking a chance on Fabregas.

The Spaniard was expected to miss a further two weeks but Wenger remained convinced that he had made the right call. He claimed: 'I feel that I did the right thing, and would do it again. You do what you think will win the game.'

Had Lampard been injured, Chelsea could have turned to Ballack, Malouda, Essien and so on. Likewise, Ferguson had several good options in most positions. But the Gunners were so dependent on a core group of three or four players and, with injuries to van Persie and now Fabregas, lasting the pace in the title race seemed unlikely.

But Wenger certainly was not throwing in the towel. That was simply not an option. Even without his two best players, he found a way to take ten points from the next four games. Hapless Portsmouth were drubbed 4-1 at Fratton Park, a victory that moved the Gunners to within four points of leaders Chelsea with a game in hand. For all the gloom and doom surrounding Fabregas' injury, Arsenal were within touching distance of the top.

The Frenchman was hugely proud as Nasri, Eduardo and the ever improving Ramsey stepped up in Fabregas' absence. A sloppy draw with Everton – a game that could easily have been a defeat – was followed by back-to-back wins over Bolton, the second of which took Wenger's men to the Premier League summit after battling back from a two-goal deficit.

But disappointment was just around the corner and the problem for Wenger was that his side tended to have three or four game slumps rather than one game blips. With the league so closely contested, the FA Cup offered another route to silverware yet Arsène opted to field a largely second string side away to Stoke in the fourth round. Wenger had Fabregas back from injury but gave opportunities to Francis Coquelin, Jay Emmanuel-Thomas and Craig Eastmond, as well as back ups Silvestre, Vela and the newly re-signed Sol Campbell. Stoke took full advantage. Ricardo Fuller scored twice in a 3-1 victory and another piece of silverware passed Wenger by.

Given the trophy drought, it was a puzzling decision but the Arsenal boss explained himself post-game, telling the press: 'I don't regret the side I put out. We had ten injuries and a very difficult programme coming up. We have four very important games now in a short space of time, that is what we are focusing on.' The message seemed clear – the Premier League and Champions League were the targets.

BACK IN CONTENTION

Despite resting nine of his first choice side against Stoke, the Gunners only managed a single point from their next three league games. A goalless draw away to Villa was hardly a bad result but any slip-ups simply provided a boost for Chelsea and United. They had missed the chance to return to the top of the table and worse was to follow at the weekend as United came to the Emirates.

Wenger had enjoyed recent success at home to United in league action, including a 2-1 win the previous year. But on this occasion, the champions ripped Arsenal to shreds, capitalising on every Gunners error and punishing the hosts ruthlessly on the counter attack. Arsenal's failure to track back was highlighted as a real flaw as United scored twice after breaking up Gunners attacks. Nani conjured a brilliant piece of skill on the right for the opener before setting up Rooney for a breakaway second. Park made it three in the second half and, despite a late rally, the Gunners could only cut the score to 3-1.

Pundits were quick to write Arsenal off after this men-against-boys outing but it was far too early for that. And Wenger agreed. Speaking of his disappointment at the defeat, he told the media: 'We gave them too much room. We were naive. It is difficult to say straight after the game why we were not at our level. It is too early to analyse but I believe there are some mental reasons. It is a massive blow and a massive disappointment. The players wanted to win, they are really down. We have to recover from that. That is part of top-level football.'

This was one of the toughest patches of Arsenal's season as they moved on from the loss to United to face first Chelsea then Liverpool. Having been blown away by the Blues at the

Emirates, the trip to Stamford Bridge was daunting and Wenger knew his team could not afford to slip further off the pace.

But with no attacking spark and a defence terrified by Drogba's all-round game, Arsenal left empty-handed. Their football was pretty at times yet there was no end product. In two games against the Blues, Wenger's players had failed to score and had conceded five.

A timely win over Liverpool improved Arsène's mood a little but he realised his team were now reliant on the top two slipping up. All he could do was keep his troops motivated and take it a game at a time. The victory over the Reds cued another purple patch for the Gunners, who won six of their next seven games and did not lose a league game for two months.

And the Frenchman had noted that the elite teams were no longer having things all their own way. It seemed likely that the champions would lift the trophy with one of the lowest points totals in Premier League history. So there was still hope.

In Europe, Arsène could not have been happier with his team's progress. As expected, they had cruised through the group stage without breaking sweat and the second round draw paired the Gunners with Porto. Wenger set about plotting the Portuguese side's downfall.

The January transfer window had been and gone and Arsène had resisted the temptation to spend some of the money available to him. With a tight run-in ahead, it might have made sense to invest in another striker but it was hard to question Wenger's wisdom when the Gunners recovered from a 2-1 first leg loss in Porto to shrug aside Sunderland, Stoke and Burnley in successive weeks.

The trip to Stoke brought Arsène to the boil again as he responded to the hosts' physical approach with the same exasperation he had reserved for Sam Allardyce's Bolton team in years gone by. His rage centred on a horrific injury to Ramsey, as a result of a Ryan Shawcross challenge. The Gunners had taken the points but Wenger was seeing red when he spoke to reporters, claiming: 'The tackle from Shawcross was horrendous. Spare me how nice he is. Did you see where the injury is? To lose a player of quality at 19 like Ramsey is hard to accept. That is not football for me and I refuse to live with it. The FA have to act.'

It was a devastating blow for Ramsey and it took Wenger some time to simmer down after the game. The physicality of opposition teams had upset the Frenchman for many years as the line between aggression and malice grew ever thinner. But his team refused to dwell on the controversy, as they had seemingly done in the wake of Eduardo's horror injury two years earlier.

A 3-1 victory at home to Burnley kept Arsenal in the thick of the title race, just two points behind leaders Manchester United. The top three had distanced themselves from the pack and it promised to be a gripping final few months. But more injury problems were dampening Wenger's spirits. Fabregas had limped off against Burnley, adding another twist in his stop-start season, and it could not have come at a worse time.

Porto, buoyed by their 2-1 first leg win, visited North London on March 9 and many Gunners fans feared the worst when Fabregas was ruled out. But Arsène had always disputed the suggestions that his team was flat without the Spaniard or van Persie and their absence allowed others to step up and show that there was indeed squad depth at the Emirates. And nobody cashed in more than Bendtner. At times derided earlier in the campaign, the Dane benefited from Wenger's faith in him and scored a hat-trick as the Gunners battered Porto 5-0.

Wenger was on his feet as wave after wave tore through the Porto rearguard. Nasri produced the highlight of the night with a brilliant solo strike but this was a night for Arsène to cherish. It was a moment that told him that his trust in youngsters – and players that played his kind of football – was not misplaced. He told the press: 'We played fluent football with a positive start and the early goals gave us the belief we needed. We were good to watch and won with style.'

This special night put the Gunners in the draw for the quarter-finals, where they were paired with Barcelona. It was instantly dubbed the tie of the round and pundits were soon salivating over witnessing two of the most stylish teams come face to face. The Spaniards would be heavy favourites, as defending champions, but Wenger refused to take a backward step. He said: 'We respect what Barcelona have done but competition is about what you do tomorrow. I believe what is important is that on the day everyone sees a good game and we win it. We are focused on us, not our opponents. In the quarter-finals you are bound to meet a good team and Barca are a good team.

'If you go to the bookmakers and try to place a few pounds, you will see that we are not favourites against Barcelona. Of course they are a good side, but so are we. For me, we have a 50-50 game – if we turn up with our best performance we have a good chance to beat them.'

Much like the tie with AC Milan in 2008, Arsenal would need to be at their best to progress. In the meantime, the Premier

League demanded Wenger's attention as he plotted an unlikely title triumph. Victories over Hull and West Ham showed the Gunners' never say die spirit. Wenger had almost given up hope at Hull until Bendtner scored a last gasp winner to put Arsenal joint top, though Chelsea had a game in hand. The Frenchman was equally on edge against the Hammers when Vermaelen was sent off but again his players found a way to win.

But the Gunners slipped four points off the pace with a 1-1 draw at Birmingham. United and Chelsea had won emphatically that day but a late Kevin Phillips goal dented Wenger's title ambitions. It was a tough blow but Arsène was soon focusing on the midweek glamour tie with Barcelona and finding a way to stop Lionel Messi. The Frenchman fancied his team's chances of passing and moving to victory against anyone and it promised to be an enthralling tie.

The first 45 minutes at the Emirates may go down as the most one-sided goalless half of football ever played in the competition. Wenger sat in sheer disbelief as Barcelona completely outclassed his team, creating chance after chance and rarely letting Arsenal string two passes together. Yet Almunia was simply unbeatable. Time and again he rescued the hosts as Messi and Xavi among others strolled their way through on goal.

Whatever Wenger said at the break made little difference and Barcelona finally found their shooting boots early in the second half. Zlatan Ibrahimovic scored twice and the tie looked to be beyond the Gunners already. Yet Arsène's players proved that their boss had instilled real character to go with the flair as they stormed back into the contest in the final 25 minutes.

First, Walcott pulled one back and then Fabregas, limping

heavily and heading for yet another enforced absence, levelled from the penalty spot with five minutes to go. Wenger had spent much of the game in dismay but even he was jubilant as his captain netted the equaliser. The second leg would still be an uphill battle but the Gunners could at least travel with hope.

Despite news that Fabregas would not play again that season, Arsène remained positive. His team had looked nervous, they had squandered possession on a frequent basis and they had been reduced to spectators at times. Yet the game had finished 2-2 and the tie was still alive. Wenger acknowledged that Barcelona's performance had been outstanding but told the press: 'We have to go for it [in the second leg]. It would be a big achievement but we believe we can do it.'

There was no let up from Arsène's men in the title race either as they beat Wolves to stay in contention. Then all thoughts turned to Barcelona again. Beating the Spaniards in the Nou Camp would quite possibly top Arsène's all-time achievements list but there could be no repeat of the sluggish, overawed start in the first leg. So a special performance was the order of the day and the travelling Gunners fans were treated to exactly that – only the show came courtesy of the peerless Messi.

For 20 minutes, everything went to plan for Wenger. His side harried Barcelona more successfully than a week earlier and then Bendtner stunned the hosts by putting Arsenal ahead. But the lead lasted just two minutes and from then on Messi destroyed Arsène's careful plans. The little Argentine completed a sublime first half hat-trick and added a fourth late on for good measure. Painful though it was to watch his side carved to pieces, a part of Wenger marvelled in Messi's performance. For once, Arsenal had been beaten by a team that simply played superior football.

The Frenchman admitted: 'I believe we lost against a team that is better than us and that has the best player in the world. Once he's on the run, Messi is unstoppable. He's the only player who can change direction at such a pace.' Almunia and several other Gunners players offered up similar sentiments. Arsenal might have lost on the night and in the tie but football had been a big winner – not that this was much consolation for Wenger.

Now it was Premier League title or bust. The probability of another trophy-less season had just shot up and Wenger was quick to stress the importance of a quick recovery from the Barcelona defeat. United and Chelsea were also out of the Champions League and so the league was at the forefront of the top three's thoughts.

Given a week to prepare for the trip to face Tottenham at White Hart Lane, Arsène felt confident his players would be rested and motivated. The chance to put a dent in their rivals' bid for fourth place was an added incentive and enough to fire up the travelling fans. But, in another example of Arsenal's hangover from disappointments, it quickly became clear that Tottenham were the hungrier team.

Admittedly, the Gunners' title hopes were already slim but the display at White Hart Lane suggested the title race was already over. Tottenham debutant Danny Rose announced himself with a stunning volley before Gareth Bale doubled the lead and, though the returning van Persie pulled one back, the hosts held on for the win. Arsenal's title bid was, if not mathematically over, then on the brink.

Post-match, Wenger was visibly hurting. He told reporters: 'We must forget the title race and try to finish as high as we can. It's unlikely but you never know. It shows that we're not mature enough because you can't afford to lose these games if you want to win the league.

'We have made progress this season but had too many players missing tonight. You need a miracle to make it happen like that. Tonight our weaknesses were exposed. We'll continue to fight but even a point wasn't enough from tonight – we needed three points.'

There was no doubt that Wenger had been dealt a rough hand on the injury front, losing van Persie, Fabregas, Gallas and Song and numerous others for key moments. But pundits argued that a title contender needed to handle these setbacks better – and that meant building a stronger, more experienced squad.

With little left to play for, the Gunners managed just one point from their next three games, throwing away a 2-0 lead to lose at Wigan, drawing with Manchester City then losing 2-1 at Blackburn. Wenger called the Wigan defeat 'the most disappointing of the season' and his players' body language in the closing minutes showed there was little fight left.

Though Arsène managed to rally his troops for an impressive 4-0 win on the final day of the campaign to seal third place, the end of season analysis focused on one predictable area. The Gunners had failed to lift a trophy for the fifth straight season. That was hardly the mark of a top European club and with City, Tottenham and Villa all on the rise, nothing could be taken for granted in the years ahead.

Taking in the past nine months, Wenger told the press: 'We

were just a fraction short this season. We want to improve in quality, but there's not necessarily a big number of players needed. We have gone beyond expectation this season but we are still frustrated because one month ago we were in touch with the championship and didn't win it.

'We have shown a good attitude and strong character this season but we conceded too many goals to win the championship. You don't win the championship if you concede 40 goals.'

A portion of Gunners fans must have groaned at the statement on transfer plans but the Frenchman had always stuck to his guns. And opinion was split over just how many new faces Arsenal needed – perhaps one or two big names would get Wenger over the hump. After all, he already appeared on the verge of signing highly-rated Bordeaux striker Marouane Chamakh on a free transfer. Plus, it was worth remembering that 2009/10 was a major improvement on the previous year and that had come despite serious injuries to Arsène's two biggest talents.

An interesting summer lay ahead for the Frenchman as he plotted the next step in his plans. The World Cup in South Africa would provide a healthy distraction and then he would refocus on tweaking a squad that he believed was on the cusp of taking the Premier League – and Europe, for that matter – by storm.

Wenger knew that the 2010/11 campaign might just be the most critical of his managerial career – but he could not wait to embrace that challenge.

ON THE OUTSIDE LOOKING IN

'The additions will be minimal but if there are some they have to be really top class.' These were Wenger's words in May 2010, as Arsenal neared the end of a fifth successive trophy-less season. With the previous summer's transfer fees for Adebayor and Touré still burning a hole in the club's pockets and stadium loans now paid off, those in the know talked of a transfer kitty of close to £40 million. Following another injury-hit season, striking cover for van Persie was seen as a top priority, as well as more of a physical presence at the back and in the middle.

Arsène's first signing was a goalscorer in the form of long-term target Chamakh on a free transfer from Bordeaux – and his arrival had seemed a certainty before the previous season even drew to a close. The 26 year-old Moroccan had hit 16 goals in consecutive seasons for the 2009 French Champions, including a strong showing in the Champions League. Wenger told the press, 'Chamakh is a striker of real quality and has all the attributes to come to England and do very well. He is very good in the air and also a good team player.'

Despite links with Everton's Jack Rodwell and Toulouse powerhouse Moussa Sissoko, a midfield addition failed to materialise. However, better than a signing for Wenger was the news that captain Fabregas would not be leaving to join Barcelona, despite another summer of intense speculation. 'I convinced him to stay,' the Arsenal boss told the media with great pleasure, 'I am confident we will keep him for a few more years.'

Meanwhile, it was all change in central defence as Wenger replaced the released quartet of Senderos, Gallas, Campbell and Silvestre with French duo Sébastien Squillaci and Laurent Koscielny for a combined fee of just over £15 million. Squillaci, 30, joined from Sevilla and fulfilled all of Wenger's criteria. The Gunners boss explained: 'We needed a centre-back of quality and experience and at the right price he was all of that'. Koscielny arrived on the back of an impressive season with Lorient and, at 24 years of age, represented a more long-term investment: 'He has shown he is mentally strong, he's a fighter and a very strong competitor.'

It had not been the major shopping spree that many fans had hoped for, but Wenger had addressed some major issues and, with the exception of newly rich Manchester City, it had been a summer of cautious spending in the Premier League. In pre-season, Nasri and Chamakh got off to scoring starts, while 18-year-old midfielder Jack Wilshere, back from a successful loan spell at Bolton, took his chance to impress with aplomb. For yet another year, most pundits had Arsenal down as an outside bet for the title, and Wenger spoke confidently: 'You always go into a season wanting to win a trophy. I am confident that we will do it.'

With Fabregas and Song still recovering from knocks, Wenger opted to hand Wilshere a first Premier League start in the tough opening day fixture away at Liverpool. Arsenal struggled to respond to a 46th minute David Ngog strike despite the home side playing with 10 men for the whole second half after a red card for Joe Cole. With the clock ticking down, a late Pepe Reina own goal gave Wenger's side a point, but it was a laboured start to the season. Van Persie's appearance as a substitute was cause for celebration but a second yellow in stoppage time capped a Premier League debut to forget for Koscielny.

For the next month, however, Wenger's side were unstoppable – and the Frenchman had extra cause for celebration after signing a new three-year contract extension. Walcott bagged his first Arsenal hat-trick as the Gunners demolished newly-promoted Blackpool 6-0 before a satisfying first away win since March against bogey side Blackburn and a 4-1 trouncing of Bolton continued the run. Song's goal in the latter fixture, Arsenal's third, was their 1,000th Premier League goal under Wenger.

The Gunners certainly seemed to be enjoying themselves, with Fabregas, Song and Arsenal Player of the Month Wilshere orchestrating the flowing, passing football that Arsène loved. Unfortunately, as in previous seasons, with his side flying high, Wenger was hit by a flurry of injuries to crucial players. Van Persie and Walcott were both ruled out for six weeks with ankle injuries, while centre-back Vermaelen ruptured an Achilles while on international duty with Belgium.

In Europe, drawn alongside Shakhtar Donetsk, Braga and

Partizan Belgrade, Arsenal sailed through their opening Champions League match against Braga, but an away match at Sunderland proved the first of several setbacks for Wenger and his fragile squad. An early Fabregas goal had Arsenal on track for another victory, but an injury to the Spaniard and the dismissal of Song rocked the Gunners, with Darren Bent equalising in the final seconds. Rather than his growing injury list, stoppage time was the subject of Wenger's frustration: 'It [the goal] was outside the four minutes.'

A second-string Arsenal comfortably despatched a third-string Tottenham in the third round of the Carling Cup but back in the league against a confident West Brom, Wenger's side looked lost without Fabregas. Two Almunia errors saw them 3-0 down until a late double from Nasri. Wenger summed it up well: 'It was a poor performance, defensively and offensively.' Arsenal found their feet again with a 3-1 Champions League victory away at Partizan Belgrade, but all attention was focused on the upcoming top of the table clash with league leaders Chelsea.

In the absence of Vermaelen, Fabregas, Walcott and Van Persie, in the words of *The Telegraph*'s Henry Winter, 'Arsenal floated like a butterfly, Chelsea stung like a bee'. For all the pretty passing, there was no cutting edge to Arsenal's play. Drogba gave Squillaci and Koscielny problems all day and opened the scoring after 39 minutes. A late Alex free-kick gave Ancelotti's side a key 2-0 win, taking them seven points ahead of the Gunners. Wenger praised his side but saw the lesson to be learned: 'At this level you can get punished. You have to be more clinical.'

After two straight Premier League defeats with five goals

conceded, Wenger welcomed back Djourou and Bendtner in a tough 2-1 home win against Birmingham. Having seen his team go 1-0 down, Wenger was pleased with the character shown to fight back through a Nasri penalty and Chamakh's fifth of the season. With Chelsea and Manchester United both drawing, it was a massive victory for the Gunners, marred only by a late Wilshere red card for an ugly tackle on Nicola Zigic. Not that Wenger was too worried about the youngster: 'He made a mistake, he came out and said I'm sorry. He's a strong character and I believe he will handle that well.' After the game, the Frenchman also gave an update on Arsenal's various injuries ahead of a very busy late October schedule – '[Fabregas] has little chance for Tuesday. Sagna is 10 days, Vermaelen is 10 days, Almunia is a question of days but van Persie looks to be a bit longer.'

There was no sign of these absentees in the Champions League but a very strong team effort saw the Gunners crush a much-fancied Shakhtar Donetsk side 5-1 at the Emirates, breaking records along the way. Chamakh became the first player to score in six consecutive Champions League matches and a total of fourteen goals in the first three games was a new competition high. Valuable minutes for the returning Fabregas and Walcott were the icing on the cake for Wenger.

And the fine form continued with a huge 3-0 win away at title rivals Manchester City. Taking full advantage of an early, last-man dismissal for Dedryck Boyata, Arsenal eased to a comfortable win that installed them at the front of the pack chasing runaway leaders Chelsea. Wenger was full of praise for his team's 'intelligent' approach to the game and reserved special mentions for man of the match Nasri, midfield duo Song and Denilson and much-criticised goalkeeper Lucas Fabianski. The buoyant spirit continued with a 4-0 Carling Cup win at Newcastle and a late Song winner against West Ham in the Premier League. Wenger was particularly delighted with the three consecutive clean sheets, with Squillaci and Koscielny now looking well-adjusted to their new surroundings.

After the early setback against Chelsea, October had proved a hugely successful month for Wenger and his team. November, however, got off to a bad start with a Champions League defeat at Shakhtar and a shock 1-0 home defeat to Newcastle. A first-half Andy Carroll header following a Fabianski error gave the Toon Army their first win at Arsenal since 2001. Even the appearance of van Persie after 60 minutes could not help Arsenal find the cutting edge to go with all their possession. Wenger later told the media 'We never found second gear'. The Gunners slipped to third, with more dropped points at the Emirates.

Arsenal were quickly back to winning ways away at Wolves and Everton. In the former, Chamakh took the plaudits with both goals. In the latter, it was the 'discipline, commitment, togetherness, desire, 100% focus' that particularly pleased Wenger, as his team returned to second place. This joy was short-lived, however, as his side stuttered at home once again, giving up a two-goal lead in a 3-2 North London derby defeat. In his post-match interview, Wenger questioned the mental toughness of his players at key moments: 'When we have to deliver we can't, that is worrying. We put ourselves in the right position and failed.' A 2-0 Champions League defeat at Braga wrapped up a horror week for the Gunners and left them needing a win in their final game against Partizan to progress.

Back in the Premier League, Arsenal saw off Aston Villa 4-2 but a second-half fightback from the home side was another worrying sign for Wenger. However, Chamakh's tenth of the season and Wilshere's first Premier League goal for the club were cause for celebration. In the Carling Cup, a strong Arsenal side saw off Wigan 2-0 to reach the semi-final and then a 2-1 home win against Fulham saw them go top of the Premier League. In the absence of Fabregas, it was Nasri again who shone with a flash of genius in each half. It was not all plain sailing, though, and Wenger singled out Djourou for praise: 'When we had to defend in the air, he was dominant. I believe he will be a very good centre-back.' In the Champions League, Arsenal got the job done against Partizan with Walcott coming off the bench to inspire a 3-1 victory. However, it meant a second place finish and, in all likelihood, a tougher tie in the first knockout round. Wenger told the media: 'I know exactly who we will get' – Pep Guardiola's Barcelona who had knocked them out in the quarterfinals the previous year. He was, of course, correct.

Switching his focus back to the Premier League, Wenger was upbeat: 'We are still in a strong position because we still have to play Chelsea, Manchester United and Manchester City at home – Liverpool as well. More than ever, we will still have our say in this league.'

All was set up nicely for the big Monday night match at Manchester United, pitting first against second. In a cagey encounter, Ji-Sung Park grabbed a fortuitous winner to send

Ferguson's team back to the summit. Wenger brought van Persie and Fabregas on for the final half hour but neither could quite engineer the necessary response. It was an unfortunate defeat, but one that meant Arsenal were without a win in their last 11 matches against Manchester United and Chelsea. With the Blues up next, Wenger told his players to 'take a lot of encouragement from the game tonight and of course bounce back on Saturday.'

And bounce back they did with a brilliant 3-1 win. Wenger was able to field his strongest side (except Vermaelen) for the first time all season, with van Persie, Fabregas, Walcott, Nasri and Song all starting. Arsenal began strongly without converting chances but goals from Song, Fabregas and Walcott in a 15-minute period either side of half-time saw off a Chelsea side on the slide. It was Arsenal's first win against their London rivals since November 2008 and kept the pressure firmly on leaders Manchester United. Arsène was delighted with his team's spirit and quality.

A 2-2 draw at Wigan, though, was an opportunity missed as a late Squillaci own goal gave the 10-man strugglers a valuable point. Wenger opted to rotate his side in the busy festive period, offering starts to Bendtner, Chamakh, Arshavin, Denilson, Rosicky and Diaby. The result was a below-par performance and two goals conceded from set pieces. 'We came back well in the first half,' Wenger told the press, 'but didn't produce enough in the second.' With the big guns back in the side, the New Year's Day trip to Birmingham proved more straightforward. Van Persie grabbed his first of the season and Nasri his thirteenth in a 3-0 win which left Wenger's side in third but hot on the heels of the two Manchester clubs. Seven points from nine in six days was no disaster but Wenger knew that defeat at home to Manchester City would be.

That clash finished goalless, with the Arsenal boss ruing missed chances. 'They came for 0-0 and got what they wanted.' Wenger's analysis was spot-on in a frustrating match where van Persie, Fabregas, Nasri and Walcott all came up empty in their attempts to break the deadlock. Arsenal had 61% possession and hit the woodwork on several occasions. Wenger expressed his frustration at not coming away with all three points: 'I feel we had the performance but not the result.' His side went into a big week of cup football in third place, four points behind Manchester United.

Fighting hard on four fronts, the last thing Wenger and Arsenal wanted was replays. But as against Manchester City, the Gunners could not find the finish to put away a resilient Leeds United in the FA Cup Third Round. In fact, it was only a last-minute Fabregas penalty that saved them from defeat. In the first leg of the Carling Cup semi-final four days later, Arsenal went one worse, losing 1-0 at Ipswich. Despite the presence of Walcott and Fabregas, the Gunners just could not get going against Championship opposition. Having rested van Persie again, goals were becoming a problem for Wenger, with Chamakh goalless since the end of November and Bendtner and Vela unprolific as back-ups.

Arsène brought his Dutch talisman back into the league side and Arsenal won 3-0 at West Ham in an uncharacteristically ruthless display. The victory left the Gunners just a point behind United and two behind City. Van Persie grabbed two and Walcott one as their partnership continued to flourish. Wenger knew much rested on keeping them both fit. After impressing in the cup, young Polish keeper Wojciech Szczesny was rewarded with a Premier League start. Arsène called it a 'good, mature performance' and spoke confidently of his team's title chances. 'It is in our hands, we play all of the big teams at home and we have a strong run at home now.' Not that the league was the sole aim; an accomplished 3-1 victory in the replay at Leeds meant Arsenal were still on course for four trophies. Van Persie was at it again in a 3-0 home win against Wigan, scoring his first Premier League hat-trick despite missing a penalty. With Fabregas also starring, Wenger had every reason to be optimistic as his team leapfrogged City into second. Three days later, a 3-0 win against Ipswich booked a first cup final appearance since 2007.

On the subject of his goalkeeping options, Wenger had this to say in late January; 'At the moment Wojciech is Number One. He's done nothing for me to take him out.' A victory over a spirited Huddersfield side in the fourth round of the FA Cup was overshadowed by a hamstring injury for star performer Nasri and a red card for Squillaci.

February began with Wenger's side showing their mental strength in recovering from a controversial Louis Saha opener to beat Everton 2-1 thanks to second-half goals from Arshavin and Koscielny. 'We are ready for the fight and we've shown that again tonight', Wenger told the media. An injury to Song was the only dampener on a third successive league win that cemented their place as Manchester United's prime challengers.

In their next match at Newcastle, Arsenal were cruising 4-0 through goals from Walcott, Djourou and a van Persie double.

What followed was one of the season's defining halves of football. First Djourou limped off with an injury, then Diaby was sent off for a moment of madness. Two penalties against Koscielny and a Best strike had Newcastle right back in the game with five minutes to go. Then a Joey Barton free-kick was cleared as far as Cheik Tiote, who hit the sweetest volley into Szczesny's bottom left corner. Cue scenes of delight for Alan Pardew and his players, and despair for Wenger and his. However, the Frenchman remained stoic after the match, telling the press 'we panicked a little bit and we were a little bit unlucky as well'. A Manchester United defeat made Arsenal's draw all the more galling.

Wenger's players responded well against Wolves, with a van Persie double earning them a 2-0 win. Djourou returned at the heart of the defence, while Wilshere and Fabregas continued to dominate the midfield areas. Rooney's spectacular winner in the Manchester derby kept United four points clear but Arsenal were within striking distance.

Next up was the first leg of the Champions League second round tie against Messi and co. At the Emirates, a David Villa goal saw Barcelona take a 1-0 half-time lead but an excellent second-half display saw Arsenal triumph 2-1. Wenger's substitutions were inspired, with Bendtner causing problems up front and Arshavin grabbing the late winner after van Persie's equaliser. The Frenchman called it 'a special night' and dedicated it to the loyal supporters: 'The fans tonight were very positive and behind the team and they played an exceptional part in it as well.' The all-important away goal meant the tie was set up perfectly for an enthralling second leg at the Nou Camp.

First, though, there were domestic matters to deal with. In the FA Cup Fifth Round, a stunning late Jonathan Tehoue strike gave Leyton Orient the replay they wanted, and Arsenal dreaded. In the league, Squillaci was the unlikely hero as his eighth minute header gave the Gunners all three points against Stoke. The injury curse against Stoke continued, though, with Fabregas and Walcott both leaving the field early. Wenger preferred to focus on the three 'very, very important' points.

The penultimate day of February was Carling Cup Final day, as Wenger looked to end his team's six-year trophy drought. Fabregas and Walcott were ruled out but Arsène chose to rush van Persie back from a knee injury. The Dutchman cancelled out Zigic's opener but was then forced off after 70 minutes. With the Gunners working in vain for the winner, an 89th-minute defensive howler gave Birmingham a shock victory. Man of the match Ben Foster launched a free-kick into the Arsenal penalty area and a mix-up between Szczesny and Koscielny saw the ball arrive at the feet of Obafemi Martins for a simple tap-in. For Wenger and his players, the mental scars would last a long time.

A Bendtner hat-trick led a second-string side to a 5-0 win in the FA Cup replay against Leyton Orient, but in the league, Arsenal could not find the goal to beat Sunderland at home, despite the return of Nasri. The poor end product worried Wenger but luckily another Manchester United defeat meant the gap remained just three points.

Fabregas and van Persie were both back for the second leg against Barcelona but neither covered themselves in glory as the Catalan side triumphed 3-1. A solid 44 minutes of defending was undone as Fabregas gifted a ball to Iniesta who played in Messi to finish in style. In the second half, a Busquets own goal gave Arsenal a brief glimmer of hope until van Persie was very harshly given a second yellow for playing on after the referee's whistle. The Dutchman complained he could not hear over the noise of the crowd.

Barcelona took full advantage with goals from Xavi and Messi. With seconds to go, substitute Bendtner had a golden opportunity to win the tie but fluffed his finish. Unsurprisingly, Wenger's wrath was aimed at the referee: 'He killed a promising, fantastic football match.' Captain Fabregas, however, took responsibility himself: 'I take full blame for the result tonight. It was one of the worst nights of my life.'

Having been kicked out of the Carling Cup and the Champions League, the FA Cup quarterfinal against Manchester United took on an extra significance for Wenger. However, a weak United side showed the clinical touch that Arsenal lacked to emerge victorious through goals from Fabio and Rooney. Arsenal, missing Fabregas but otherwise at full strength, had plenty of possession but yet again no end product. Wenger's message of 'we were not outplayed' was beginning to sound like a broken record. Arsène's thoughts switched to the league after seeing his team dumped out of three cup competitions in a fortnight. 'Now we need to respond quickly and win our next games,' Wenger told the media.

Back-to-back draws against West Brom and Sunderland was not what Wenger had in mind. Arsenal may have extended their unbeaten run to 13 Premier League games, but this was four valuable points dropped. A 3-1 win at Blackpool kept the title hopes alive but Manchester United were now seven points clear.

A 1-1 draw at home to Liverpool, however, all but doused the burning embers of hope. After 90 minutes of goalless toil, eight minutes of injury time were signalled for a head injury to Jamie Carragher. In the last of those eight minutes, van Persie converted from the spot but after 102 minutes, Kuyt converted an equalising penalty. Wenger chose not to focus on the extra four minutes: 'We cannot do anything about it, we have to continue to fight...We have dropped two points – that's the reality today.'

Arsène saw the return North London derby as an opportunity for revenge but also a must-win game with his team's title challenge hanging by a thread. In an end-to-end first-half, Walcott, Nasri and van Persie struck to give the Gunners a 3-2 lead. A second-half penalty pulled Spurs level and despite the pace of Walcott creating a succession of chances, Arsenal again could not find that winning goal. With nothing else to play for, Arsenal's Premier League season had well and truly stuttered and stalled with five draws in six matches. All a despondent Wenger could say was: 'We will fight like mad for the next game.'

Unfortunately, against a relegation-fighting Bolton, Arsenal did not show the necessary fight. Van Persie cancelled out a goal from on-loan striker Daniel Sturridge but a 90th minute Tamir Cohen header gave the Trotters all three points. Mental fragility, set piece vulnerability, possession without end product – it was the same old story for Arsenal. But Wenger jumped to his squad's defence, telling the media: 'If there's somebody to blame it's me, it's not the players. The players have been outstanding the whole season.' The Frenchman reluctantly added that the Gunners' title chances were 'very minimal now'.

With four games remaining, a resurgent Chelsea were odds-on for second and Arsenal were left looking over their shoulders at Manchester City in fourth. Wenger hoped that his players could raise their game for the arrival of league leaders Manchester United. He was not disappointed, as Ramsey celebrated a Premier League start in place of Fabregas by scoring the game's only goal. 'We'll keep fighting' was Wenger's post-match message.

Sadly, this turned out to be the last fight from his tired team, as Arsenal took just a single point from their final three games. In their defeat to Stoke it was the aerial threat, against Aston Villa it was the pacy counter attacks; even with the return of Vermaelen, Arsenal's defensive vulnerabilities saw them pass the 40 goals conceded during the previous season, much to Wenger's annoyance. Only van Persie's goals kept the team going, and his strike in the 2-2 draw with Fulham on the final day saw him equal Ronaldo and Henry's Premier League record of scoring eighteen goals from 1 January onwards. Arsène needed more from his supporting cast.

Arsenal finished the 2010-11 season with eleven points from the final ten matches. For a sixth successive season, Wenger's team had got close to several trophies, but come away with nothing. 'We are frustrated, disappointed but as well we have not to go overboard and think that our team is not good', was Wenger's analysis. 'We have to rectify some things in our squad and we will try to do it but it's not easy, even with money. We can't buy players for £50m. If we find the right players we will spend money.' It was not the strong, daring statement that Arsenal fans were hoping for, but at least Wenger had confirmed that there were issues to be dealt with.

Arsenal's league season was a case of too many draws (11), brought about by a combination of a brittle temperament, poor defending and a lack of clinical finishing support for the injury-prone duo of van Persie and Walcott. Chamakh had added just one to his 2012 Premier League tally, Bendtner and Vela struggled to make an impact and only Nasri contributed enough from midfield. Having scored fifteen the previous season, Fabregas managed just three league goals this time around. The major positive for Wenger to take was the development of younger talents like Nasri, Djourou, Szczesny and Wilshere. Over the summer of 2011, Wenger's number one priority was holding on to star trio Fabregas, Nasri and van Persie. Getting these players and others fully fit, and keeping them that way, were numbers two and three.

BOUNCING BACK FROM THE EXODUS

Without an international tournament for distraction, the summer of 2011 was a long slog for Wenger. Barcelona continued their dogged pursuit of Fabregas, while Manchester City continued their raid on the best of the rest. In July, Clichy was the next to join Toure and Adebayor at Eastlands in a deal worth £7 million. The emergence of Kieran Gibbs had certainly softened the blow and Wenger told the media: 'Gael leaves with our respect and best wishes'.

With Denilson heading back to Brazil on loan and Eboue signing for Galatasaray, Wenger was doing a good job of trimming his squad. Contract rebel Nasri, however, remained a key part of Wenger's plans: 'I'm willing to keep him for another year, even if it means we risk losing him for nothing in a year's time. Our goal is to win the championship and we need good players to do that.'

In terms of arrivals, Arsenal were once again linked with the same authoritative types: big central defenders like Christopher Samba and Gary Cahill, powerful defensive midfielders including Scott Parker and Yann M'Vila, and skilful creators such as Eden Hazard. In the end it was Hazard's teammate at Lille, Gervinho, who became Wenger's first big summer signing for £10.5 million. The versatile Ivorian forward had helped the French club to a League and Cup double and Wenger was pleased with the business: 'Gervinho is a player that can play in a number of positions up front. He is good one against one, he is strong and was the best provider in the French League with assists and he scored 15 goals.'

As opening day approached, Wenger's only other investments had been in future stars Carl Jenkinson and Alex Oxlade-Chamberlain. The latter, signed from Southampton, was certainly a coup for the Gunners but not one that addressed the fans' more immediate concerns about a fragile defence and star players with their eyes on the exit. Wenger asked for patience but a bad injury to Wilshere in pre-season only raised more concerns. Ankle surgery would keep the young Englishman out for at least five months. There was light, however, amongst all the gloom, in the form of a fit and free-scoring van Persie. Arsène was relying on his star striker to lead the team this season.

The Premier League season began with a damp squib of a goalless draw at St James Park. Wenger left out both Fabregas and Nasri, and the Gunners certainly missed their creativity. The Arsenal manager called it a 'solid performance' but his new-look side lacked a cutting edge. Gervinho's frustrating debut went from bad to worse late on when he was sent-off for a spat with Newcastle's Joey Barton.

Two days later, the mood at the Emirates darkened as Fabregas completed his long-protracted return to Barcelona for £35 million, but Nasri was back in Wenger's side for the visit of Liverpool. Despite an early injury to Koscielny, Arsenal more than held their own until the dismissal of Emmanuel Frimpong midway through the second half. A Ramsey own goal and a late Suarez strike then gave the Reds their first win at Arsenal in eleven years. It was cruel luck and Wenger was right to feel aggrieved at some of the refereeing decisions. With the pressure mounting, the Arsenal boss told the media: 'There is no chance I would walk away.'

Nasri, however, completed his £25 million move to rivals Manchester City. Wenger defended the psychological reasons for letting the midfielder leave: 'What kind of commitment can you have when the player is not there long term?' With the season underway and the transfer window closing in under a week, Wenger had to act quickly, especially with his team through to the Champions League group stage. Van Persie and Walcott scored the goals to give the Gunners a 3-1 aggregate win over Italian side Udinese. Arsenal Supporters' Trust spokesman Tim Payton called for 'significant use of the £80 million in the transfer account to strengthen the squad'.

These calls became angry demands after a humiliating 8-2 defeat at Old Trafford, the club's worst result since 1896. Due to injuries and suspensions, Wenger handed starts to the inexperienced trio of Jenkinson, Francis Coquelin and Armand Traore and a confident Manchester United side took full advantage, with Rooney grabbing a hat-trick and Ashley Young a brace. Wenger was hurt by his side's shocking display, admitting 'we collapsed in the second half'. In *The Guardian*, Kevin McCarra called it 'relegation day for Arsenal', arguing that the Gunners had conceded their elite club status – and 17th position in the league certainly seemed to support this verdict.

In a chaotic final two days of August, Wenger loaned out Bendtner to Sunderland and brought in Brazilian left-back Andre Santos, South Korean striker Park Chu-Young, German defender Per Mertesacker, Spanish midfielder Mikel Arteta and Israeli winger Yossi Benayoun. Arsenal had spent only a third of that £80 million kitty but Mertesacker and Arteta in particular were seen as shrewd and experienced signings. These two were thrown straight in against Swansea as a freak Arshavin goal gave Wenger's side their first win of the season. In the Champions League, Arsenal took a valuable away point against a Dortmund side featuring Mario Götze, Shinji Kagawa and Robert Lewandowski.

However, any settling of nerves was quickly undone as a Yakubu double inspired Blackburn to a 4-3 victory in Arsenal's next league match. Wenger's side dominated possession and Gervinho grabbed his first Premier League goal, but three goals in twenty second-half minutes, including two own goals, saw Arsenal capitulate again. 'Defensively we are fragile because the confidence is gone', Wenger admitted afterwards, before thanking the fans for their fantastic support through troubled times.

Arsenal got straight back to winning ways with a 3-1 Carling Cup win over Shrewsbury and then a 3-0 league win against Bolton, where van Persie picked up his 99th and 100th Arsenal goals. Afterwards, Wenger was quick to praise his leading man; 'it's difficult to imagine at the moment our team without him'. The Dutchman, who was named club captain after Fabregas' departure, was entitled to feel stranded after the summer departures. The Gunners made it three wins in a row against Olympiakos as 18 year-old Oxlade-Chamberlain became the youngest Englishman to score in the competition.

The recent recovery leant a better atmosphere to the celebrations surrounding Wenger's 15th anniversary at Arsenal. He talked of feeling 'proud', 'grateful' and 'very lucky' to be in charge of such a great club with such strong values.

But two days later, his team suffered yet another setback as Tottenham won an entertaining North London derby. Arsène pushed Song back into defence due to injuries and the Cameroonian was greatly missed in the midfield battle against Parker, Luka Modric and Rafael van Der Vaart. Again, the Arsenal defence succumbed, with Szczesny at fault for Kyle Walker's late winner. Wenger's frustration was clear as he told the press 'we lost a game we should not have lost'. The result left the Gunners 15th, just two points above the relegation zone.

The international break allowed the Arsenal squad to leave domestic troubles behind and return with new confidence and hunger. In a 2-1 defeat of Sunderland, it was van Persie again who came to the rescue, revelling in his injury-free start to the season. Despite the Dutchman's contract expiring in 2013, Wenger was keen to focus on the 'now': 'What is important is how he plays'.

A late Ramsey goal gave Arsenal a 1-0 win at Marseille and top spot in Champions League Group F at the halfway stage. And there was no sign of the usual European hangover as Gervinho and van Persie goals despatched usual bogey side Stoke City. A trip to London rivals Chelsea represented a massive challenge at the end of an encouraging month and a superb team display suggested Arsenal had turned a corner.

Trailing 2-1 at half-time, Wenger and his backroom staff celebrated in style as the Gunners fought back to claim a 5-3 victory that saw them rise to seventh. Hat-trick hero van Persie took the headlines but Ramsey and Walcott were also constant threats in attack. At the other end of the pitch, however, Arsenal's defensive frailties remained clear for all to see, with a worrying 21 goals conceded in their first 10 league matches. Wenger needed Mertesacker to adjust to the fast and physical English game quickly – and more additions might be necessary in January.

November began with consecutive cleansheets in a goalless draw against Marseille and a convincing 3-0 win over West Brom. With Arteta, Song and Ramsey bossing the midfield and van Persie and Walcott finding the net regularly, things were certainly looking up for Wenger and his team. 'We are getting stronger', he told the media. The 2-1 win at Norwich was a tenth in twelve games, with van Persie's double taking him to 31 goals in 2011. Arsène had nothing but praise for the 'good attitude and spirit in the squad', as Arsenal wrapped up their Champions League group with a 2-1 defeat of Dortmund to progress to the knockout stage for the twelfth consecutive season.

With positivity reigning supreme, the scene was set for another Arsenal slip-up. A late Vermaelen own goal gave a disciplined Fulham side a point at the Emirates and four days later a breakaway goal from Sergio Aguero knocked a young

Arsenal side out of the Carling Cup. Wenger couldn't fault the effort of his players but saw a few lessons to be learned – 'It was an unfair result but I felt we were a bit naïve.'

A dominant 4-0 away win at Wigan was the perfect response to a disappointing week. Wenger was happy to see Arteta, Vermaelen and Gervinho joining van Persie on the scoresheet. 'There is a difference between the team at the start of the season and now, and we can still improve.'

Arsenal celebrated their 125th anniversary with a 1-0 win over Everton that took them into the top four for the first time all season. A sensational van Persie volley yet again made up for chances squandered by Walcott, Gervinho and Ramsey. It was a seventh Premier League win in eight games, achieved despite Wenger fielding four centre-backs due to injuries to Clichy, Gibbs and Sagna. Next up was a trip to title challengers Manchester City. In an even and absorbing game, a second-half Silva strike proved the difference as City maintained their 100% home record and reclaimed top spot. Afterwards, Wenger bemoaned the defensive reshuffle caused by an injury to Djourou, as well as questionable decisions, including a van Persie goal that was ruled offside.

Again, Wenger's side fought back valiantly after a major defeat. In a busy Christmas schedule, Arsenal rarely convinced but took seven points from a possible nine against Aston Villa, Wolves and QPR. Van Persie ended 2011 with a phenomenal 35 Premier League goals, 50 in all competitions. After a horrible start to the season, Arsenal went into 2012 in fourth place, 'a fantastic achievement' as Wenger was quick to remind everyone. In fact, the Frenchman was not ruling out a title challenge.

January began in style with the return of the prodigal son, Henry, on loan from the New York Red Bulls. At 34 years of age, Henry was hardly Wenger's typical transfer target but the Arsenal manager knew his old striker's goals and experience could be crucial: 'I am sure during these two months he will be a massive asset to the team in the dressing room and on the pitch.'

But Arsenal's year began with a poor 2-1 defeat at Fulham, where a Djourou red card led to two late goals. Walcott and Gervinho should have put the game to bed in the first-half but Wenger was particularly incensed by a penalty not given and the nature of Djourou's second yellow card. 'We had some bad decisions from the referee today,' he complained. Henry made his return debut in the FA Cup against Leeds, adding 'even more to the legend' as Wenger described it, by grabbing the only goal of the game.

However, in the league, Arsenal continued their poor start to 2012 with a 3-2 defeat at Swansea. More goals scored by van Persie and Walcott, but more importantly more goals conceded. It was not ideal preparation for the visit of second-placed Manchester United and, in the end, Arsenal were undone by a late goal from Danny Welbeck. After a poor first half, the Gunners dominated the second with van Persie equalising after 70 minutes. Wenger's unpopular substitution of Arshavin for Oxlade-Chamberlain backfired badly as the Russian's poor defending against Antonio Valencia allowed Welbeck in to score.

Afterwards, the manager was quick to defend his decision, saying 'I've been a manager for 30 years and have made 50,000 substitutions. I don't have to justify every one.' Wenger did admit, though, that the defeat left the club in a difficult position.

After three defeats in a row, the last thing Wenger's side needed was to go 2-0 down in their next game against Aston Villa. And yet van Persie and Walcott combined once again to pull off a magnificent second-half comeback. Wenger was pleased with the resolve: 'The players showed a lot of character.'

The Arsenal manager needed February to be a better month for his team but it started with a 0-0 draw at Bolton. Arteta's return from injury was the one positive in another game where Arsenal's poor finishing cost them dearly. 'Every game in the championship is a cup final now', Wenger told the media. His players responded to this rallying cry in style by thrashing Blackburn 7-1. Van Persie scored a hat-trick and Oxlade-Chamberlain grabbed his first Premier League goals. Wenger was quick to commend the young Englishman's progress but his general message was all about consistency.

Arsenal moved back into fourth place with a battling 2-1 win at Sunderland. Wenger welcomed Sagna back into his side but then saw Mertesacker hobble off in the second-half. Henry grabbed a late winner in his farewell match to make it a very useful tally of three goals in six games. It was the team's 'exceptional spirit and quality' that impressed the manager most and he urged his players to maintain that level in their Champions League tie at AC Milan. Sadly, it ended up being 'our worst performance in Europe by far' according to Wenger. The ruthless Rossoneri punished defensive mistakes to hand Arsenal their heaviest ever European defeat. 4-0 was a massive mountain for the Gunners to climb at the Emirates.

Wenger watched yet another Arsenal season falter in February. In the FA Cup Fifth Round, a strong Arsenal side could not recover from their European embarrassment and Sunderland took full advantage. Injuries to Coquelin and Ramsey compounded what was another terrible day for the Gunners. Arsène did, however, have some sympathy for his tired players: 'the schedule was just too difficult for us'.

A week later, Arsenal found themselves 2-0 down once again, this time in the North London derby. But in 27 breath-taking minutes either side of half-time, Wenger's side found the net five times. Against all odds, Arsenal had secured a third consecutive league win, earning Wenger another Manager of the Month award. He was proud of the character shown by his players, and singled Rosicky out for particular praise.

The win seemed to galvanise Wenger's players. Despite an early Koscielny own goal, the Gunners fought to a brilliant away win at Anfield. Van Persie's goals took him to 25 league goals for the season. Wenger also had praise for his other man of the match, Szczesny, who saved an early Dirk Kuyt penalty. No one gave Arsenal much hope in the Champions League second leg but Wenger's side very nearly pulled it off. With Oxlade-Chamberlain a danger throughout, the Gunners found themselves 3-0 up in the first-half but Milan defended stoutly in the second. It was his squad's lack of depth that frustrated Wenger most: 'When we tired in midfield, we had no opportunities on the bench'. To hear the Arsenal manager admit that his team needed strengthening was an exasperating blow for the legions of fans who had been demanding January signings. It was to be yet another trophyless season for Arsenal.

But with the race for third place still on, the Gunners had plenty to play for. A 2-1 win against Newcastle left them just one point behind Tottenham with ten games left. Vermaelen scored the winner in the 95th minute, just reward for 'our relentless effort to win' in Wenger's opinion. It was the fourth consecutive league match where Arsenal had fought back from behind – how Arsène would have loved some of that new-found resilience earlier in the season.

A sixth consecutive Premier League win, away at Everton, saw Arsenal move into third. It was Vermaelen again who popped up with the winner. With a settled backline of Szczesny, Sagna, Vermaelen, Koscielny and Gibbs, the Gunners finally looked capable of defending leads. 'In January, we had four full-backs out', Wenger emphasised. 'Now, to have our defenders back, it changes the game.'

It was left-back Gibbs who opened the scoring in the next match, a comfortable 3-0 win against Aston Villa. Wenger was pleased to see Walcott and Arteta taking the goalscoring burden off van Persie for once. But just as Arsenal looked at their most solid all season, they slipped up again at relegation-threatened QPR. This time Arsène had no complaints about the result: 'Our performance was not good enough to win this kind of game.'

An admonished Arsenal turned in a much better performance at home to title challengers Manchester City. Roberto Mancini's side were frustrated as the Gunners had the best of the chances. Arteta won the game with a late long-range strike and Mario Balotelli was sent off late on. It was a massive win but, as Wenger told both players and supporters, 'The job isn't done yet.' A comfortable win at Wolves saw Arsenal open up a five point lead over Spurs. Van Persie equalled Ian Wright's record of scoring against 17 of the 19 other Premier League teams, and Walcott got his eleventh of the season.

But the consistency that Wenger sought was still yet to be found. In their next game, the Gunners failed to recover from a horror start and lost 2-1 to Wigan Athletic. Yet again, the other attackers failed to step up with goals when van Persie was struggling. Wenger had already acted to thwart the problem, securing the signing of experienced German striker Lucas Podolski from Cologne for next season.

In the meantime, Arsenal failed to find a winner in games against Chelsea, Stoke and Norwich. With the Blues involved in a Champions League semi-final, Roberto Di Matteo's second-string side played for the point. A frustrated Wenger concluded 'They killed the game and we were not quick enough to open them up.'

Following the Stoke draw, the Frenchman admitted his side was over-reliant on van Persie's goals. With his side ending the season in indifferent form, Wenger again incurred the wrath of the Arsenal faithful. His reaction was defiant: 'It's easy to sit in the stand and insult people. It's the easiest sport in the world.'

A 3-3 draw at home to Norwich did little to change people's minds. While Wenger complained about a lack of penalties given at home, Gunners fans despaired at their team's inability to hold on for the win. Suddenly, Tottenham were two points behind again with a game in hand.

Arsenal finished the season with an unconvincing 3-2 win at West Brom, which proved enough to secure third place as Spurs faltered. It was an exciting game to mark Wenger's 600th Premier League match in charge, but the Frenchman was not pleased with the defensive errors. His team had conceded 49 goals in 38 games, six more than in the previous season, despite the experience of Mertesacker and Vermaelen. In front of goal, Wenger also had issues to resolve. Golden Boot winner van Persie aside, Arsenal had only managed to score 44 goals with Walcott contributing eight and Vermaelen and Arteta six apiece. In terms of finishing, Gervinho's debut season had been a big disappointment and Chamakh had managed just one goal in 19 games.

However, Wenger was quick to put everything into perspective. After all, Arsenal had finished one place higher than the previous season, with two extra points. Ramsey and Walcott were fulfilling their potential after injuries and older players like Rosicky and Arteta looked rejuvenated. 'I'm proud of the season. The mental solidity, the unity and solidarity inside the club has been tested...We were 17th in the league and in the first seven games we had lost four of them. When you have played seven games, there are 31 to go. It's very difficult to imagine you can finish third.' The problem was that the main reason for their recovery was still to sign a new contract. With the best year of his career ending without any silverware, van Persie was keeping his options open: 'I love this club. Whatever happens that will never change.' Wenger was facing another summer of distracting transfer talk.

With the Podolski signing already secured, Wenger turned his focus to fitness. In the 2011-12 season, Arsenal massively benefited from getting more than double the number of games out of van Persie, Walcott, Song and Vermaelen. 'The second part of our signings will be to take care of the players who are injured and get them back for the start of next season,' Wenger told the press, referring mainly to the talented midfield duo of Diaby and Wilshere. With a full and healthy squad, the Arsenal manager believed the Gunners could mount a genuine title challenge.

THE DROUGHT GOES ON

O n 4 July, van Persie confirmed Arsène's worst fears. 'I've thought long and hard about it', the Dutch talisman wrote on his website, 'but I have decided not to extend my contract.' The transfer saga lasted well into August, when Manchester United eventually beat Juventus and Manchester City to his signature. To see his leading goalscorer leave for Premier League rivals was a bitter pill to swallow but Wenger remained composed. 'It's never great to lose players of that quality but he only had a year contract so we do not have a choice.'

Fortunately, the Arsenal boss had already acted to revamp his strikeforce. To the proven finishing ability of Podolski he added the height and strength of French international Olivier Giroud. A £12 million signing from French league winners Montpellier, Giroud would offer a different attacking threat for the Gunners: 'He has a very good physical presence and is exceptional in the air.' The sale of Vela to Real Sociedad was a further sign that Wenger was content with his attacking options.

In early August, Spanish playmaker Santi Cazorla became Arsenal's third summer signing for £15 million. A small and highly technical type, the former Malaga man was the classic Wenger signing. He would certainly entertain in forward positions but what worried fans most was the paucity of defensive-minded midfielders.

This worry became all the more pronounced when Song followed van Persie out of the Emirates in a £17 million move to Barcelona. With Diaby and Wilshere as the talented but injury-prone alternatives to Arteta, the Gunners certainly looked vulnerable over a busy season. Wenger, however, had no such concerns. 'It's always frustrating losing great players, but we have plenty of players in midfield.' Another summer, another two key players sold, but in Podolski, Giroud and Cazorla, Wenger had acquired world class replacements. Hopes were high for a successful season.

Wenger included all three in his squad for the visit of Sunderland. Sadly, the new-look side struggled to gel in a frustrating goalless draw. A repeat result away at Stoke and Arsenal certainly appeared to be missing van Persie greatly. Walcott's decision to reject a new £75,000 a week contract didn't help matters, although it seemed to be the least of Wenger's concerns. 'He is not obsessed by money', he told the media, 'I think Theo loves the club.'

The one positive for the Arsenal manager was two clean sheets for Vermaelen, Mertesacker et al. Against Liverpool in their third game, the Gunners finally scored their first goals of the season in a 2-0 win. It was new boys Podolski and Cazorla who found the net in a dominant display that pleased Wenger: 'The sharpness gets better from game to game.' His players returned from international duty to hit promoted Southampton for six with Podolski, Walcott and Gervinho (2) on the scoresheet. Four games in, Diaby was still fit and the Gunners remained unbeaten; their manager was quietly confident. 'We have a chance for the title but first we must show consistency.'

Arsenal opened their European campaign with a 2-1 win away at Giroud's former club Montpellier. In an unconvincing victory, Podolski and Gervinho got the goals. Back in the Premier League, Wenger knew a trip to champions Manchester City would be the first big test for his team. Arsenal took a well-deserved point thanks to a late strike from Koscielny, in for the unwell Vermaelen. Once again it was his team's spirit that Wenger found most encouraging: 'We refused to lose the game today.'

A 6-1 Carling Cup win over Coventry gave Wenger some nice attacking dilemmas, as Giroud grabbed his first goal for the club and Walcott scored a brace from his preferred central position. 'His time will come for that', the Arsenal manager told the media, 'and at the moment we have to be a bit patient.'

Three days later, Arsenal spoilt a solid September with their first defeat of the season. At home to Chelsea, Gervinho grabbed an equaliser but a second-half Mata free-kick won the game. Wenger was unimpressed with his side's defending from set pieces, with Koscielny particularly culpable. 'It is unacceptable to give away goals like that in the big games. We can only blame ourselves.'

His players responded well in the Champions League with a 3-1 victory over an injury-hit Olympiakos side. Gervinho made it five in five games, with Podolski and Ramsey also finding the net. A 3-1 win at West Ham saw Cazorla impressing once again, setting up goals for Giroud and Walcott before adding one of his own. 'I hope every young football player in England watches him' was Wenger's response. After seven league games, the Gunners sat fifth with twelve points, a few points off the leading pack but a marked improvement on the seven points won the previous season which had seen them languishing in 15th place. Arsène saw reasons to be positive.

The international break seemed to upset Arsenal's rhythm. Away at Norwich, they lacked urgency and ideas as the Canaries secured their first win of the season thanks to an early Grant Holt goal. Giroud and Podolski were still very much finding their scoring touch in English football, while Gervinho seemed to be back to frustrating form after his goal glut.

The good news for Wenger was that Wilshere was fit enough to make the bench; the bad news was an injury to Oxlade-Chamberlain. Against Schalke in the Champions League, Wenger sat frustrated in the stands as he served out the last of his three-match touchline ban. With no attacking threat and a vulnerable defence, the Gunners slipped to a 2-0 defeat. Arsenal's form was a real concern for Wenger in the middle of the season's busiest time.

A late Arteta goal gave the Gunners a vital win at the end of a bad week. Wilshere made his first start for seventeen months but it was not enough to inspire an Arsenal goal until a sending off for Stéphane Mbia. Afterwards, Wenger defended his goal-shy strikeforce, putting it down to a short-term lack of confidence. Three days later in the Carling Cup, goals were no problem as Arsenal won a twelve-goal thriller at Reading. A second-string side found themselves 4-0 down inside 40 minutes but a Walcott hat-trick inspired the ultimate comeback, completed with three goals in extra time.

November began with a massive trip to van Persie's new club Manchester United. The Dutchman stunned his old club with an early opener and Patrice Evra added a second to condemn Arsenal to their worst start to a league season during Wenger's reign. Three defeats in the late six and fifteen points from ten games was far from title-challenging form. The manager's post-match analysis was all too familiar: 'We had a lot of the ball but we were not very efficient.' Santos' decision to swap shirts with van Persie at half-time was seen by fans as a symbol of Arsenal's losing mentality, and signalled the beginning of the end for the left-back's poor spell at the Emirates.

In draws against Schalke and Fulham, Wenger's side showed slow signs of recovery. The front three of Walcott, Giroud and Podolski found the net five times but defensively, the Gunners looked devoid of confidence. The first North London derby got off to a terrible start with another Adebayor goal against his former club. However, moments later the Togolese striker was dismissed for a tackle on Cazorla and Arsenal seized the initiative in spectacular fashion. Goals from Mertesacker, Podolski, Giroud, Cazorla and Walcott gave Wenger's side a morale-boosting 5-2 win. 'It's important to rebuild the belief of the team and that result will help', he acknowledged. It certainly seemed to, as Arsenal secured qualification for the second stage of the Champions League for a thirteenth consecutive season. Goals from Wilshere and Podolski were enough to see off Montpellier, but Wenger was focused on securing top spot in their final group match against Olympiakos.

Back in the league, Arsenal slipped to seventh with two more draws. In a goalless game at Aston Villa, Wenger blamed fatigue for his team's lacklustre performance. In response to criticism for replacing Giroud with Coquelin as they chased a much-needed winner, the manager added 'I will not explain every decision I make'. Against Everton, the Gunners were lucky to emerge with a point. Arsenal's season was in desperate need of a boost as Swansea arrived at the Emirates on 1 December.

Instead, their season reached crisis point as two late Michu goals saw them drop to 10th, 15 points off leaders Manchester United. Chasing a breakthrough, Wenger replaced the ineffective Gervinho and Podolski but Giroud and Oxlade-Chamberlain could do no better. Despite pressure mounting for Wenger to be replaced as Arsenal manager, the Frenchman remained focused on the task at hand – rallying his dejected troops. 'We are in this job to turn things around and I am confident we will [because of] the quality of the players and the spirit we have in the team.'

With his first-choice players looking jaded, Wenger sent out a second-string side against Olympiakos. A 2-1 defeat saw Arsenal take second spot again, setting up a difficult tie with in-form German giants Bayern Munich. Arsène desperately needed his players to find form before February. A 2-0 win against West Brom was a good start. Wilshere and Oxlade-Chamberlain dominated the midfield as two Arteta penalties secured three league points for the first time since mid-November. A shock cup exit to League Two side Bradford, however, was a setback. A late Vermaelen equaliser took the game to penalties but Cazorla, Chamakh and Vermaelen all failed to convert. Afterwards, Wenger refused to call it an embarrassment, saying 'I think they'll be more disappointed and frustrated.'

With the Carling Cup gone and the Champions League campaign on hold until February, Wenger's focus was firmly on moving up the league table – and Arsenal did so in style. A 5-2 rout of Reading, which included a Cazorla hat-trick, took them to fifth and a hard-fought 1-0 win at Wigan put them back into the hallowed top four for 24 hours.

Wenger's side ended a strong December in spectacular fashion with a 7-3 victory over Newcastle. It was their fourth consecutive league win and saw them head into the New Year on the tail of fourth-placed Tottenham. A hat-trick against the Magpies took Walcott up to 14 goals for the season and increased the pressure on Wenger to tie him down to a new contract. A brace for Giroud suggested he was beginning to fulfil his promise in English football. After a tough spell, things were looking up for Arsène and his team.

As the transfer window opened, the papers were full of speculation surrounding potential Arsenal signings. Wenger, however, stuck to his guns and refused to spend money for the sake of it: 'If everybody is fit we have a strong squad, but in certain areas we are a bit short because we cannot rotate.' This perceived deficiency didn't stop Wenger from loaning out squad men Chamakh, Djourou and Frimpong. A New Year's Day draw at Southampton halted Arsenal's late 2012 progress. After a bright start, Wenger's side faded badly and were fortunate to emerge with a point.

Against Swansea in the FA Cup it was a case of a poor first half and a better second half but it was not enough to get the win. In a frantic final ten minutes, Podolski equalised and Gibbs put the Gunners in front but Danny Graham forced a replay Arsenal certainly did not need. With the lack of silverware becoming ever more worrying, Wenger was happy just to remain in the competition. 'If that's the choice between going out or staying in the hat then I would rather take the replay at the Emirates.' At home, Wilshere inspired Arsenal to a 1-0 win.

Arsenal's mixed start to the year got a whole lot worse when they welcomed Manchester City to the Emirates. Koscielny was sent off after just ten minutes and the champions were cruising at 2-0 with half an hour gone. Arsenal never recovered and slunk to yet another defeat against top four opposition. Wenger was disappointed by his players' response to the red card: 'We gave away two cheap goals, at 10 men you keep it 0-0 and you never know.' The one positive was 60 minutes from Diaby who would be of vital importance at the heart of the midfield with Arteta sidelined for three weeks.

Arsène's players had little time to wallow; up next in the league was a tough trip to Chelsea. At Stamford Bridge, Arsenal were far too slow out of the blocks and found themselves 2-0 down. With Wenger sending his team out early for the second-half, Walcott pulled one back to justify his big new contract, but the equaliser proved elusive. The Gunners had taken just one point from a possible nine in 2013 and, although still sixth, they sat just one point above ninth.

THE DROUGHT GOES ON

Wenger needed a good response from his underperforming players and he got it against West Ham. Arsenal scored five in a match for the fifth time in the season, with Podolski, Giroud (2), Cazorla and Walcott on the scoresheet. The goals all came within a 30-minute period after the Gunners had gone 1-0 down. Wenger was pleased to see his players gelling: 'We have many new players and it takes some time to get to know each other very well.' The comeback spirit was on display again in a 3-2 FA Cup win at Brighton and in a 2-2 draw at Liverpool. 2-0 down at Anfield, Giroud grabbed his fifth goal in three games and Walcott pulled them level. This newly prolific strikeforce went some way to alleviating the continuing defensive frailties. With Gibbs out injured, Wenger finally ventured into the transfer market just as it closed, spending £10 million on Malaga left-back Nacho Monreal.

February began with two 1-0 wins, indicating an improving solidity at the back. Against Stoke, the Koscielny-Mertesacker partnership looked impressive; against Sunderland, Wenger was forced to play Jenkinson and then Sagna alongside his tall German centre-back but the Gunners held on admirably. With his side back into fifth, Arsène had his sights firmly set on success: 'The target is to be in the top four and to focus on the two cups we are still in.' How quickly things can change. In the FA Cup against Blackburn, Arsenal struggled to create, let alone convert, chances and suffered a humiliating 1-0 defeat. 'It is very painful to lose a game like that', Wenger told the press. 'What is important is to focus on the next one. The season is not over.'

Three days later, a Bayern Munich side starring Franck Ribery,

Bastian Schweinsteiger and Thomas Mueller outclassed Arsenal in their first leg tie at the Emirates. Podolski grabbed a consolation goal but a 3-1 defeat left the Gunners with a mountain to climb in Germany. With many questioning Wenger's position yet again, Wilshere was the first of the Arsenal players to take responsibility for the failure. 'The boss has been here for 16 years and he's been doing a great job so you can't question him.'

Back in the league, the team backed their manager with a 2-1 win over Aston Villa. It was Cazorla yet again who made the difference with a strike in each half. In his post-match interview, Wenger was quick to dismiss the criticism aimed at him. 'I am not 30 years in this job at the top level and going to be destroyed by people saying I don't know what I'm doing.' In fact, three league wins had earned him the February Manager of the Month award.

The North London derby in early March pitted fourth against fifth, adding extra drama to the grudge match. Arsène knew what victory would mean to his players in the closing months of the season. But in the first-half, Arsenal's defence failed to cope with the electric pace of Bale and Aaron Lennon. They emerged stronger in the second-half but failed to add to Mertesacker's early effort.

The defeat left the Gunners seven points behind their biggest rivals and five points off fourth-placed Chelsea. 'We have to fight and it will be difficult now', Wenger admitted, 'because we dropped points we couldn't afford to drop.'

In the Champions League second leg in Munich, Arsenal put in a spirited performance to only lose out on away goals. Goals from Giroud and Koscielny made a real match of it but Wenger rued the 'many regrets from our first game.' It would be an eighth consecutive season without a trophy for the Gunners. Afterwards, their manager had interesting things to say about the absence of English teams in the quarter-final draw. 'The rest of European football has caught back on us and we have to take that into consideration when we think about the future of the Premier League.'

Wenger and his players now had ten league games – and zero distractions – to secure a fourth place finish. The challenge began well with a 2-0 win at Swansea and a 4-1 thrashing of Reading. At the back, Koscielny and Mertesacker looked increasingly assured, while up front Gervinho and Giroud were back amongst the goals. 'The team has found a better balance maybe between attack and defence', Wenger acknowledged with relief.

As they entered April, Arsenal sat just two points behind Chelsea. For the trip to West Brom, Wenger recalled the recovered Rosicky to his midfield. It proved an inspired move as he grabbed both goals in a 2-1 win. Even when Mertesacker was dismissed with over twenty minutes left, the Gunners refused to give up their lead. The performance left Arsène in confident spirits: 'Can we finish fourth? I believe we will do it.'

A 3-1 win over Norwich saw Arsenal go one better, temporarily leapfrogging Chelsea and Tottenham into third. It was a fourth consecutive win but one that needed an incredible comeback in the last ten minutes. Wenger brought on Podolski, Walcott and Oxlade-Chamberlain and this time, they had the desired effect. A fortunate penalty was converted by Arteta before Giroud and

Podolski secured the three points. 'We just have to keep winning' was Arsène's message.

A goalless draw at home to Everton slowed Arsenal's late season charge but they were back to winning ways at Fulham. A Mertesacker goal following Steve Sidwell's early dismissal proved the difference between the two sides. Although his team were unbeaten since early March, Wenger feared that caution was creeping in. 'We played with the handbrake on and tried to keep the lead without taking risks. We didn't give them enough problems.'

An excellent April ended with the arrival of Manchester United, fresh from wrapping up another league title. Ever the good sportsman, Wenger made sure his players formed the traditional guard of honour for van Persie and his teammates. On the pitch, Arsenal took an early lead through Walcott but United equalised just before half-time. Ferguson's side were more threatening in the second half but the Gunners held on for a valuable point.

The first of the final three matches was a trip across London to QPR. Walcott scored the fastest goal of the Premier League season, making it 20 for the season for the first time in his career. Arsenal held on for an unconvincing but valuable three points that saw them rise to third. Chelsea had two games in hand but as Wenger was quick to point out, 'You can only win your games and see what happens elsewhere.'

A tired Wigan side, still recovering from their amazing FA Cup Final win, were despatched in more comprehensive fashion, with a Podolski double and strikes from Walcott and Ramsey. On the last day of the season, a Koscielny strike was enough to beat Newcastle and pip Tottenham to fourth place by a single point. Against the odds, Wenger's side had secured Champions League action for a 16th season in a row. It was now eight years since Arsenal had won a trophy but with 26 points from their final 30, the Gunners had turned their season around in remarkable fashion. 'The fantastic resilience of the team has been rewarded', the manager proudly told the media. 'Not only this but I think the consistency we've shown in the recent three months is a good springboard for next season.'

Arsène had good reason to be optimistic. In defence in particular, his side had made significant progress, conceding just 16 goals in their 19 league matches in 2013. In Mertesacker and Koscielny, Wenger now had one of the Premiership's most formidable centre-back partnerships. In midfield, it was another solid season for Arteta, and a combined 113 appearances for the gifted young trio of Ramsey, Wilshere and Oxlade-Chamberlain was a massive plus.

Despite the mid-season problems, Wenger's side had finished with three more points than they had the previous season and three fewer defeats. Ten draws, however, hinted at ongoing problems with converting chances and closing out games. Walcott had finished with an impressive 21 goals in all competitions but Giroud and Podolski's Premier League totals of 11 apiece were not what Arsène had hoped for. Gervinho's total of seven in 26 games suggested he could soon be deemed surplus to requirements. Cazorla was named Arsenal's Player of the Year after a fantastic debut season in English football with 12 goals and 10 assists. He looked a good bet to join the likes of Bergkamp, Vieira, Henry and Fabregas as one of Arsène's best ever signings.

Following Ferguson's shock retirement in May, Wenger was now the Premier League's longest-serving manager by a long shot. All three of Arsenal's major title rivals were on the lookout for new bosses. Was Moyes the man Sir Alex wanted as his replacement? Having missed out on Pep, who could Manchester City bring in to replace Mancini? And would Mourinho end up back at Stamford Bridge? The 2013-14 season was set to be a fascinating one.

Wenger knew from experience that new managers usually meant big expenditure on new signings. 'I'm afraid of what Chelsea can do in the summer', he said. 'We have to be prepared for them to be one of the biggest movers in terms of investment once the window opens.' Luckily, according to Arsenal chief executive Ivan Gazidis, the Gunners were now in a financial position where Wenger could compete with the big guns again. A £70 million transfer kitty was mentioned. Arsenal's transfer record still sat at £17.6 million, paid for Spanish winger Reyes in 2003.

Would the notoriously cautious Wenger splash out big to turn his promising Arsenal side into genuine title contenders?

SILVERWARE AT LAST

Gonzalo Higuaín, Rooney, Karim Benzema, Luis Suarez – these were the kind of high-profile forwards being linked with Arsenal during the summer of 2013. And Wenger was not denying the attraction: 'They are all realistic quality-wise, [although] not all of them are available to join us. The fans, the players, everybody is reassured by big names always. But what is important is that we don't need numbers, we need quality.'

In fact, Arsène decided that his squad needed its annual trim before any additions arrived. Arshavin, Squillaci, Santos, Mannone and Denilson were all deemed surplus to requirements, while Djourou, Coquelin and Miquel were sent out on loan. In August, Wenger made room for young Frenchman Yaya Sanogo from Auxerre by selling Gervinho to Roma and Chamakh to Crystal Palace.

With the new Premier League season just around the corner, it was looking like another quiet, disappointing transfer window for the Gunners. At Manchester City, Manuel Pellegrini had spent £90 million on the likes of Fernandinho, Álvaro Negredo and Jesús Navas; at Chelsea, the returning Mourinho had given his squad an expensive revamp in the form of André Schürrle, Samuel Eto'o and Willian; at Tottenham, Andre Villas Boas had spent much of the record transfer fee paid by Real Madrid for Bale on players like Roberto Soldado, Erik Lamela and Paulinho; at Arsenal, Wenger had only added to his reported £70 million transfer kitty. A cheeky £40,000,001 bid for Suarez was rejected, while Higuaín chose to join Rafa Benitez at Napoli. Wenger remained patient, but the fans were growing impatient.

On the opening day of the season, Arsenal entertained Aston Villa. Giroud continued his strong pre-season form with an early goal but a promising start soon turned to disaster. A Christian Benteke double and a Diego Luna strike gave the Gunners their first opening day defeat at home in 20 years. Injuries to Gibbs and Oxlade-Chamberlain, plus another red card for Koscielny, made it the worst possible start to Wenger's 18th season at the club.

'What hurts me is to disappoint people who love the club,' the Arsenal boss said afterwards. 'I'm here to make them happy and when I do not I can only say sorry, come back and make them happy in the next game.' On the subject of signings, Arsène remained coy: 'I'm there to buy players. If we find them, we'll do it.'

The Arsenal manager demanded a quick response to this humiliating defeat. In the Champions League qualifying round, his players travelled to Turkey and beat Fenerbahce 3-0 thanks to goals from Gibbs, Ramsey and Giroud. Job all but done, Wenger had his sights set on signings. 'The transfer market really starts now, a lot of activity will happen between now and 2 September. We have 12 days, a lot will happen.'

Meanwhile, back in the league, Giroud made it four goals in three games as a slick and clinical Arsenal despatched Fulham 3-1. August ended with a 2-0 second leg win over Fenerbahce thanks to a double from the in-form Ramsey. His side had certainly recovered from their opening day wobble, but Arsène knew a landmark signing was needed.

Flamini was certainly not that landmark signing, but he was a familiar face who would bring experience and steel to the Arsenal midfield. Having impressed in training, the Frenchman became Wenger's second signing of the season. With one day left of the transfer window, Arsenal welcomed Tottenham for the North London derby. Without Bale and with the batch of replacements yet to gel, Spurs looked short of ideas. Another goal from Giroud was enough to give the Gunners all three points.

Wenger was delighted with his French striker's improvement, but also the solidity in defence, where Mertesacker and Koscielny were carrying on where they left off the previous season. It was an attacker that Arsenal needed, a creator but also a goalscorer. On transfer deadline day, Arsène finally got his man. The signing of Mesut Özil from Real Madrid – for a fee of £42.4 million – smashed the Arsenal transfer record by an incredible £27.4 million, and made the whole of the Premier League sit up and take note.

Özil got off to a great start with an assist in a 3-1 win at Sunderland. Arsenal's two shining lights got the goals again,

Giroud with his sixth of the season and Ramsey with his fourth and fifth. It was a third straight league win and Wenger was delighted to see his players playing with such confidence, especially with a tough Champions League group ahead of them.

Arsenal started at expected whipping boys Marseille and joined Napoli at the top of Group F with a solid if unspectacular 2-1 win. Ramsey was once again on the scoresheet, as he was four days later in a victory over bogey side Stoke. Özil had a hand in all three goals, as Arsenal climbed to top spot. With 18-year-old prodigy Serge Gnabry given a first Premier League start and Arteta returning from injury, it all looked very promising for the Gunners. Wenger's only concern was keeping his team fit and healthy during the most hectic part of the season, with Walcott already dealing with injury problems. The Frenchman explained: 'We hope we haven't lost Walcott for a long time. We have a game on Saturday and a game against Napoli after that so we will have to rotate.'

True to form, Wenger fielded a second-string side against West Brom in the Capital One Cup. The Arsenal boss was proud to watch his youthful team emerge victorious in a penalty shoot-out. Back in the league, Gnabry grabbed his first goal for the club in a tough 2-1 win at Swansea. Ramsey, the Premier League Player of September, grabbed the other to cap an incredible, 100% winning month for the Gunners. A club record 12th consecutive away win was particularly pleasing for Wenger on his 17th Arsenal anniversary, as was the September Manager of the Month award. Swansea played like his team of old, all possession and no end product. Arsène's team were now looking like genuine title contenders.

October picked up where September left off for the Gunners, as Özil scored his first for the club in a 2-0 Champions League win over Napoli. 'We're just lucky to have got him,' Wenger told the media with great satisfaction. A 1-1 draw at West Brom saw the Gunners drop their first points since the opening day but spirits remained high. Wilshere's first Premier League goal in nearly three years was a great response to a difficult week for the England midfielder, which saw him caught up in a smoking scandal.

Wenger's firm hand in dealing with the matter – 'I disagree completely with that behaviour' – had had its desired effect. Wilshere made it two in two as he opened the scoring in a 4-1 rout of Norwich. The culmination of a breath-taking move involving Giroud and the returning Cazorla, it was the perfect demonstration of Arsenal's swift and flowing brand of football. Wenger described it as 'certainly one of the best goals, one I enjoyed the most because it was a team goal.'

Norwich at home was one thing; Dortmund was quite another, as it proved. A late Lewandowski winner handed the Gunners their first defeat since mid-August. Giroud scored his eighth of the season but Arsenal missed Flamini in midfield against the German side's quick, pressing football. On his 64th birthday, Wenger was in no mood to let things slip. 'We put ourselves on the back foot with the first goal and were naïve for the second. We can only look at ourselves as not being mature enough in those situations. If you can't win the game, don't lose it.'

Arsenal were back to winning ways four days later. Away at managerless Crystal Palace, Wenger enjoyed his side's resilient performance as they held on despite playing with 10 men for the last half hour following Arteta's dismissal. With a settled backline of Szczesny, Sagna, Koscielny, Mertesacker and Gibbs, the Gunners had conceded just six goals in their last eight league matches. In the Capital One Cup against Chelsea, Wenger kept only Koscielny from his winning defence and Arsenal paid the price. Two goals down with half an hour remaining, Özil and Giroud came off the bench but it was too little, too late. With his team fighting hard on two other more important fronts, however, Wenger knew that this cup exit was not the worst news.

Arsenal's favourable early season fixture list was a favourite topic amongst the critics. And so the visit of Liverpool at the start of November was widely seen as the first big test of Wenger's side's credentials. The Gunners passed with flying colours, thanks to another solid defensive performance and the attacking nous of Cazorla and Ramsey. With his team now five points clear at the top, Wenger was focused on consistency: 'We have plenty of big games coming up and we have the ability to deal with them. I am always confident but there is a long way to go.'

Next up was a trip to Champions League finalists Dortmund, where Arsenal avenged their earlier defeat with a mature 1-0 win. Ramsey again popped up with the winner, his total of 11 goals now equalling the sum of his previous six seasons combined. The result left Arsenal joint top of the group and in a strong position to progress.

Wenger knew a trip to Old Trafford was a test of any team's strengths. Under David Moyes, United were sitting in fifth after three defeats but with players like Rooney and van Persie, they were not to be underestimated. Unfortunately, an illness in the Arsenal camp ruled out Mertesacker and Rosicky, while Arteta managed just a half. On the big stage, Wenger's players seemed to freeze: 'We were just too nervous in the first half. We rushed our game too much and lost too many balls.'

A van Persie header was enough to end Arsenal's run of 15 away games unbeaten. It was another big game lost for Arsenal but Wenger knew there were plenty more challenges to come and plenty of time to make amends. Against Southampton, his team benefitted from an Artur Boruc howler to secure 'a difficult win against a very good team'. A fourth clean sheet, two goals from Giroud and the return of Walcott after two months out were all further positives for Wenger to take. As was his side's league position: four points clear of Liverpool and Chelsea.

In the Champions League, Arsenal got one foot into the next round with a 2-0 win over Marseille. Özil missed a penalty but two strikes from Wilshere spared any blushes. Wenger was pleased to see his midfielder injury-free and adding goals to his repertoire. It was another of his young midfielders who proved the difference against Cardiff. Ramsey grabbed two against his old club to make it ten wins out of 12. 'He was phenomenal – he keeps surprising me', Arsène admitted. 'He can still develop.'

At home to Hull, Arsenal recorded a fourth successive clean sheet. Wenger shuffled his pack a little, giving Bendtner a rare start. The Dane took his opportunity well, opening the scoring before Özil made sure of the win. The Arsenal boss had nothing but praise for his players: 'I have a squad that is quite broad with quality, very even, fantastic spirit.'

It was a sign of how high expectations had become that a 1-1 against a strong Everton side was viewed as a setback. 'We are disappointed to get caught out but it's still a point', Wenger told the press. Özil added a fourth goal to his six assists so far for the season but the defensive effort was undone by a late equaliser from Gerard Deulofeu. Arsenal had not been at their attacking best, although Walcott's lively substitute appearance gave Arsène a welcome selection headache.

In their final Champions League group match, Arsenal needed to avoid a three-goal defeat to ensure a second round place. Wenger fielded a strong side that looked largely untroubled for the opening 65 minutes. However, the removal of Ramsey followed by the dismissal of Arteta saw the Gunners succumb to a 2-0 defeat. It meant another second-place finish and a troublesome tie against reigning champions Bayern Munich, now managed by Arsène's old European nemesis Pep Guardiola.

Before then, however, there was a Premier League title to pursue. A trip to Manchester City represented a massive challenge; Pellegrini's side had won all seven of their home games, scoring 29 goals in the process. Wenger's side came in 2-1 down at half-time, still very much in the game.

But in the second-half, the Gunners totally capitulated. Mertesacker and Vermaelen struggled to re-establish their partnership, Szczesny made uncharacteristic errors, Özil and Giroud were mere spectators, and Flamini found himself overrun by the power of Yaya Touré and Fernandinho. Walcott was the one bright spark, scoring two on his return to the starting line-up. A 6-3 thrashing and suddenly the Gunners did not look like such serious challengers. Wenger attempted to play down the significance afterwards: 'They are one of the teams to beat, but no more than any other we have played until now.' He did, however, admit concerns regarding the panic at the back: 'Our strength until now has been our defensive discipline but we lost that as the game went on.'

Arsène's team finished 2013 with three games in seven days. The first of these saw a solid Chelsea side play for a draw at the Emirates. In a scrappy stalemate, Mourinho extended his unbeaten record against Wenger to ten games. Despite his team being unable to penetrate the Chelsea defence and lone striker Giroud remaining goalless since November 23, Wenger chose not to make any substitutions.

The creative talents of Cazorla and Podolski never left the bench. Afterwards, the Arsenal manager refused to write his team off in the title race: 'It will be very tight, very interesting, it will go down to the team who is most consistent.' Arsenal were back at the summit on Boxing Day, as a Walcott double saw off West Ham. Cazorla and Özil were at their best but all was overshadowed by an injury to key man Ramsey. 'The Christmas period is certainly over for him,' Wenger confirmed.

But with a 1-0 win at Newcastle, Arsenal held on to the New Year top spot for the first time since the 2007-08 season. Giroud's first goal in eight games put the Gunners ahead and Mertesacker and Koscielny held firm for the three points. It was the kind of hard-fought victory that pleased Wenger most. 'We are determined to give our best absolutely and to turn back on this season at the end and think we have given our best. I hope it will be enough but it's a long way to go.' With the transfer window opening for business, Newcastle midfielder Yohan

Cabaye was the name on many lips but not Wenger's it seemed. Most agreed that a back-up for Giroud was the priority for Arsenal but Arsène would not be pressured into an ill-advised signing.

The Gunners began 2014 with a win over Cardiff, although Bendtner and Walcott left it late to secure the result. Wenger was pleased with his side's clinical form at the Emirates: 'We know we have to play 10 home games and we want to make this place a fortress and take the points no matter what the others do.' In the FA Cup Third Round, North London rivals Tottenham were despatched 2-0. Arsène fielded a strong side and was made to rue this decision when Walcott was stretchered off with ruptured cruciate knee ligaments. The injury was a devastating blow, ruling the England forward out for the rest of the club season and the World Cup. In Walcott, Wenger had lost a game changer and a goalscorer. Strong rumours linked Arsenal with Schalke's wunderkind Julian Draxler, but in the end no transfer materialised.

Walcott's absence was not felt too strongly at first. The Gunners went one point clear at the top with a 2-1 win at Aston Villa. Oxlade-Chamberlain played his first minutes since the opening day and Wilshere scored one and set up the other. Wenger was impressed: 'He is coming back to his best'. Asked if he was feeling the pressure, the Arsenal boss replied, 'The only way you can give an answer to that is to win the games.' And the Gunners continued to do just that, beating Fulham in the league and Coventry in the FA Cup, making it seven consecutive victories with only two goals conceded. With Ramsey and Walcott sidelined, Giroud, Podolski and Cazorla had picked up the scoring slack with ten goals between them. But just when Wenger thought his side had discovered that title-winning grit, the Gunners were held to a 2-2 draw on the South Coast against a plucky Southampton side. As well as the late dismissal of Flamini, the Arsenal manager criticised his players' performance: 'We played in second gear and Southampton in fourth.'

With the transfer window about to close, Wenger reacted to the bad news of a Ramsey injury setback by securing experienced Swedish international Kim Källström on loan from Spartak Moscow. Two days later, Arsenal's medical team confirmed the new midfielder would miss six weeks with a back injury. For once Wenger had panicked in the transfer market, with disastrous consequences. 'I wouldn't have signed him if we had another two or three days', Arsène admitted, 'but it was on Friday at 5pm'. Not that his team seemed too concerned, as a rejuvenated Oxlade-Chamberlain scored both goals in a comfortable win over Crystal Palace. With 24 games played, the Gunners were refusing to surrender top spot.

A decisive four-week spell began with a daunting trip to Anfield. Liverpool were undefeated in 2014, having taken 11 points from a possible 15. At home, Brendan Rodgers' side had won 11 out of 13 league matches, scoring 38 goals. Wenger knew it was a massive test for his team, on a parallel with the Manchester City match in mid-December that had ended in a 6-3 defeat.

Sadly, Arsenal fared even worse this time, finding themselves 4-0 down after just 20 minutes on their way to a 5-1 defeat. The Gunners had no answer to the aerial threat of Skrtel at set pieces and the pace and skill of Raheem Sterling, Suarez and Sturridge. In terms of an attacking response, Özil and Giroud looked to have nothing left in the tank. Another humiliating away defeat against a title challenger left Wenger worried but not despondent. 'It raises questions that we have to answer on Wednesday night. I still think we can win the league because mathematically it is possible.'

Wednesday night was a home tie against a struggling Manchester United, a brilliant opportunity for Wenger's players to respond to the criticism. But despite the attacking triumvirate of Giroud, Özil and Cazorla, the Gunners failed to make the breakthrough. And with the match stumbling towards a goalless draw and his biggest stars looking jaded, Wenger opted not to use substitutes Podolski and Bendtner. Instead, the Gunners seemed to settle for the draw which left them a point behind leaders Chelsea.

After the final whistle, the Arsenal manager was already looking ahead: 'It is important to recover physically and prepare for the next game as we want to stay in the FA Cup.' And stay in the competition they did, avenging the recent league defeat at Liverpool. Oxlade-Chamberlain was the star man in an exciting cup tie, scoring the first and assisting the second for Podolski. What was particularly pleasing for Wenger was the manner in which his team held firm against a second half onslaught.

Three days later, Arsenal welcomed reigning European champions Bayern Munch to the Emirates. With Sanogo starting up front in place of Giroud, the Gunners made a very positive start and won a seventh minute penalty, which Özil failed to convert. Unable to find the goal their play deserved, Wenger's side found themselves reduced to ten men after 36 minutes when Szczesny brought down Arjen Robben. Playing Guardiola's brand of total possession football, the German giants took full advantage of their numerical advantage on the way to a 2-0 victory.

Midfield maestro Toni Kroos in particular was outstanding, scoring the first and completing an astonishing 147 passes. Rather than the missed penalty, Arsène not for the first time focused his anger on a red card decision. 'The referee made a decision that killed the game,' he lamented before suggesting Robben had made the most of Szczesny's challenge. Attempting to overcome a two-goal deficit in Munich looked another impossible task for the Gunners.

Next, Wenger and his players switched their attention back to the league, where a title challenge was still well within reach. Giroud and Rosicky celebrated their returns to the starting line-up with goals in a 4-1 thrashing of relegation-threatened Sunderland. Wenger delighted in an assured performance and an important three points that kept the Gunners right on Chelsea's heels.

Next up was Stoke, Arsenal's stylistic opposite and bogey side. As ever, the Potters were physical and tireless; but on this occasion, the Gunners lacked their usual creative spark. A second half Walters penalty gave Stoke the three points and left Wenger's side four points behind the league leaders. The manager called it 'a massive setback' and once again questioned his side's ability to perform under pressure. It was a bad start to March, as always one of the crucial months of Arsenal's season.

The build-up to the FA Cup quarter-final against Everton was hampered by news that Wilshere would be out for six weeks with a foot fracture. Not only would he miss around 12 club matches, but his World Cup dream was also hanging in the balance. His Arsenal teammates, however, showed solidarity in the face of yet another injury blow. Wenger watched with pride as his team pulled out a strong second-half performance to win 4-1 and progress to the semi-finals. With the European campaign all but over and the Premier League slipping away once more, the FA Cup became more and more significant as Arsenal's best bet for that long elusive trophy.

Wenger knew the Champions League second leg in Munich was a long shot at best. As expected, Arsenal struggled for possession as Guardiola's side locked down the game. An injured Özil struggled through the first half before being replaced by Rosicky. The match opened up a little in the second half but a Podolski equaliser was as much as the Gunners could manage, as they exited in the second round for the fourth year in a row.

Afterwards, Wenger rued the Szczesny red card in the first leg but also his side's failure to dominate: 'We never got them really under pressure. We still have regrets over the two games.' Arsène's focus returned to domestic matters, both league and cup. The Gunners started by making it three North London derby wins out of three for the season. A second-minute stunner from Rosicky was the difference, but Arsenal's lead never really looked under threat. 'It was a must-win game,' Wenger admitted. 'We maintained the focus not to make the mistake that would cost us.'

The trip to Chelsea was a massive occasion in every sense; not only was it a battle between title contenders but it was also Wenger's 1000th game in charge at Arsenal. The Frenchman joined Matt Busby, Dario Gradi and Ferguson on a very illustrious list of managers to have reached the target with just one club.

Arsenal were hoping for further reason to celebrate; instead they left Stamford Bridge with reasons to despair. Within 20 minutes, the Gunners were 3-0 and a man down, with Gibbs wrongly dismissed instead of Oxlade-Chamberlain. Arsène opted for Arteta as the sole holding midfielder and watched as another powerful midfield ran riot. When Flamini came on for the second half it was all too late. In their three away games against the other title contenders, the Gunners had taken zero points and conceded 17 goals. The statistics spoke for themselves as to where their title challenge had gone wrong. Wenger took full responsibility for the humiliating defeat and demanded an immediate response from his players. In the build-up, Arsène said that every defeat 'leaves a scar in your heart that you never forget'; this game more than most.

Against Swansea, Arsenal demonstrated the after-effects of a huge defeat. Having gone behind, goals from Podolski and Giroud had the Gunners in the lead with minutes to go, until a calamitous Flamini own goal gave the Welsh side a share of the spoils. Arsenal were down to fourth and suddenly Wenger was looking over his shoulder at Everton. 'I think at the moment [the title] is not the biggest worry we have. We have to be realistic.'

This was especially true with Manchester City up next at the Emirates. This time Wenger chose to employ both Arteta and

Flamini and the midfield coped well with Touré and company. A Flamini equaliser gave the Gunners a well-deserved point, but it was another big game where Giroud had failed to fire his side to victory. Afterwards, Wenger chose to reflect on how far his team had come during the season. 'Overall, if you listen to what people said after the first game against Villa and where we are today and the quality we showed today, I just think we are not as bad as people say or think we are,' he said.

Sadly, any sense of recovery after the City draw was lost at Goodison Park. Roberto Martinez out-thought Wenger, as Steven Naismith and Romelu Lukaku helped to power Everton to a 3-0 win. It left the Merseysiders just a point behind Arsenal with a game in hand. It also left Arsenal with more issues to resolve; Mertesacker's lack of pace was exposed, Monreal looked weak defensively, Szczesny made uncharacteristic errors, Cazorla never got going and Giroud looked jaded throughout. The only positive was Ramsey's return from injury. 'I'm 100% committed to fight to make the top four but it will be difficult', Wenger admitted. 'We need to go back to basics. The heavy defeats away from home have taken some of our charisma away.'

After two points from a possible 12 in the league, a return to cup competition was something of a relief. Fabianski in for Szczesny and Sanogo in for Giroud were Wenger's only changes against a Wigan side full of confidence after beating Manchester City in the previous round. The Gunners looked sluggish and jittery in a poor first half. When the Championship team took the lead through a Jordi Gomez penalty in the 63rd minute, suddenly Wenger's side were up against it.

Arsenal threw everything at Wigan in search of an equaliser and were rewarded when Mertesacker headed in with ten minutes to go.

A winner eluded both sides in normal and extra time. In the penalty shoot-out, Fabianski was the hero, saving from Gary Caldwell and Jack Collison to set up a final against Hull. While it was perhaps not the trophy that the Arsenal fans treasured most, it was a golden opportunity to lift some silverware. Relief was Wenger's main emotion after watching his side struggle through. 'We have a target in the FA Cup final but now we have a period where we can concentrate on the Premier League,' he admitted.

With five matches to go, Arsenal sat two points behind Everton and in real danger of missing out on Champions League football for the first time since 1995. A strong finish was essential and Wenger got exactly what he asked for. West Ham took the lead at the Emirates but Podolski and Giroud made sure of three crucial points. Then in a rehearsal of the FA Cup Final, Ramsey grabbed the opener against Hull in his first start back from injury before Podolski made it four goals in two games.

With Everton losing to Crystal Palace and Southampton, Arsenal opened up a four point lead with a 3-0 win over Newcastle. It was a third straight win for the Gunners and a sixth straight defeat for the Magpies. Koscielny, Özil and Giroud grabbed the goals and Wenger singled out his German playmaker for particular praise. 'Mesut Özil is getting stronger in every game now. He is refreshed. Over Christmas he suffered physically. Now he looks physically sharp.' Against West Brom, it was his French hitman that did the damage. Giroud's 22nd goal of the season secured fourth place and Champions

League football yet again. But any relief was mixed with regret for Arsène: 'We are frustrated because we were top of the league for 128 days then dropped off. If you look at our overall performance, we've done well in the cups and the Champions League. We didn't fail anywhere. But we missed something to be decisive in the Premier League.'

The Gunners finished the league season with a trip to all-but-relegated Norwich. A phenomenal Ramsey volley and a first senior goal for Jenkinson gave Arsenal their fifth consecutive win and fourth straight clean sheet. To the delight of the travelling fans, Wenger brought on both Wilshere and Diaby after long spells out. Injuries to others including Walcott, Ramsey, Oxlade-Chamberlain and Özil had also played a massive part in the club's season, as their manager was keen to point out. 'At the very important moment of the season we had many players together out and we were a bit unlucky with that.'

The Arsenal squad's total of days missed due to injury was an incredible 1,716 days, by far the most in the Premier League. Despite this, however, Arsenal had finished just seven points behind champions Manchester City with 79 points, their highest total since the 2007-08 season. Plus, 17 clean sheets was a great achievement for Wenger's oft-criticised backline and, taking out the 20 goals conceded in the away games against the top five, they let in just 21 in 34 games. Goals remained something of an issue for Arsène, especially in the absence of Walcott. Despite barren spells, Giroud had stepped up to score 16 league goals but Podolski's eight, Özil's five and Cazorla's four were just not enough.

The season, though, was not quite over. On May 17, Wenger

took his team back to Wembley for the first time since 2011 with the aim of winning a first trophy since 2005. With the Gunners installed as firm favourites, the pressure was really on to end the infamous trophyless streak. Steve Bruce's team, however, had other ideas, shocking a nervy Arsenal with two early goals.

A stunning Cazorla free-kick put the Gunners back in contention but they struggled to find the equaliser against a stubborn Hull defence. On the hour mark, Arsène sent on Sanogo in place of Podolski and the Tigers' concentration slipped, as Koscielny bundled in from a corner. Arsenal went in search of the winner but Gibbs blazed a glorious chance over. In extra-time, Hull looked exhausted and Giroud's influence was growing, hitting the bar with a header. Then, after 108 minutes, the Frenchman played a neat backheel into the path of Ramsey who poked home. There could not have been a more deserving match-winner than Arsenal's Player of the Year. As the final whistle was blown, Wenger could finally celebrate a major trophy again.

It had been a tougher test than many expected, but Wenger had won his fifth FA Cup trophy and the burden had, at least in part, been lifted. 'It was an important moment in the life of this team', the Arsenal manager told the media. 'To lose would have been a major setback but to win will be a good platform to build on.' Most felt that a winning mentality was the missing ingredient in this young and talented Arsenal squad. Now that they had tasted success, surely the sky was the limit.

However, their leader's presence remained an integral part of the project. And finally, after months of speculation, Arsène committed his future to the Gunners, signing a three-year extension that will keep him at the Emirates until 2017. He explained: 'It was never a question of leaving. It was a question of doing the right job for this football club.'

With his job secured, the Arsenal manager moved on to a summer of transfer activity. 'It will be busy, but the main thing for us will be to keep the stability because we feel we are close. We want to add something that makes us even stronger, but, number wise, it will not be massive.'

A centre forward appeared to be the priority, with Bayern Munich's Mario Mandzukic and QPR's Loic Remy among those rumoured to be on the Gunners' radar. Spaniard Javi Martinez stood out as another potential target and the type of presence who would bolster the Arsenal midfield, if available. Money certainly appears to be no object for the right quality player; Wenger's budget is rumoured to be as high as £100 million. But with Chelsea and Manchester United likely to come back much stronger next season, the question remains: can Arsenal fulfil their promise and make a sustained title challenge? Arsène certainly believes so.

FUTURE PLANS

As Wenger looks back on his time at Arsenal to date, he will undoubtedly be flooded with positive memories. From the Double in 1998, to the Invincibles to an array of special European nights. However, he craves another Premier League title almost as much as he longs to win the Champions League – and he is aware that time is running out to make these dreams a reality.

As Wenger heads into the next stage of his lengthy spell at the club, he can be proud of the way in which he has safeguarded Arsenal financially for the future – not only through balancing the books but by nurturing a group of hugely talented youngsters. United might have unleashed the likes of Beckham, Giggs and Scholes in the early 1990s but Arsenal are now leading the way in bringing young talents into the first team squad.

Despite some of the unease during the trophy drought, there

is plenty for Gunners fans to smile about. Having signed the contract extension, Wenger is ready to guide his young squad towards more silverware.

Arsène – a keen swimmer and runner – is in excellent health and manages the stress of management better than most bosses. This means that the Frenchman may have several years in football ahead of him. His enthusiasm remains as high as ever, despite all that he has achieved, and he appears to get no end of enjoyment from his job.

The Champions League is one hurdle that the Frenchman is yet to overcome and this will no doubt be in his plans, regardless of how much he claims to favour the Premier League. Falling short in 2006 proved very painful and he yearns to make amends.

Yet one day, Gunners fans will have to come to terms with Arsène's departure from the club. Wenger has loved his time at Arsenal but will eventually seek a fresh challenge. His stint in England is already easily his longest managerial spell and so the recent extension could be his last at Arsenal.

Managing elsewhere in Europe could be an option if Arsène leaves the Emirates in 2017. Top clubs in Spain and Italy have constantly shown an interest in acquiring Arsène's services.

International management is another alternative. He has frequently been linked with the England job and is thought to be one of the men that the FA most covets. Wenger has resisted the temptation thus far but, with England rebuilding, the Frenchman might eventually take on the challenge of restoring some pride to the nation that he has called home since 1996. Though some cynics at one time suggested that he might find the idea of being obliged to select English players too restricting and against his usual principles!

The French national team job may also appeal to Arsène. He has allegedly been approached several times by the French FA. One of those occasions was back in the summer of 1997 when he was asked about becoming manager after the 1998 World Cup but turned down the chance due to his commitment to Arsenal. He told the press: 'I am under contract for two more years and I do not want to move, not to become French coach or to take any other job.'

But that is not to say that he would respond in the same way given another opportunity to manage his native country. He is such a knowledgeable figure within the game that he would instantly earn the respect of any group of players. It would be a proud task for Arsène and might just be the perfect way to bow out of management. He has always enjoyed the buzz of major international tournaments and could be the man to lead France back to the glory years of 1998 and 2000.

It is hard to think that Wenger could ever fully retire from football. He has been involved in the game for so many years that even when he decides to quit management, the Frenchman might choose to take on a different role within a club. Perhaps he would take on a scouting post or fulfil a role as an ambassador because he has always enjoyed the countless hours of analysing opponents and watching videos of transfer targets. Arsène's knowledge would be a huge loss if he did not pass it on to young bosses when he ends his own managerial career.

His work in several different countries makes it hard to guess where Wenger might settle when he retires. London has been a happy home for him but he will probably prefer a change of scene when he walks away from the Emirates Stadium. He has a wife and daughter to think of and so clearly he will make the choice that is in their best interests. He has mentioned a desire to return to Japan at some stage but this may take the form of an extended holiday rather than a full-time post.

Retiring from management would at last give Arsène a chance to catch up on all the sleep that he has missed during his career. The Frenchman has admitted in the past that football rarely escapes his thoughts: 'You sleep for one or two hours and then you wake up and it's in your mind. Perhaps I don't step away from football enough. That's always been my problem, but I would say that I do it better now than ten years ago. At least I am always very optimistic, so that helps me to relieve the tension.'

Whatever Wenger might claim, the strain of the job has taken its toll on him. Arsène, 65 in October, must think carefully about how managing is affecting his health. But he is stubborn: 'Football will not kill me. When you start the job, the tension is high because you think you will never make it. I still feel horrible after defeats because I feel responsible. It's a normal feeling for every manager.' He has certainly got better at dealing with bad results but he remains unable to simply go home and forget about them. Instead, he has learned to live with it so that it does not impose on family life.

Perhaps the greatest achievement of Wenger's time in England is the way that he has managed to keep his private life separate from his job. To this day, he remains a mysterious figure – even after all these years at Arsenal. He honours his commitments to the media by always attending press conferences but he is reluctant to indulge the press with one-on-one interviews. As James Cowley noted in the *Observer* prior to the 2006 Champions League final: 'The essential unknowability of Wenger – the mystery and fascination of him – is heightened by his refusal to play the media game or embrace celebrity. This is a shame because it means we shall never know him as he really is.'

By all accounts, Arsène can be lively company, full of wit, but other Premier League managers rarely see this side of the Frenchman's character. So seemingly the only people to sample the real Arsène are his players and coaching staff – and the conclusion there is overwhelming. No team can achieve what the Gunners have managed under Wenger over the years without total admiration and respect for their boss.

Whatever Wenger decides to do in the future, it will be a very sad day for English football when 'The Professor' finally leaves Arsenal.

APPENDIX: ARSENE'S ALL-TIME BEST ARSENAL XI

W enger's years at Arsenal have been memorable for both the glorious style of play and the trophies that his players have won. His dealings in the transfer market have generally unearthed some excellent talents and his ability to sell top players at the right time has helped to keep the side fresh and motivated.

With so many classy and committed footballers gracing Highbury and the Emirates during Arsène's tenure, it is a thankless task to pick a dream team from the Arsène years. There are plenty of options for every position but, after hours of consideration, I have reached my conclusions.

GOALKEEPERS

There is little doubt here. While **Jens Lehmann** impressed during the unbeaten league run, few in the world can compete with **David Seaman** in his prime. The former England keeper produced consistently excellent performances as the Gunners won the Premiership title in 1997/98 and 2001/02 and will be remembered for some phenomenal saves, including his superhuman stop from Paul Peschisolido in the FA Cup semi-final in 2003. Lehmann, meanwhile, had some excellent moments but a string of high profile errors will always be remembered by Gunners fans. Seaman is without doubt the best goalkeeper of the Wenger era.

DEFENDERS

There is far more competition here, especially with the Gunners' defensive reputation in the 1990s. **Tony Adams** captained the side brilliantly in the early Wenger years. He led by example and never backed down from a challenge. Arsène never had a more committed player and Adams deserved the 1997/98 Double as much as anyone at the club. Other prominent centre-backs have included the dominant **Sol Campbell** who was so strong in the air, the speedy **Kolo Toure** who slotted seamlessly into the heart of the defence and the powerful **Martin Keown** who never stopped making life difficult for opposition front men. Plus, **William Gallas** was a major factor in Arsenal's strong 2007/08 campaign. Campbell, in his prime, narrowly shades the rest of the pack and partners Adams at the heart of the back four.

Lee Dixon, who, like Adams, figured in the earlier successes of Wenger's tenure, has been the pick of the right backs. He turned in reliable displays that earned him international caps for England and his positional play was almost flawless. Adams and

Dixon were both part of the back four that were famous for their 'arms up' offside appeals. **Nigel Winterburn** and **Ashley Cole** have been the two outstanding candidates at left back. Winterburn offered strong tackling and no frills distribution while Cole combined lightning pace with an eye for the counter attack. Cole, though, has the edge because he established himself as one of the world's best full-backs during his time at Highbury.

MIDFIELD

Wenger's teams have always blended steely ball-winners and creative geniuses in the midfield areas. No team can field four attack-minded players in these positions and so the mix had to be right. In the centre, **Patrick Vieira** stood head and shoulders above the rest as a combative ball-winner. At his best, he could dominate midfield single-handedly and his presence alone intimidated opponents. He was also the captain as the Gunners completed the Double in 2001/02 and embarked on the unbeaten Premiership run two years later. **Emmanuel Petit**, his midfield partner in the early Arsène years, also oozed class and had a terrific left foot. Together they outfought all comers – except perhaps Roy Keane.

Of the more creative talents, **Robert Pires** was simply unstoppable at times with his deceptive pace and eye for goal, and he was particularly prominent during the 2001/02 season. His ability to assist *and* score earns him a place on the right wing. Although he spent most of his time as a left winger, he is naturally right footed and narrowly pips **Freddie Ljungberg**. Ljungberg chipped in with vital goals too and became very popular with Gunners fans. His clever runs in behind defences caused no end of problems and he regularly found the breakthrough when Wenger needed it most. Going further back, **Marc Overmars** destroyed defences with his searing pace and played a major role in the 1997/98 Double. He possessed the skill to change the game in an instant and helped make the transition from the 'boring Arsenal' days to the Wenger era. **Cesc Fabregas**, who captained the Gunners before returning to Barcelona, blossomed under Wenger and will go down as one of the club's greatest ever talents. With his range of passing and composure in possession, he earns the second midfield slot, alongside Vieira.

FORWARDS

This is another position in which Wenger has been spoilt for choice. **Thierry Henry**, the club's leading goalscorer, enjoyed some sensational seasons at Arsenal. Arsène helped develop him into a world class striker and Henry rewarded his manager with a collection of magical moments. His clinical finishing and lightning pace made him impossible to mark when he was on top of his game. **Dennis Bergkamp** spent many years with Wenger at Arsenal and his vision allowed him to play on well into his thirties. The Dutchman's best campaign was probably the 1997/98 Double-winning season when he scored a batch of spectacular goals. Other leading candidates include **Nicolas Anelka**, whose brief Arsenal career was very successful before an acrimonious exit, and **Ian Wright** – the best natural goalscorer that Wenger ever had. **Robin van Persie** spearheaded the Gunners attack for several years, including some extremely prolific campaigns. But his move to Manchester

United in his prime counts against him when selecting this team.

Seaman

Dixon   Adams   Campbell   Cole

Pires   Vieira   Fabregas   Overmars

Henry   Bergkamp

While no members of the current squad feature in my line-up, that speaks to the frequent changes in personnel at the Emirates, with big names often choosing to chase silverware elsewhere over the past five years.

This dream team blends the heroes of the 1997/98 campaign with those who took leading roles in the triumphs of 2001/02 and 2003/04. Bergkamp, of course, was at the club throughout and has the silverware to show for it.

If these eleven stars had had the chance to play together, who knows how long Arsenal's unbeaten run would have stretched!